The Only Child and His Brothers

Troy Lyndon Hanson

Dedication

This book is written for my children and their descendants. I would hope that it would give them some insight as to the trials and tribulations their ancestors faced in developing a new nation and existing without some of the creature comforts provided by our present-day development and technology.

I would hope that my future family will appreciate the hard work and persistence of the past generations in bringing the advanced, comfortable existence of life that was founded in the United States of America a few hundred years ago. I share my life with you to make awareness of the goodness of the human race and to show my hope and prayers that you will manage to keep the cohesiveness of the American people who have produced the finest quality of life in the world. My story is a small part of the big picture of the development of America as I know it today.

Acknowledgment

I would never have authored this book without the encouragement of my lovely spouse, Elizabeth Ann. Thank you my dear. I love you much.

Our super daughter-in-law, Lorna Charlson Hanson, really inspired me to find my birth family and used her great skill in genealogy to drive the search to discover my maternal family. Her daughter, our grand- daughter Elissa, and her husband Stephen then stepped in and introduced us to the modern science of Biotechnology Genetic Genealogy through the company called 23andMe.

Then came our grand-daughter, Christiana Hanson, who taught me how to use a computer for writing and then edited the work. My Publisher came along with great patience to put the book into print. Finally, I would never have started the book except for the urging of Ms. Ferris Frost, a Colorado Springs College instructor who told me when I was 80, "I better get started writing as I did not have much time left!" I am personally amazed that the Good Lord has given me enough time to complete the book. Thank You All.

Contents

Page Blank Intentionally

Preface

I recently received an interesting article from a friend who informed me that I am a 1%er. This came from the internet, the author is unknown, but the subject relates directly to my story.

1%ers

99 % of those born between 1930 and 1946 (worldwide) are now dead. If one was born in this time span, he is one of the rare surviving 1%ers of this special group. Their ages range from 77 to 93 years old, a 16-year gap. (I am currently 88 years old).

Here are some interesting facts about the 1%ers:

- They are the smallest group of children born since the early 1900s.
- They are the last generation, climbing out of the depression, who can remember the winds of war and the impact of a world at war that rattled the structure of our daily lives for years.
- They are the last to remember ration books for everything from gas to sugar to shoes to stoves.
- They dealt with the black market for sugar.
- They saved tin foil and poured fried meat fat into tin cans.
- They can remember, unless you grew up on a farm, milk being delivered to your house early in the morning and

placed in the "milk box" on the porch.

- Discipline was enforced by parents and teachers and close relatives and neighbors.

- They were the last generation who spent childhood without television. Instead, you "imagined" what you heard on the radio.

- With no TV, you spent your childhood "playing outside".

- There was no Little League.

- There was no city playground for kids.

- The lack of television in your early years meant that you had little real understanding of what the world was like.

- You got "black and white" TV in the early 50s that had one or two stations and no remote.

- Telephones were one to a house, often shared (party lines), and hung on the wall in the kitchen.

- Computers were called calculators and were hand cranked.

- Typewriters were driven by pounding fingers, throwing the carriage, and changing the ribbon.

- 'INTERNET' and 'GOOGLE' were words that did not exist.

- Newspapers and magazines were written for adults, and news was broadcast on your radio at noon and in the evening.

- Most highways were two lanes (no interstates).

- You went to town to shop, and you walked to school.

- The radio stations you could receive in the daytime

numbered about 3.

- You weren't neglected, but you weren't today's all-consuming family focus.
- They were glad you played by yourselves.
- You entered a world of overflowing plenty and opportunity, a world where you were welcomed, enjoying yourselves.
- You felt secure in your future, although the depression and poverty days were deeply remembered.
- Polio was still a crippler. Everyone knew someone who had it.
- You came of age in the '50s and '60s.
- You are the last generation to experience an interlude when there were no threats to our homeland.
- World War 2 was over, and the cold war, terrorism, global warming, and perpetual economic insecurity had yet to haunt life.
- Only this generation can remember a time after WW2 when our world was secure and full of bright promise and plenty.
- You grew up at the best possible time, a time when the world was getting better.
- More than 99% of us are retired now, and we should feel privileged to have "lived in the best of times".

As I have grown older, I have started looking at memories of my past, particularly my adoption and the circumstances around it.

How fortunate I was to be brought into the home of two loving people who gave me everything they had, to see me launched into what I hope was a patriot who loved his country, and to be one who wanted the best for everyone. As you read this history, remember the list of things at the beginning of these paragraphs, and I think you will understand why I think I am truly a 1%er. Enjoy!

Chapter One

Life Begins

January can be bitterly cold in West Central Wisconsin, and so it was in 1935. I was only 10 days old when Hanna Borge, Probation Officer and County Nurse of St. Croix County, picked me up at my birth mother's parent's home at 535 East 1st Street in New Richmond. I was born there at 5:00 p.m. on a Monday, January 7, 1935. The birth had been kept very private as my mother was divorced and single and already was raising two boys from her previous marriage, and my birth father was married and had a family and did not want his identity known. Consequently, the State of Wisconsin had impounded my original birth certificate. I was going to be a foster child.

The Great Depression was affecting the whole US population, and I suppose in my birth mother's and her parents' eyes, they felt it was going to be difficult to feed another mouth. Mother had moved back in with her parents when her previous husband, Darrel Olsen, had walked out on the family, leaving her alone with a 2-year-old and an infant and many miles from her parents' home. Now, she was living with her parents, trying to support herself and her boys by working as a typesetter at the local New Richmond newspaper and doing seamstress work. Her parents were retired, and money was tight. She had now been living with her parents for about three years before I was conceived.

My birth mother met with Hanna before my birth, and they worked with Lutheran Welfare Services and completed and signed the papers to place me in the foster child program of St. Croix County. Now, on this cold, snowy Thursday in January, I am on my way to my new home and life. I am sure that my birth mother is sad and my new parents very happy.

The above information was not known by my adoptive parents as my birth certificate was impounded. I only found this information about 20 years ago using DNA ancestry technology.

When I left New Richmond on Thursday, January 17, 1935, my birth certificate showed my name as Troy Linden Olsen. That was to be my name for three more years. My birth mother had made a good decision. I was going into the best family on earth. My new parents desperately wanted a child to care for and love, and I was that truly fortunate baby.

My new foster parents, Everett and Letty Hanson, were living in a white two-story house on the Rush River farm South of Baldwin, Wisconsin, where Everett was born. It was his father Louie's 200-acre farm near which the Rush River flowed. The farm boasted a thirty-foot windmill, a large barn, and some outbuildings, which were all painted red. A dirt road running North-South was on the East side of the farm, and St. Croix County Road N, an East-

West Road, was about one-mile North of the house. Rich dark river bottom soil and slightly rolling hills made the farm a productive venture. Lauritz (Louie) and Helen Hansen, my new foster paternal grandparents, purchased the farm in 1892, and their children were all born there.

In 1920, they retired from farming and moved to the Village of Baldwin. After their move to Baldwin, the farm was run by Everett and his younger brother Rex. Rex, his wife Lillian, and their son Robert also lived on the farm in another house near my new dwelling.

The mid days of January would see snow deep on the fields of the Hansen homestead, and the road next to the farm drifted full of deep snowbanks. After a cold, 15-mile ride on rough, snow-covered roads starting in New Richmond, Hanna stopped her car, most likely a 1930 plus Chevy or Ford, in the Village of Baldwin to purchase some clothing and supplies for me to use in my new life with the Hansons.

The wind was blowing, and it was slow going on that final five miles from Baldwin down to the farm in Rush River. As we arrived at the corner of County Road N and the road that passed the farm (Nelson's Corner), it was determined that the car would not be able to negotiate the deep drifts of snow blocking the southbound road. Everett had anticipated the problem and had hitched up a team of horses to a straw-filled double box bob sled and had driven the team across the fields and picked me up at the corner. The last mile of my arrival trip was on a sled pulled by two farm horses. I did not know it then, but I was to have other trips at our Wilson farm in the same sled some years later.

Rush River – The Hansen Homestead

The first three years of my life were spent living on Grandpa Louie's Rush River farm, which now was MY farm. I don't remember a great amount about my early Rush River farm life, but I do have pictures of me around the big white house with my parents and farm machinery pulled by horses and mules. I also know that my grandparents, both paternal and maternal, stand out in my memory.

Lauritz Christian Hansen (my Grampa Louie) was born on December 15, 1867, and grew up near Merton, Waukesha County, Wisconsin, between Madison and Milwaukee. His father and mother and his father's parents had immigrated from Denmark some years earlier. He came to Rush River in about 1890 and, in 1892, purchased our farm. On December 27, 1893, he married the girl next door, Helena Hanson, who was born July 22, 1870, and raised on a farm about one-half mile south of his land. By marrying their daughter, his new in-laws gave the new couple the south 40 acres of our farm. His new in-laws were Christian (Aasetton) and Christy

(Kjerstie) Hanson. Please note that two families came together with similar names, i.e., Hansen-Danish heritage and Hanson-Norwegian. The fact that two of Louie's boys decided to spell their last name using "son" (my father Everett and his older brother Vernie) has caused some confusion. I was told that it just was the way it was. So…

Helen and Louie raised three boys – Vernie, b 1894; Everett, b 1897; Rex, b. 1900; - and two girls – Lynda, b 1905 (who died at age 3 from eating aspirin); and Carol, b 1910 - on the Rush River farm. Louie and Helen first moved into a small house that was built on the farm in its earliest days, and the boys were born there.

Grampa Louie had a brother, Peter, who had homesteaded a farm nearby, and in 1900, Louie and Peter contracted Jens Hanson, a close family friend but no relative, to build each of them a farmhouse on their respective farms. That year, Louie moved the family into this lovely, towering, stick-built house, and their two girls, Lynda and Carol, were born there. That was the house that my new parents were living in when I arrived on the scene in 1935.

I would imagine that Grampa was a good farmer and businessman. His farm was rich river bottom that produced abundant crops, livestock, and dairy. His brother Peter was a steam locomotive engineer on the Soo Line between Milwaukee and St. Paul. This gave Louie insight into how to use the railroad to market cattle and produce.

As Everett and Rex grew into manhood, Louie had them working the farm and raising stock and milking cows. My dad, Everett, and his brother, Rex, both loved horses, and horsepower was the business end of a productive farm. Louie, during his early days farming, had horses with sore feet shipped in from his old home in southeast Wisconsin, so there were several teams of horses for the boys to use for fieldwork. They even had a team of mules to do the heavy work.

By the late nineteen-twenties, the boys had reached manhood. Vernie, the oldest brother, had served in the Army in WWI and came home (with PTSD or shell shock, as they called it back then) to move away and farm on his own. Rex and Lillian were married, living in the original Rush River farmhouse with their young son, Bob, who was born on the farm on May 6, 1926.

In 1930, my Aunt Carol was in Nurses Training in the twin cities – St Paul and Minneapolis - and my dad and mom were about to marry. Louie and Helen had moved off the farm in 1920, purchased a small home a few blocks south of Main Street in Baldwin (1250 Oak St.), and Louie had started a new career selling kitchen cook stoves (ranges) while also working as a railroad shipping agent. He had set up a stockyard in Baldwin where he was shipping the area's farmers' livestock to be sold at the Milwaukee and Chicago Stock Yards.

The country was starting to recover from the Great Depression. Things were starting to look up.

The Rush River Early Years

Everett and Letty Hanson were married in Baldwin on June 11, 1930. They moved into Louie and Helen's big house on the Rush River Farm while Everett's brother Rex, his wife Lil, and son Bob lived in another nearby house.

Everett was born on May 4th, 1897, in the first house Louie had built on our farm. He was educated through 6th grade in the Palmer Grade School, a mile east of the farm. He was then sent to a "Normal" school in Menomonie to study agriculture, including Black Smithing and Horse Shoeing.

World War I was winding down, and, at the very end, he was drafted in 1918 and spent 90 days in the US Army stationed at Camp Douglas north of Madison. He was a Doughboy. After the Army, he spent some time living with relatives in Texas, building oil storage tanks. His Aunt Bertha, his mother Helen's sister, had married a Texas oil man from the Houston area, which was the source of this employment. Now that he had been educated, had military service, and had wandering behind him, he was ready to settle down. He had met a lady in Baldwin who was employed on the main street making ladies' hats – millinery.

Letty Lund was born in Stillwater, MN, on 19 July 1889. She was the oldest of five girls and two boys. Her parents immigrated from Norway around 1887 and were married in 1889. Hans and Olava Petterson Lund had originally settled in Stillwater, MN, and they then homesteaded a farm south of Hammond and finally purchased a large home in northwestern Baldwin just south of the railroad tracks, which would become known as the Lund home.

Letty and Everett were married in Baldwin on a warm June day in 1930 in the yard of the Lund home. I remember the house well as my Grandfather Hans would hear the approaching train whistle and would pick me up and run out the front door and about 200 feet up near the tracks to watch the train speed through, whistle screaming, with smoke and steam flying all around. Grampa Hans died in 1937 when I was just two years old. I find it interesting that I would remember something like that as young as I would have been.

I also remember large family gatherings at the Lunds. Mother's spinster sister, Pauline, had been a cook for the famous Pillsbury family in the twin cities when she was young and was a gourmet cook. Now, she lived with her parents in this Lund house and would prepare the most delicious meals for our family. I was introduced to many fine Norwegian foods (some, such as goat cheese), which I never learned to like.

The Only Child

My early years with my new parents were very warm and happy. As an "only" child, I was doted on and was, I am sure, quite spoiled. I certainly was a lucky boy to be taken into Everett and Letty's home and into their families. The grandparents, aunts, and uncles on both sides of the family also unconditionally accepted and loved me. I experienced something similar many years later, which will be covered in the latter part of this book.

Baldwin, which was then called "The Biggest Little Town in Wisconsin," became my hometown. My doctor was Dr. Kunny of the Baldwin Clinic. I have evidence of him giving me several examinations and giving me a Wassermann test in 1936. I also have an appointment card showing an appointment with Dr. S. D. Arnquist, a dentist whose office was close to the Baldwin Clinic.

Church-wise, I was baptized by the Reverend H.P. Nordby, a beloved Lutheran Pastor of the Baldwin Evangelical Lutheran Church. He had also married my new parents. Most of the Lunds were members of that church. For many years, he also served as the Pastor for the North Rush River Lutheran Church, where Louie and Helen's children - my aunt and uncles – attended. So, he was the Pastor for both sides of my new family. Reverend Nordby followed my religious life all the way through my confirmation, upon which, he sent me an autographed picture with his personal congratulations written on the back. He was truly my first Pastor. The Christian faith has been a major part of my being ever since I was a young child.

After his move to Baldwin, Grampa Louie continued his entrepreneurial spirit. An article in the April 28, 1922, Baldwin Bulletin stated that "L. C. Hansen, who has been traveling for the Art Stove Co. of Detroit, MI, is now on the road for Monarch Malleable Range Co of Beaver Dam, WI." I am guessing that this was the first job he took after moving from the farm to Baldwin. Sometime after that, he started his stockyard venture, and a few years later, in the 1930s, Grampa Louie again changed jobs and was now running the Baldwin branch of the "J.D. Larson McCormick Deering - International Harvester - Farmall Tractor Implement Company," which had its main shop in nearby Hammond. His shop was only a few blocks north of his home in the Village of Baldwin.

I have fond memories of sitting in the driver's seat of the bright red tractors with their big black rubber tires in Grampa's shop. The machines were so high I needed to be lifted onto the seat. I would spend much of my time pretending to drive them while Grampa waited on the local farmers who needed parts for their machinery and were always in a rush when they came to town.

I remember Grandma Helen placing me on the sidewalk in front of their Baldwin home and pointing me north to walk, all alone, the three blocks to Grampa's tractor shop. It was a fun time, and my

Grampa Louie was my best pal.

Baldwin was about five miles from the Rush River farm. I remember riding the family Model T Ford car into town with Dad driving. The village had about 700 residents, and it was our major shopping town with a creamery, elevator, retail stores, barber shops, and even an opera house that started out showing silent movies and was where I saw my first talking movie. The village had a tall, large water tower with "Baldwin" painted on the side and a sewage plant. Its residents had electricity, indoor plumbing, and sewers. A modern town indeed! I remember Grampa's house had a flush toilet and bathtub, push-button light switches, and a large octopus-type coal-burning furnace in the basement. His neighbor's house even had an attached garage and a method of opening the garage door electrically from the car.

We farmers would not have running water and electricity in our houses for many more years. The outside hand water pump and outhouse were standard equipment in our lives, and as a child, these town luxuries were not missed – I didn't know any better.

In 1936, Mother and Dad started looking for their own farm; and the next year, we moved to the 40-acre farm where I grew up.

Chapter Two

Cady Township

Everett's old Model T Ford Coupe was like all Model T's - black. Dad was the driver. Mother had no interest in driving cars, horses, or machinery. He and Mother would ride up front, and I had the cramped back seat to myself. Sometimes, I would sit on Mother's lap as we bumped down the dirt and gravel roads. The car had no heater, so one learned to bundle up when going to town in the winter months. Also, it had no electrical system, so it was cranked by hand to start, and the lights only worked if the little four- cylinder engine was running.

One warm fall day in 1936, I remember driving east on County Road N. I was standing between the seats as we turned into a narrow driveway on the south side of the road. Standing there was a house, barn, and outbuildings. The house was painted a green color, and Mother said, "Oh my, this will never do. I hate that color." We never even got out of the car, and to this day, when I see that shade of green, I don't care for it. We were a family looking to buy a farm, and I was about to be a permanent part of that family. My formal adoption was completed on June 28, 1938. I had been a foster child for three and one-half years. Wisconsin law requires a child to live as a foster child in the prospective adoptive family's home for more than six months and, among other requirements, have the consent of the birth mother and the Wisconsin State Board of Control for the adoption. Everett and Letty were listed on the petition as being inhabitants of the Township of Rush River, St. Croix County, so this event must have occurred in the last months of our living on Grampa Louie's Rush River farm.

I have in my references for this book a Bill of Sale dated 1936 transferring the title of the 40-acre John Thompson Cady Township farm to Everett Hanson for the sum of $2,500. This is the amount Dad paid to the widow Thompson and her daughter. Everett and Letty had saved for many years and probably had assistance from Grampa Louie to now own one of the prettiest little farms in the Township of Cady. I was now, by court order, Troy Lyndon Hanson and now was also part owner of this small piece of Wisconsin farmland.

The farm, my farm, was situated in rolling hills of West-Central Wisconsin about fifty miles straight east of St. Paul, MN. The farm's east boundary had a north-south road called the Wilson Road that ran 2 miles north into the Village of Wilson and three miles south to State Highway 29. County Road N, an east-west road, was near the farm's southern boundary. If one followed N about twenty miles west, you would be close to Grampa Louie's Rush River Farm and the intersection where my new father met me when I arrived as a 10-day-old infant. My farm was across the road from the Wilson Norwegian Evangelical Lutheran Church. The church cemetery, lying south of the church building, was directly across the road from our driveway. The white church was atop a hill, and it and its steeple could be seen for miles around the countryside. Our short driveway came west from Wilson Road, passed the house about ten feet on the north side, and then went down a small hill to the barn.

The farmhouse was an older structure and had shiplap siding that was painted white. It had a porch facing south and a parlor room facing east. You could see the church and cemetery from the parlor through a large, fixed pane window with a multi-colored window above it. A kitchen was on the west side and had a "Monarch" wood-burning kitchen range with a warming oven on top and a water reservoir on the side. An upright wood-burning heating stove was in the parlor, and from a corner of the parlor, steep stairs went up to two bedrooms above the kitchen and parlor. A grate in the floor of the bedroom above the parlor was the bedroom's only source of heat in the winter. On the west side of the house, there was a small multipurpose room, which we called the Back Room, which was also used as the house's rear entrance, which we used as the main entrance. One would take off work shoes and clothes and hang them over the wood box. It was the location of the cellar entrance with a small door on the floor. The cellar was under the kitchen, and the base of the brick chimney was there. It was about 6 feet high, 8 feet wide, and 12 feet long. It had a dirt floor and shelving on both sides to hold the many jars of canned food my mother would make during the Fall harvest and canned meat from our own animals. The cellar never froze, even with temps as cold as minus 50 degrees during the winter and was a cool place to store food in the Summer.

Mother used many green-blue Ball canning jars. One ate very well on a farm. The back room was the location of the ice box (which did not appear until I was 7 years old). It held a two-burner kerosene stove that was used to heat water in copper boilers for washing clothes and baths. A Maytag upright wringer washing machine powered by a noisy, smokey gasoline engine was also located in this room. A long flexible metal pipe was used as an exhaust pipe and was stuck through a hole in the south wall to get rid of the smoke and noxious fumes generated by the engine.

I suppose the "back room" was an early version of a modern-day "mud" room. The room had a small table with a mirror over it and a metal wash pan for hand washing, teeth brushing, and Dad shaving. A razor strap hung on the wall as Dad used a straight razor. The wastewater was simply thrown out the door at the base of a large lilac bush about ten feet from the house.

The kitchen had a counter with a tall cream bucket under it that was called a "slop" pail. It, too, was emptied by dumping it under the lilac bush. At the back of the house, across the driveway, was a combination woodshed/outhouse. A single-car garage, granary, chicken coop, machine shed, and well house all lined up on the north side of the driveway. A cistern, where all the fresh pumped well water would be stored, was in the ground to the west of the well/pump house. The cistern had a hand pump on top where the water was drawn and carried to the house in milk buckets about 150 feet away.

The house did not have electricity until after WWII when I was 11 years old. We used kerosene lamps and lanterns. We had one lamp that used a mantle instead of a wick and burned much brighter. This lamp was used for reading and sewing.

About 300 feet down a small grade to the west of the house, a newer hip-roofed barn and silo stood. All the buildings were in good condition. The barn had running water. A one-cylinder gasoline engine with two big flywheels was connected by a flat belt to the well pump. It was used to pump great-tasting, clear, cold water into the cistern adjacent to the well house. Gravity flowed water to the barn and into drinking cups for the cows. A long-handled cast- iron hand pump that stood atop the cistern would take about 15 full swings up and down on the handle to fill a three-gallon pail with water. The house was about 150 feet from the pump, and as I got older, one of my chores was carrying in water. A water bucket and dipper were always in place in the kitchen, and many buckets of water were heated in copper kettles on the kitchen/back-room stove for bathing and clothes washing, and the warm water reservoir attached to the wood-burning cook stove had to be filled. I grew up on the farm and in this house from age 3 to 18. During these years, I never felt deprived of anything. Grandpa Louie had a modern house in Baldwin with electricity, running water, and a furnace. We were just as comfortable in our 1910 farmhouse.

Chapter Three
The Rural Setting

There were trees around the house and more trees across the road in the cemetery. A small, wooded area was located on the west side of the farm in the pasture area. The fields were on rolling low hills. The whole farm setting was beautiful, with splendid views to the south, west, and east. It was a dairy farm with a dozen Jersey cows, a few pigs, two dozen chickens, a sheep or two, two workhorses, some cats, and a dog. The farm housed and fed the three of us. We raised crops to feed the livestock - hay, corn, oats, and grass pasture for the cows and horses during the Summer. We always had a garden and fruit trees, a rhubarb patch, and we picked wild strawberries in the roadside ditches for a special dessert. We bought gasoline, dry goods, building materials, spare parts for the machines, and, once in a while, ice cream, which had to be consumed quickly as we had no refrigeration until the last few years of my farm life.

My father once told me that one year, we spent a total of $300 cash on farm and living expenses. We traded labor with the neighbors and milk, cream, and eggs, too. Our neighbors were like us. This is how I grew up. My adoption was truly a blessing.

The neighborhood

It has been said that it takes a village to raise a child. This applies to the children of farmers. Cady Township was the first- or second-generation settlement home of many farmers with Norwegian heritage. Most were Lutheran and members of the church next to the farm. The township north of us, around the Village of Wilson, was the settlement of farmers with Irish heritage, and they had the only Catholic church for miles around. The township south of us held the German settlers, and they had a German Lutheran church. All these townships were only a few miles from our farm. There was minimal interaction with these distinct groups as each had first-generation immigrants who still spoke their native language, and a few did not yet speak English.

The Township of Cady boasted names like Brandvold, Sather, Smith, Ing, Halderson, Jensen, Steiro, Johnson, Christenson, Thompson, Matson, and Hanson. These names identified us as Scandinavian.

Other neighbors were Brandt, Miley, Krueger, Timm, and Weinke, which indicated a German heritage. The village of Wilson became my hometown and our trading center. It held our Post Office. The town had about 300 residents and was named after a lumberman. It had a State Bank; two grocery stores – Brandvold's and Teeters; 3 bars - the one on Main Street owned by an Irishman named O'Keefe; a railroad depot; a Hardware Store owned by Steve Cave; Paul Walhood's automobile garage with a hand pump glass gasoline dispenser (a gallon of gasoline cost 17 cents); a large building across from the Bank that had some kind of a store in the front and a pool hall in the rear; a grain elevator and the American Legion building housing Wisconsin Post 330 and Boy Scout Troop 150; next to the Legion building was Frank Meredith's Barber Shop with the Wilson Telephone Central switchboard in the shop and he and his wife's living quarters in the back. It also had two churches, a Catholic and a non-denominational. Several houses were east of the central part of the village, and the Wilson Grade School stood among these homes.

U.S. Highway 12 connecting Minneapolis/St. Paul, Minnesota, with Chicago, Ill, and the Northwestern Railroad tracks ran east to west along the south side of the village. An automobile cabin motel/bar type operation owned by Joe Carl stood along Highway 12 east of town (this was also the Greyhound Bus Depot), and the Wilson Night Club stood at the intersection of Wilson Road and Hwy 12. Two other bars/eateries – Shady Rest and Pleasant View Bar and Grill - were west of the village on the south side of Highway 12. The Village of Knapp was down the highway about eight miles to the east, and the Village of Hersey was about 4 miles west, just north of the highway. A small limestone quarry was just on the east side of town. The railroad and highway were very busy. The trains, like the highway, ran between the Twin Cities and Chicago. A fast-diesel-powered train, "The 400", came through twice daily, aptly named as it took 400 minutes to travel between St. Paul and Chicago. It had an air horn with a distinct piercing Mumm sound.

I remember the sounds of the Cady countryside - steam train whistles that could be heard clearly on cold winter days on our farm, and when the tracks became ice-coated, you could even hear the steam engines Puff, Puff-Puff as the wheels on the locomotives slipped as the train pulled the steep westbound grade that passed by Wilson. Wilson Road, which ran in front of the farm, was about fifty feet from the house, so one could easily hear the old cars shifting down gears as they pulled the steep hill up to the church. On a windless day, one would hear the rural sounds – cows lowing, chickens crowing, cackling and clucking, pigs squealing and grunting, sheep bleating and horses whinnying, plus the infrequent airplane overhead. The bell in the steeple of the church could be heard for a good mile on a quiet Sunday morning. The countryside was very peaceful - a great place to grow up.

Farm Life

Life on a dairy farm is quite laid back and routine. Rise early, have breakfast, and milk the cows. Each cow was hand-milked into a metal bucket. The person doing the milking would sit on a short stool about a foot high. I remember my dad using a "T" stool on which he had to balance. In the first years, my mother would go to the barn with Dad to help with the milking, and I would be left in the house by myself. I had a brown-brindle medium-sized bulldog mix by the name of Jiggs to keep me company. We both would get into some mischief at times, and there were some spankings. I remember crawling behind the old wood-burning kitchen range with Jiggs to stay warm - we both would take naps back there. I don't ever remember burning myself on the back of the stove, but I certainly did on the hot top and oven from time to time.

One morning, while Mother was out milking, I took the drinking water dipper, scooped the dirty water out of the Slop Pail, and poured it on the kitchen floor. Even Jiggs knew we were in big trouble after that caper. I can't exactly remember the punishment, but it was unpleasant. I don't think I ever did it again. What is a slop bucket? Remember, we had no plumbing, so when the pots, pans, and dishes were washed in a dish pan, the dirty dish water was poured into the tall pail along with scrapings from the dishes and dregs from the coffee cups, etc. As the pail would fill, it was simply dumped outside on the edge of the backyard or taken to "slop the hogs." The slop bucket was not generally used for chamber pot contents. Dumping the chamber pot (there was one in each bedroom at night) was an unpleasant job that involved taking the filled pot very carefully to the outhouse and disposing of the odiferous contents there. I think that was the most unpleasant task I had to do on our 1940s farm.

As I matured, Dad had me doing more farm work. My first main chore was to raise the new chicks. Each year, in early spring, the old chickens would be slaughtered, and the chicken house would be cleaned and whitewashed (sanitized) with a lime solution. New chicks would be mail-ordered, and the mailman would bring them in boxes with small holes on the sides. They were just days old when they arrived, and I had to see they were kept warm and fed. We used kerosene heaters that spread the heat close to the floor, and food (chicken feed) and water were supplied in small feeders. The chickens grew rapidly, and as the weather warmed, they were allowed to "free range" outside the coop, pecking on the ground for small pebbles to help digest the chicken feed in their crops. My tasks were to make sure they were inside at night as we had many foxes roaming our fields and to see that they were healthy. Chickens are strange creatures. When they are some months old, they peck at each other to the point that blood is drawn. As soon as the red blood is visible, the wounded creature is severely attacked - mainly by young roosters - and could be killed. My job was to catch the attacking roosters and put tiny red lens glasses on them. Now everything looked red to them, and they stopped their attacking. These roosters did not know it at that time, but they would later be the main course at Sunday dinner. We were interested in the hens that laid eggs. I had a daily job of gathering, washing, and placing eggs in crates to take to town and sell. Milk and eggs were the main cash crop on our farm. I was taught farming from an early age.

Farming involved a lot of heavy work. Dad had a team of workhorses that were used to pull machinery. I was taught how to harness and drive horse teams as soon as I could lift the leather harness and manage the horses. These draft horses were mostly gentle, muscular giants. Their backs were broad and were about five feet from the ground. The driver called them by their name – Topsy and ???? - but ours did not respond to "Gee" or "Haw" like their predecessors, but they did respond to "Giddyap" and "Whoa." The driver held the reins and slapped them gently on their backs to make them move forward and pulled back on the reins to make them back up. I was about 10 years old when I started driving our team. I learned how to plow using a hand-held single bottom "walking" plow. Handling it and the horses simultaneously was quite a feat. Dad gave the instruction, and Mother watched the first time when I used that rig to plow the garden on the south side of the house.

As I got more confident driving horses, I used them while I rode on a larger plow when I mowed, raked, and loaded hay and then when I cultivated corn. This was the age when I was helping by milking cows by hand, feeding the animals, fixing fences, repairing machinery, painting buildings, and picking rocks from the fields.

There was always work to be done on a farm. That was the way it was. I learned early on that the farm would house, feed, and clothe you. A farmer was self-sufficient.

Maturing

It did not take me long to figure out that I did not like milking cows. It needed to be done two times a day, seven days a week. There was never a break. I loved the outdoors, using machinery to work in the fields and fixing things. If you were a farmer, you did not hire carpenters, mechanics, or plumbers - you did that yourself. Dad had been trained as a blacksmith and had the forge, drill press, anvil, and tongs to repair the machinery. He strongly encouraged me to use these tools and learn how to make things work. My imagination ran wild. I would spend hours drilling holes, bending metal, pounding nails, sawing boards, and fixing or playing with gasoline engines. The shop was mine to use in any manner. I had no trouble amusing myself, which was good because an only-child farm kid generally does not have playmates, and I had no brothers or sisters and really did not miss them. I built things. I built a shack with old boards and tar paper behind the granary. I even built an airplane with wooden boards and could sit on it and pretend I was flying. My imagination ran wild.

I had much freedom as I grew. My parents were older when I came to them – Mother was forty-five, and Dad was thirty-seven when I arrived on their doorstep. They both were very caring, loving, and somewhat laid back. They gave me space to explore and dream, and if I showed interest in any particular subject, they would try to expand the experience. We always had books and magazines, weekly papers, and even the Sunday paper as I grew up.

I remember a battery-powered tube radio that used an outside long-wire antenna. It required a six-volt automobile battery to power it. A propeller-driven generator (wind charger) was mounted on the chicken coop to keep the battery charged, and it needed weekly charging, which generally took a day the wind was blowing hard enough to turn the propeller.

We would listen to the news at noon on WCCO from Minneapolis with Cedric Adams as the newscaster. I also listened to Jack Armstrong, Little Orphan Annie, Amos and Andy, and the Scary Squeaking Door. I would send away decoder rings and other amazing things that required box tops from Wheaties, Post Toasties, Corn Flakes, Rice Krispies, or Cheerios. Imaginations were developed via radio in those days.

Evenings would have the whole family gathered around the radio, listening to newscasts and special live entertainment programs. Kate Smith singing "God Bless America" and swing bands performing at various ballrooms in the large cities were also high on our listening lists. These days were the early days of radio, and programming was not sophisticated. This small electronic box was our connection to the world. Some of the radios even had a shortwave band that would allow us to tune into broadcasts from around the world. I was fascinated by this device, and the fascination carried through into my adult life.

Grade School

Cady Creek Grade School was located about a mile south of the farm on Wilson Road. My parents made sure that I had started reading about the time I turned five years old. Bernice Knutson (later Mrs. Lester Jensen) was the teacher of this one-room eight-grade school at that time and was a friend of our family. The normal age for a child to enter first grade was six years old. School started in August, and I would be five years and eight months old at that time. Bernice was persuaded by my mother to allow me to start early. The school was a one-room school with eight rows of school desks lined up in front of the teacher. The first-grade row was to the teacher's far right, and that year, 1940, there were about five first-graders enrolled - Mary Christenson, Beverly Brandt, Lillian Thompson, John Matson, and the youngest one, me.

We walked down the dusty gravel road to school and back each day. The older kids kept an eye on us young ones, and I don't remember any problems with this method of transportation. We also had one of the school fathers, Harold Johnson, modify an old

Chevrolet panel truck with two benches, and he would take us to school and back in his "School Bus." I believe he charged 50 cents each month for this service. I was the youngest kid in the school that

first year and continued to be one year younger than my classmates all the way into college. I wonder to this day how different it would have been to be one more year more mature while learning. There were about twenty students in Cady Creek. They were spread out from grades one through eight and all taught by one teacher.

The schoolhouse.

The schoolhouse was built on an acre of land purchased from a Norwegian neighbor, Hartwick Steiro, in the mid-1920s. It had a cloakroom where the coats were hung and a wood-burning furnace in the basement. The typical Girls'/Boys' outhouses with privacy screens and a storage shed stood behind the school. A merry-go-round and two swings stood in the schoolyard. There was no well, so the water was carried in a tall shotgun can (a metal can about 3 feet tall and 12 inches across with a carrying handle) from one of the close by neighbor's farms. Inside, an upright piano was against one wall, and bookcases, blackboards, and a round-faced, wind-up school clock were on the wall behind the teacher. An American flag was in the corner.

The teacher was omnipotent and had authority. She would start lessons with the first grade and move up the grades as the others studied. School started at 8:00 and was over by 5:00. We carried our lunch from home, and if we had a hot lunch, it was brought from home in green Mason jars and then set on a metal grid in the floor over the furnace to stay warm. Recess was spread out through the different grades, so it was unusual for the whole school to be outside playing, and the recesses were unsupervised. I learned how to get along with others at recess. I, as an only child, did not have much other interaction with other kids except in school. The school truly was a broad learning experience.

Early Rural Social Life

Rural social life was centered around the church and the school. Most of the farm families in our school area belonged to the Wilson Norwegian Lutheran Church next to our farm. The church was a large white building with a tall steeple sitting atop a hill across from the northeast corner of our farm. It was built around 1891. Inside, on the east end of the building, was a large hand-crafted wooden altar with a ceramic statue of Jesus with his arms spread in a "come to me" pose. A round pulpit and baptismal font were placed to the side in front of the altar. Two rows of 14-foot-long wooden pews faced the altar. A choir loft seated about 30 singers was about ten feet off the floor in the back of the sanctuary. The loft also held a full-sized pump organ, the only musical instrument in the sanctuary.

The main doors of the church were on the west end, with wide concrete steps and a landing leading to them. Two single doors on the church's south side entered the basement. The basement held many tables and chairs and a kitchen with a range at one end. A long flight of outside stairs allowed the preacher to climb and come in behind the altar if he desired. A pair of outhouses stood behind the church. The cemetery was just south of the church and was about a block long, so it was across the road from our front lawn and driveway. I was churched there from the day we moved onto the farm, and Mother was a Sunday School Teacher for many years.

In the early days, the first service each Sunday was spoken in Norwegian, and there were two sets of hymnals, one of which was in Norwegian. I remember the Reverend Lewis, who spoke Norwegian and English with a Norske accent, standing in the pulpit giving long sermons. We kids did survive by attending the English service. I also remember that a list was published annually that showed the amount of money each family had donated to the church annually; some of the donations were less than one dollar. The offering was received by everyone walking around the altar and placing the money on the altar. Later, I learned how to sing in church. Many of the kids who were in my confirmation class had musical talent. Mary Christianson had taken piano lessons and was able to sing solos and accompany herself. Roy Johnson and John Matson were good singers, and we three soon learned how to read music and sing the tenor and bass parts. The Brandt kids all could sing. The congregation enjoyed the musical abilities of their youth.

After WWII, we got a new pastor- Edwin Gunderson. The first time he came into the church, he was dressed in his Army officer uniform as he was just being discharged and had been a Lutheran Chaplain. The uniform impressed me. He and I became friends, and he was the pastor that confirmed me. He worked for two churches. The Woodville congregation was larger than ours, and they were only 7 miles away. Pastor's salary was made up from the two churches and gave him a living wage.

At Christmas, a large twelve-foot Christmas tree stood in the front corner of the sanctuary with wax candles placed in metal clip holders on the tree. The candles were lit, and an usher stood by the tree with a stick with a wet rag on it to put out any fires that might get started. Later, the church had a Kohler electric generator installed in the basement to provide lighting in the church. Rural Electricity would not come to Cady until after WWII.

Another memory was the annual Vacation Bible School taught by some young Evangelical teens of the Steiro farm family, just south of our farm. They really taught us about Jesus and the Christian religion - it was not to be missed. That and my confirmation class was the basis of my Lutheran church education. I still remember parts of the instruction today.

Over the years, I got to perform many duties during the church services, such as ushering, ringing the bell, and taking the collection when we finally got collection plates. I remember dropping a plate one Sunday. There were mostly coins in the collection, and the plate and coins hitting the wood floor made quite a noise! Ladies Aid, Luther League, church suppers, weddings and receptions, funerals, and many festivals kept the church busy. The whole congregation pitched in to clean and maintain the buildings. I even got the job of keeping the cemetery mowed in the Summer. Folks would come across the road to use our long-handled cistern pump to get water for the flowers on the graves. We all knew and supported each other in our farm area. It was a great way to live.

Social Activity

My father was a WWI veteran and had joined Post 330 of the American Legion which had its building in Wilson. This post was a center of social activity over the years as I grew up. I remember reciting the poem "Flanders Field" for an Armistice Day celebration when I was about five years old. I would play TAPS for their Memorial Day cemetery ceremonies in my later years. The Wilson American Legion Post was another activity center after the war. There were dinners, dances, and special patriotic programs there.

At one time, Dad was the Treasurer of the post, and I

remember a small floor safe that Grampa Louie gave Dad to secure the Legion's money. It stayed in our home for many years. The top front of the safe had "L.C. Hansen" lettered on it. I still know the combination to the safe, which now sits at Cousin Bob Hansen's farm.

Cady Creek Grade School was another center of activity. The school students would put on special programs throughout the school year, which included plays, recitals, patriotic events, and fundraisers. All were well attended to by parents and neighbors. I remember "speaking a piece" at many of these gatherings, as did many of my classmates. One event held at the school stands out in my memory. It was the BOX social. The whole neighborhood attended, and it was a fundraiser for the school. The ladies and young women of the community would place a delicious lunch in a shoe box and then decorate the box, making it beautiful. Everyone would gather in the school, and a person acting as an auctioneer would then sell the boxes to the highest bidder. Generally, no one knew who the woman was who had made the lunch; however, some of the bachelors were given hints as to a box they would be interested in bidding on. The lady would, of course, sit and eat with the lucky bidder. Some of my female classmates also entered their boxes in this social. It was a fun time and my first experience at auction bidding.

By the time I was in the fourth grade, things had changed for me. The first was the "Oak Lane" school, which was about three miles north of us, closed, and the students were consolidated into our school. Our name changed then to Cady Lane Grade School. Two kids started school that Fall who had a lasting impact on my life – Duane Henry and Darlene Bertha Wienke. Darlene was a grade ahead of me, and Duane (Dewey) was a grade behind. Dewey and I quickly became like brothers. He was two weeks younger than me – remember I started school one year too early - and we are buddies even to this day (as this is being written, we are both 88 years old!). I really never felt like an only child, even though some of my classmates called me one. I had always known that I was adopted but had not been told that, before me, my parents had taken another foster child with the intention of adopting him. His mother reclaimed him sometime after he arrived at the Hanson home.

But now I had a make-believe brother and sister plus another mother and dad. Dewey and I got to do things together in school such as carrying the water from the Halderson farm and helping the teacher with other tasks. I was delighted, and the rest of my school years saw us kids running around the neighborhood together and maturing together. I truly believe the Lord had his hand in putting us together.

Chapter Four

Special Memories of Living in Cady Township

I lived on the Cady farm until I was seventeen years old. Those seventeen years were filled with many experiences and events that would shape my life. I was fortunate to have my parents, relatives, neighbors, teachers, pastors, and friends beside me as I went through these life lessons, challenges, and experiences. I need to share some of these with you now so you can understand how I came to be as I am today.

WWII 1941: December 7th

Mother, Dad, and I were invited to Sunday dinner at Mother's sister's, my Aunt Alyce Hanson's home in Baldwin. Alyce had married Chris Hanson - no relation - who was an auto mechanic at a Dodge garage there in town. They had one girl, my cousin Youland, who was seven years my senior. They were town folk and probably had more money and a nicer house and car than their farmer relatives. But it didn't matter as we all were in the same family and enjoyed each other. We were all sitting in the parlor after dinner and listening to radio station WCCO from Minneapolis on a large floor- model radio. The announcer was saying that President Franklin Delano Roosevelt was about to address the nation.

At this time, the President's voice announced that our

military base in Pearl Harbor, Hawaii, had been attacked by the Japanese Navy and that the United States was now at war. A moment or two later, my mother said, "Oh my" (one of her favorite exclamations), I hope Troy does not have to go into the Army." The talk then moved on to how our lives would be changing during a war. Aunt Alyce came to me and told me that she was going to give me a bugle and that I should learn how to play TAPS so I could take part with the Wilson American Legion Honor Guard when the military funerals would start in the cemetery across from our farm. She got me the horn, and I taught myself how to play TAPS and later participated in a number of funerals for our neighbors who lost their lives in WWII. I turned seven years old one month after this event. (Tonight, 2-29-2016, I used that bugle to play TAPS, as I try to do each night here at our Senior Park, our winter home, – Rancho Bonitos in Yuma, AZ).

Music was part of my life from that point on. I was given a toy violin for Christmas that year because we had two neighbors, Simon Halderson and Stuart Smith, who were fiddle players, and I liked their music. A year or so later, Simons' wife, Tillie, who was our church organist, started giving me piano lessons. We did not have a piano for practice, so I would go to Oscar Brandvold's farm-up the hill just on the other side of the church to practice using their parlor piano. My teacher, Tillie, was Oscar's sister, and the Brandvold's - Oscar, Dorothy, and their children, Don, Janice, Bob, and Pete - were our closest neighbors, and we looked out for each other, so I was welcomed there without even knocking.

After a year of having to use Brandvold's piano for practice, I stopped the lessons. All was not lost as I did a concert for my parents plus some neighbors at Tillie's home and played a solo piece, which mocked a fiddle called "Uncle Si." It was chosen because my piano teacher's husband was named Simon or Si. I believe I can still play it from memory and know that the song sheet is still in our collection of piano music today. After that experience, while in grade school, I continued to play my bugle and then, as a sixth grader, was given a cornet by a shirttail cousin on my mother's side, Morris Peterson.

I played that cornet all the way into my freshman year in high school and then switched to a baritone horn (euphonium- small tuba), which I played through high school and my first year of college. In 1953, I went back to the cornet playing in "Bobby Art's Swallows," a Polka Band in Eau Claire, WI, and then again in 1955 when the "Cadets of Note", a Cadet Club dance band made up of Aviation Cadets and led by a Flight Instructor, was organized at Spence AB.

I took a hiatus from music during the rest of my military career but picked it up again in 1973 when I became a member of the Al Kaly Shrine Band in Pueblo, Colorado. I was Director of

Community Relations for the North American Air Defense Command (NORAD) when I was stationed in Colorado Springs in 1973 and had the NORAD Band as part of my responsibility. I was too busy to sit down and play my baritone horn with them. Too bad. Now, I would have loved to say that I played with the NORAD band.

Electricity

Our farm had no electric service until the Rural Electric Association came into being after WWII. I was eleven years old when the local REA association out of Baldwin came through, stringing power lines and bringing electricity to each farm in our area.

My parents hired a local company to wire the house, well house, chicken coop, and barn with lights and electrical outlets and also put a yard light on a tall pole by the well house. We finally got rid of the kerosene lamps and lanterns and the fire hazards they presented. Each room in the house had only a single light on the ceiling and a wall plug to keep the installation cost down, and each fixture was a single bare bulb. Table and floor lamps were used in the parlor. A minimal application but a significant improvement in our lives.

I immediately took to repairing electrical plugs and gadgets. I found out what an electrical shock was all about while experimenting with some charged (hot) wires. One evening, my dad was sitting in his easy chair reading, and I was "fixing" an extension cord near his feet. I put a new outlet on the cord and, not worrying about crossing wires, proceeded to plug the cord into a live outlet. A small explosion and blue ball of fire erupted from the poorly wired plug, which was now very close to Dad's feet. He almost went over backward, and my eyes got really big. The lights in the house went out when the fuse blew, and Mother came running saying, "Oh my." I did not even get into trouble as I knew as much about wiring as my parents. We all arrived at a new age.

Electricity changed things on the farm. The well house now had an electric motor instead of the old gasoline single-cylinder big fly-wheeled chug-chug. The barn got an electric milking machine, a Surge brand. Each cow still had to be milked one at a time, but the teat pulling was minimal. Tool grinders no longer had to be hand cranked. A small electric motor now did that work, and cooking in the kitchen was better with an electric refrigerator replacing the old ice box, which put the fellow who delivered the blocks of ice out of business. Even the milk was cooled by a water cooler that pumped chilly water over the milk cans.

The fuse box for the farm was on the wall in my room. One night, we had a bad electrical storm, and lightning came in on the power line and blew the fuses to pieces right next to my bed. That got my attention. That same lightning strike carried down to the barn and knocked down some of our cows by traveling through the metal stanchions. One cow had to be sold to the fox farm because she went insane after the electrical shock. That was a tragedy as our income was reduced due to lower milk and calf production.

We did not quite arrive in the new century with electricity as it did not give us running water in the house or indoor plumbing. I never enjoyed that pleasure the whole time I lived in Cady. The closest I came was when I was 14 plus, driving up to the Wilson Greyhound Bus depot and paying Joe Carl 25 cents for the use of a shower in one of his automobile tourist cabins. (He also sold me a small bottle of brandy to drink on the way back down to the farm). Life was good. Electricity finally introduced my family to appliances such as an electric frying pan, mixer, portable water heater, radio, and, years later, television.

Country Socializing

One advantage to living in the country came with getting a driver's license at age 14. The license was good for limited daylight driving for things like going to school and other farm-related trips. I purchased my first vehicle when I was about 12 years old when our neighbor Harry Hanson (no relation) decided to part with his 1929 Model T truck. It had been parked in the machine shed for many years and was really dirty. I bought it from him for $15 and pulled it back to our farm with our Farmall C tractor. The front tires were rotted away, but the back ones still held air. I had a lot of help from my friends – Dewey Weinke, Harold Moe, and Roy Johnson - in trying to get it running. None of us knew anything about the three pedals on the floor or the levers on the steering column, but Dad, having owned one when I was little, taught us about the coil system that fired the spark plugs and the magneto that activated the coils. We pulled it around the fields until we finally solved the problems, and it started. Many pleasurable hours were spent taking turns driving it on bare front rims around the pastures and fields. After I left for the military, Dad made the truck into a saw rig, and it ended up in the pasture next to a rock pile. I salvaged the steering wheel and windshield and still have the steering wheel today. It was a fancy truck with electric headlights, kerosene parking lights, and a two-speed rear differential operated by a lever next to the driver.

Dewey's folks had a 1931 Model A coupe with a rumble seat on the back. Dewey got to drive it around the countryside even though he was only 12 or 13. It only had one wheel with a brake – the left rear, but it worked very well. He would load up his sister Darlene and cousins Jeannine, Shirley, and me, and we went everywhere except to town.

One evening, we all went to an abandoned church down in a lonesome valley about five miles from the farm. It was dark when we got there, and after parking in the overgrown front yard, we dared each other to go inside. The front door was locked, but those old churches had that long steep stair in the back that allowed the preacher to enter the church from behind the altar. We slowly made our way up the rickety staircase. We five, one behind the other, led by Dewey with the flashlight at the top, found the door unlocked. Dewey slowly opened the door, and we slipped inside and found ourselves behind the altar. Just then, a flock of nesting pigeons flew right over our heads out the door. Dewey turned around, yelling, "Get Out!". I have never seen the look of terror on a face like that. We stumbled down the stairs and ran for the car. No one fell – amazing. It was an exciting experience that was never to be forgotten or repeated.

Our small gang hung together for the next few years. Many Monopoly games were played at kitchen tables in our homes. We also played with the Ouija board which predicted interesting future lives for us. I guess we learned how to interact with others and always had our parents nearby to give us guidance if needed. I did not know how to dance, but I borrowed my folk's 1937 Chevy one year and took Dewey's cousin Jeannine to a prom. She was older than me, but we had a fun time.

When I was 13, my dad and I bought a 1940 Chevrolet Club coupe. This was to be my car when I turned 14 and could legally drive. It needed lots of work to be road-worthy. I paid $50 for it, and had it stored in a neighbor's machine shed while I worked on the brakes and transmission. This car was newer than Dad's. His was a 1937 Chevrolet two-door sedan, and he and my mother had purchased it soon after we moved to the Cady farm in 1938. The cars were similar in mechanics, so I, with lots of help from Dad, had little difficulty in getting mine running. Dewey purchased an identical 1940 Chevy a year or so after I had been running mine. We both used these cars for the next four years. They both had loud "Hollywood mufflers" and radios. We put outside visors on them and blue jewels in the taillights. We tied squirrel tails to our antennas and were cool dudes. Mine took me to college in Menomonie and on a trip one Christmas to see a girlfriend in Michigan. I don't know how many miles we put on our Chevys, but we sure had a great time running around. I never had an accident or got a traffic ticket in that little black car.

Snippets

Living across from an old cemetery had its moments. Dewey and I would walk by it at night and keep a wary eye out for the supernatural. Never did see any ghostly glowing lights or hear any moaning sounds, but did have one experience that bears retelling:

I would sometimes practice my piano lessons at the Brandvold's in the evening. This dark night, I was returning home and riding my bike. I had just passed the church and was coasting down the hill on Wilson Road with the cemetery on my left. About 100 feet from our driveway, I saw a white object flying across the cemetery fence toward me. My imagination ran wild, and I sprang into action, pedaling as hard as I could straight down the road. I passed our driveway at high speed, but the white thing was right behind me. We went another thousand feet, now approaching the speed of sound, when I realized my white collie dog was chasing me. My fear now turned to frustration as I now realized I would have to push the bike back up the hill to our driveway.

Winter

Winter in Cady was always cold and sometimes snowy. A blizzard moved in one day after the kids were in school at Cady Lane. Harold Johnson's old bus would not be able to deliver the kids back to their homes. My Dad realized what was happening, hooked up our horses to the sled that had been used some years earlier in Rush River to take me home the first time, put lots of straw in the box, came down to school, and took the Brandt kids and me home. I still remember snuggling down in the box while the snow blew around us with Dad in his heavy clothes driving the horses. A day or two later, we kids were walking atop the drifts that were so high we could step on the telegraph lines that ran along County N.

When I was much younger, I remember Dad trying to drive our Model T Ford car on top of the snow drifts to get to County Highway N, which was plowed before the side roads. He got about halfway down Wilson Road to the corner, and the car fell through the snow. He and the neighbors then had to shovel out the road so the car could be driven to the main highway. A revolting development. He would have to haul out our milk to N so the Milk Hauler could pick it up, and the Mail Carrier would leave our mail in the empty cans left by the Milk Hauler. He used the same heavy box sled that had delivered me to Rush River in 1935 and had hauled the Brandt kids and me home from school in a blizzard a few years before this storm.

The North-South roads like Wilson Road would have deep drifts of snow that would require special rotary plows to clear. The stretch of road between the church and our driveway was a particular problem and sometimes would not be cleared for a week or more. Some of the blizzards would have winds of 50 mph and chill factors of minus 50 degrees or more. It was dangerous trying to walk from the house to the barn. Some neighbors would tie a rope between the two to guide them along when the visibility was zero.

I had a pair of Norwegian flat wooden skis that I used to go over the fields to visit Dewey and the neighbors. It was slow going, but I got a lot of exercise.

Fishing

During the Summer, Dad and the neighbors would organize a fishing trip to one of the many lakes within an hour's drive from our farm. They mostly fished sunfish and crappy and would rent 12-foot row boats to get out on the lake. They always seemed to bring a milk can full of live fish back. They would then clean the catch, and we would have a fish fry.

Later, Dewey and I were allowed to take our bikes down in the valley east of the farms to fish for brook trout in Gilbert Creek. We used worms for bait. There were some large fishing holes on the creek, which attracted some older fishermen who would drink beer and spit on the bait. They did catch more fish than us. We learned lots of fishing tricks on these outings. We would leave his house before sunrise and ride our bikes about five miles east on Highway N to Gilbert Creek, a spring-fed stream that ran along the road. We would stay most of the day, eating a brown bag lunch and drinking water right from the stream, pushing our bikes up the long hill that took us into the valley. We always brought fish back.

Field Work

The most enjoyable part of farming for me was working the fields using various pieces of machinery. Summer weather in Wisconsin was warm and very comfortable. Many days, I would be out all day without a shirt. At age 11, I was old enough to take the team of horses and mow and dump rake hay. The team was docile and easy to drive and probably knew more about where to go than I did.

The smell of the new-mown hay was sweet, and the old machinery was quite reliable, so my job went quite smoothly. I would mow a hay field one day and then, a few days later, when the hay had dried, would go out with the dump rake and make fluffy wind rows of cured hay. We would then hook the team to a large rectangular racked hay wagon and an awkward-looking hay loader, and I would drive the horses while Dad loaded the wagon. One fine day, we were making our way down the windrow of hay when a nest of bees came up the hay loader and into the wagon. The bees were upset and flew around, stinging whatever got in their way. The noise and excitement in the wagon scared the horses, and they started to gallop, pulling the wagon loader and the two operators down the field at a high rate of speed. Dad managed to throw the bees' nest out of the wagon, come and grab the reins, and stop the show before we all crashed. No damage except for some bee stings, and our laid-back horses made the day again.

A very boring job that was all mine was cultivating corn. The horses pulled the cultivator down each row of corn as the operator (me) sat on the back with my feet on pedals that would move the diggers left and right. The idea was not to dig up the corn but to destroy weeds growing between the rows. The horses knew to walk between the rows, so all the driver had to do was start and stop them and then, at the end of the row, turn them into the new row. It was slow, hot, boring work. One day, while I was cultivating, a neighbor who owned a small airplane flew over. I had always wanted to fly and got excited and forgot my job. The horses did not even slow down, but I tore out about 20 feet of young corn plants. I had to stop, get off the machine, and hand-plant them back into the ground while hoping that Dad did not see. Cultivating corn was not without danger. One day, a distant neighbor came riding back to the barn slumped in the seat of the cultivator. He had been cultivating during a thunderstorm and had been struck by lightning. His horses survived and simply brought him back to the barn. Dead.

When I was about 12, Dad decided that the time had come to retire the horses, and we purchased a shiny new red Farmall C model tractor. It had large wheels on the back and two small front wheels close together on the front. It was a row crop tractor designed for multiple uses on a small farm. A four-speed manual transmission and a very modern hydraulic lift system. We bought it from the company that Grampa Louie had worked for some years earlier, Larsen Implement in Hammond. The mighty machine came with attachments such as a two-bottom plow, mounted hay mower, and cultivator. I was in my glory! Gone were the smelly, slow horses, and now I would do the fieldwork driving. If I couldn't fly, I could drive a tractor. I soon mounted a radio up in front of the steering wheel, and now I was set - music while working.

Plowing

One Fall Day, I was plowing a future corn field with the Farmall C. I was trying to see how fast I could complete the field and was whipping the tractor around at the end of each furrow. I got too rambunctious, and the tractor's front wheels left the ground and came down with the front wheels crossways. Both wheels snapped off the tractor, and we came down with a grinding thud. It took a truck with a crane to lift the front end of the machine and lots of demanding work to replace the broken shaft. Fortunately for me, the dealer found a bubble in the casting where it broke and paid for the entire accident. Our Farmall did a lot of work around the farm with me at the wheel. I was very happy.

Flying

I seemed to have an inherent love of and a desire to fly airplanes. When even one flew nearby, I would run out to watch, and, even at age 8 or so, I built my own airplane out of wood scraps and would sit in it and pretend to fly. I started building model airplanes a bit later and had some hanging from the ceiling in my bedroom. I got the balsa wood kits from the Baldwin drug store and had glue and sharp knives to cut the small pieces and put them together. I don't believe I had much luck flying them as I did not have the guidance to set up the balance so they would glide properly.

Around age 10, the fellow who owned the Wilson Night Club (Roger Litchfield) brought his Aeronica two-place red airplane to Joe Peterson's field just south of Wilson. He kept it tied down there, and I would admire it as we drove to town. He invited Dad to go on a ride with him one day, and a few weeks later, I got to go. I sat in the back, and we bumped down the field and into the air. We flew around the farm and admired the church from 1,000 feet in the air. He did not let me try to fly it as I suspect he was not very confident in his own pilot abilities. We made a smooth landing on the hay field and taxied back to the tie-down spot. Dad was waiting for us and was grinning. He knew I was hooked.

About a year later, Lester Jensen - my first-grade teacher's husband - learned how to fly at an airport near Elmwood. I got to fly with him in a yellow two-place tail dragger – I think it was some type of Piper aircraft. We flew around the area for an hour and then landed. I don't recall my reaction, but I suppose I was as excited as before. Lester and I became friends, and later, when he was driving a semi-truck delivering produce around the area, I went with him one cold winter night and stayed up all night helping him with the crates of lettuce, carrots, and other produce he delivered to the grocery stores in Baldwin, Spring Valley, Glenwood and other towns within a 50-mile radius. I remember being cold and very tired from that experience, but just being with a pilot made the trip worthwhile. Maybe I would get to go flying with him again? Didn't happen. I didn't know it then, but my next flight would be in an Air Force T-34 training aircraft many years later.

I did have one experience that I still remember. I was about 10 and out in the yard with Dad when we heard a high-pitched sound of an airplane just to the north of us. We saw an Army Air Corps B-25 bomber flying low with smoke trailing. Evidently, the aircraft was in trouble and about to crash. Dad and I jumped in the car to follow it when it hit the ground near a small town named Hersey, a few miles to the northwest. By the time we got to the scene, the fire had subsided, and we were able to walk up to the wreckage. The pilots' bodies were still strapped in their seats, and they were still smoldering from the fire of the crash. It took a long time for officials to arrive, and we left before they got there. I picked up a piece of a machine gun sight and kept it as a souvenir. I can still see the bodies of the crew strapped in their seats. Apparently, it did not negatively impact me enough as I continued to want to fly. We did not have newspapers to tell us about the crash, so we did not know what or why about that accident.

Guns

I had always had a fascination with guns. All our neighbors had some, and most went unused. Dad had a 16-gauge single shotgun that he used to dispatch pigs and steers when he butchered. Grampa Louie would come to visit mostly on Sundays, and when I was about eight years old, he started bringing a Daisy air rifle BB gun for me to use. He generally had the gun fully loaded with BB shots. I would take it around the farm, mainly trying to shoot sparrows. Most farms had an abundance of these birds, and if a couple came up missing, no one would care. I also tried to shoot squirrels but had little luck. If I hit one, it would just run away, probably smarting from the little BB. This went on for a few years, and I never got to keep the gun. Grampa would always take it home with him. I looked forward to those Sunday visits so I could improve my marksmanship.

When I was eleven, Dad came home one day with a small 22-caliber single-shot rifle. It had a very short barrel - only about 20 inches long - and a block of metal that closed when a bullet was placed on the barrel. The hammer then could be cocked, and the gun fired. It was about as foolproof as a gun could get, and I learned to be very accurate with it. I was now able to kill anything that would hold still long enough for me to take careful aim. I brought home some squirrels, which Mother promptly fried for me to eat (after I skinned them and dressed them), and I even shot a pheasant that would fly straight away from me so I could get an accurate airborne shot. I then shot a Blue Heron, which I found wading in a nearby pond. Stewart Smith, our taxidermist neighbor, mounted it for his collection of Wisconsin birds, which he displayed in his well house shop. Years later, State of Wisconsin Game Wardens came to him and confiscated many of his birds and animals because they were placed on the no-kill list due to their rarity.

I did try my hand at deer hunting when I was in my early teens, using the 16-gauge shotgun with lead slugs, but I never got close enough to a deer to kill it. I did get to kill the steers we butchered and even had to put my own dog down when he went blind and could no longer be around farm machinery. All of this was part of growing up on the farm.

Gun safety was taught by Grampa and Dad using common sense. Never had an incident myself, but I was present when Dewey's dad, Hank Wienke, committed a boo-boo. The birds, the Starlings, were starting to become pests as there were too many of them. Hank kept a shotgun in the kitchen of his house to thin out the population. When a flock would land in the backyard, he would slowly sneak the gun out of the screen door and then shoot. Dewey and I were in the basement that day when we heard the screen door squeak open. Nothing happened. The birds had flown before Hank could get a bead on them. He had cocked the gun as he was pointing it out the door. Now, as he brought it back in, he had to release the hammer. As he got it in the door and was pointing it at the floor, his finger slipped off the hammer, and the gun discharged, blowing a hole in the kitchen floor. Dewey and I were about 10 feet from the hole and were properly scared. Dewey's Mom, Bertha, really gave Hank the dickens over that escapade. More fun.

George Menter lived North of Dewey's farm and had a few nice apple trees. One Fall night, we decided to go "coon" some of his apples. We apparently were a bit noisy because we found that George also owned a shotgun. One loud blast and hearing the shot going through the tops of the trees got us running – we never did go back.

During my first year of college, some of us were out running around the countryside one dark night using the spotlight I had on my 40 Chevy to spot or shine deer. Little did we know that the Game Warden was lying in wait for someone to shine and shoot a deer at night – it was illegal. Next thing we knew, the red lights were behind us, and after we stopped, the Warden came up and asked if we had any guns. I told him yes, as I now possessed the famed BB gun, which was in the trunk. The look on the Warden's face was priceless when I opened the trunk, and he reached in and pulled out an air rifle. No arrests that night.

Chapter Five

High School and Beyond

The village of Spring Valley was about 8 miles south of the farm. From its inception in 1894, floods dominated the town's history. There were bad floods in 1907, 1934, and 1938, and three in one year, 1942. The September 1942 flood wiped out the town. The Wisconsin Governor visited and was asked about a dam for the Eau Galle River and stated that "Spring Valley isn't worth that much money."

I started my freshman year at Spring Valley High School in the Fall of 1948. A red and white school bus came down Wilson Road and picked us up at the end of our driveways.

The school building had managed to withstand the floods with damage to the interior during each flood because the river flowed about 200 feet just behind the main building. It was a multi-grade school with some of the elementary grades housed in the lower level. The high school occupied the two upper floors. There was an agricultural building with a large shop across the street, and the whole campus was only one block east of the main street. The football field was just to the north of the school, and the gym was just to the west. I spent a lot of time in the Ag building learning how to be a modern farmer and in the shop learning woodworking, welding, metalworking, and auto mechanics. The shop was open in the evening to anyone in the area who needed to use the machines. Searle Smith and I would go down after milking and work on our own special projects. I had an interesting encounter with a jointer/planer when I was planing off some wood using my left hand to push it across the cutter. My pointer finger got ahead of the wood, and I lost part of the end of the finger. Lots of blood, and I thought the shop teacher, Wally, was going to faint. My left pointer finger today is shorter than my right from this accident.

Music & Typing

I was in the band immediately after school began during my high school Freshman year and was playing the coronet that my cousin Morris had given me. Spring Valley High School was a particularly good school and produced some great athletes, musicians, and farmers. I did not find the studies too trying and ended up taking all the math and science courses offered over the four years I attended. I also took a typing course. I was one of only a few boys to complete the course, and I never regretted it. I participated in the Future Farmers of America organization and went on some fishing trips to Canada with our Ag instructor, Wally Hansen. I also sang in the choir and took part in a stage play directed by my favorite English teacher, Miss Lu Rice.

When I turned 14, I got my driver's license by taking our principal, Syver, for a ride around the block in Dad's 1937 Chevy. I also participated in Senior Skip Day, where we drove the Chevy to Prescott and drove down the circular bridge there. A driver's license also allowed me to try dating. I took a classmate, Nola Madsen, to our junior prom and another classmate, Mary Lou Olsen, to the Senior Prom. I had hesitated to ask Mary Lou because she was a city girl and very pretty – the daughter of a friend of my dad's. Dad had bet me a small sum of money I did not have the nerve to ask her, and I cooked up my courage and found that she would go with me. I suspect the other guys were afraid to ask her since she was blond, very pretty, and a popular cheerleader. I dated some other girls from our farm neighborhood but never had more than one date with them. I just did not have time for girls at that time of my life. I think I did the proms and other dates at the urging of my parents who wanted to be sure that I did like girls.

Farm kids in high school generally rode the bus to and from school each day. The bus would take us home as soon as school was out, so we country kids did not get to participate in many after-hours events such as sports, but I was not much of an athlete, so that did not bother me. Band, chorus, and drama generally met during the school day, so that allowed us farm kids an opportunity to do extracurricular activities.

I enjoyed high school and remembered one event that probably changed my life. Major Richard Bong was a WWII flying ace. He flew over Spring Valley one day in a P-38 Lightning and buzzed the school, did aerobatics over the town, and, in general, put on a great air show. I had always wanted to be a pilot, but that did it. I was convinced that I should pursue that goal but did not know how I was going to do it. A year or so later, God showed me a way.

College

I was just seventeen years old when I graduated from Spring Valley High School. I guess my parents were planning on sending me to college, but I think I feared leaving home and moving into academia as I did not consider myself a particularly good student. We talked about my future, and the folks wanted to know if I had considered farming. I believe my answer was that I did not like dairy farming as it tied one to the farm 24/7, and I did not see enough financial reward for staying on the farm. As neighbors over the years, we had some Norwegian bachelor farmers, and I was not impressed with their lifestyle. They did little to enjoy life, and I was just coming into my own, discovering girls and beer, so I decided to try college life.

I enrolled in Stout Institute, a Wisconsin State teacher's college for Industrial Arts and Home Economics, located sixteen miles east of the farm in Menomonie. The tuition was about $1,000 each semester, and I could live at home and drive to attend classes. Living at home was quickly voted down as winter would bring many days that the roads may not be passable, and we still did not have running water or a bathroom in our farmhouse. So, I rented a room in Lynwood Hall, the men's dormitory on Wilson Ave., right in the center of the college campus. I soon had a roommate, Don Koch, and many new friends from the surrounding states. I set up my part of the room with a bed, desk, and a high-fidelity music system consisting of a 45-rpm record player and a two-tube amplifier with a speaker. I could park my 1940 Chevy close by, and life was good.

Our dormitory supervisor was a middle-aged Psychology professor, Dr. Salyer, and he and his wife had an apartment just down the hall from my room. They were both great with ready advice about campus living and even studying. There was a cafeteria for food and a few beer joints that were student hangouts. I even pledged to the local FOB fraternity, which had its own house near my dorm. My study habits were extremely poor, and after the first semester, I had a session with the Dean, who advised me to get with it during the next semester or I would not be welcomed back. I managed mostly C and D grades, except for music, where I was pulling an A.

I was a member of the Stout Concert Band and even traveled with a brass quintet on an advertising tour for the school. I had a girlfriend, Mary Seppenan, a Catholic Finlander from Iron Mountain, Michigan. She was a sophomore who was living in the women's dorm off campus, about a mile from our dorm. The Chevy came in handy.

Living was getting expensive, so I took a job at Wally's Pure Oil filling Station in Menomonie. I was Wallace Lowery's only employee. It was a great job greeting the customers, filling their tanks, washing their windows, and collecting the money. I also got to change and repair tires and service the vehicles. The job looked great on my resume, as it showed I was responsible and honest. The station was close to campus on busy Highway 12 and Cresent Ave. I worked for a semester and then found a better-paying job with Wisconsin Dairies, the local creamery, as a cheesemaker's helper, making and packaging cottage cheese.

During that Summer, I continued working for the dairy, but this time as a raw milk input person, dumping and weighing milk as the milk hauler brought it in milk cans from the farmers. I had moved back home by then and had a long drive early in the morning to be to work on time. I sometimes got little sleep but was having a great time.

Another job I had during my time in Menomonie was with Anderson Dry Cleaners as their route driver, picking up and delivering cleaning using the business's Pontiac station wagon. I think Floyd Anderson was hoping I would become part of his business because I was dating his daughter, Carol, but I did not see the clothes cleaning service in my future.

Vocational School

The Only Child and His Brothers

My friend Dewey had now graduated from high school and was working in Minneapolis and courting the daughter of the Ford Dealership owner in Glenwood City, so we did not see much of each other. I decided that I would not go back to Stout and instead enrolled in a vocational school in Eau Claire, which was about thirty miles from home. I rented a room in a rooming house on 309 Dodge Street there and started to learn radio and television electronics at the Eau Claire Vocational School, which was just down the road from the Leinenkugel Beer Brewery. Very convenient.

Television was just coming into rural Wisconsin and Minnesota. There was WCCO TV in Minneapolis and WEAU TV in Eau Claire. I had only been in my course a few months when Reggie Meyer of Meyer Music at 412 South Barstow in Eau Claire hired me to help him sell and service TV sets to the farmers around the area. I took that as a part-time job setting up a portable crank-up TV antenna on his panel truck and running the antenna wire into the farmhouse where we had set up three 12-inch black and white round tube TV sets of different brands – Muntz, RCA, and GE were the most popular. The farmer would move the antenna clip from one set to the next, trying the three sets for about a week. Then the wife would pick the one she wanted, and I would put up a permanent antenna atop the house pointing to the single TV station, WEAU TV, in Eau Claire or the station in Minneapolis, whichever came in clearer. Those sets had many vacuum tubes that would fail, so I also got to go out on service calls, changing tubes and other parts. The farm wives loved TV - it was the best entertainment they experienced living out in the country. Reggie's marketing was foolproof. If the farmer would let him bring three TV sets into his house, the farmer's wife would only allow two to be removed. I was busy going to school and working for Meyer Music & TV.

Air Force Aviation Cadet

Life was interesting while I lived in Eau Claire. I was learning electronics and assembling the Heath Kit line of radios, televisions, electronic organs, test equipment, and ham radio equipment. I was living in a rooming house and eating most of my meals at a small diner downtown where the owner sold weekly meal tickets and monitored my eating habits, just like another mother.

I was now 18 years old and somewhat restless and still dating the young lady whose father owned the dry cleaner business located in the center of the Stout Institute campus. Carol, an only child, was still in high school but was a mature person who loved to look ahead at life's possibilities. Her parents were probably looking for her future husband to step into the family business, and I was uncomfortable with the prospects. One day, it all changed.

I was in the Menomonie Post Office one pretty morning in mid-February of 1954 when a young fellow in an Air Force Uniform approached me with one question. "Have you ever thought about becoming a pilot?" he asked me quite nonchalantly. He had my immediate attention. "I have" I replied, remembering Richard Bong and his Spring Valley airshow a few years prior, "but I have no idea how to go about being one." He smiled and said, "Do you have at least a year of college?" I replied that I did, but the grade point average was nothing to brag about. He said that did not matter. "Would you like to see if you qualify for the United States Air Force Aviation Cadet Program?" We discussed the requirements and how I would proceed to Chicago to take a battery of written and medical exams to see if I could qualify to enlist in the program. He said he would set me up for a train ride on the famous "400-passenger train" which made a stop in Menomonie to go to the Armed Forces Induction Center in Chicago for my testing. I did not take long to think about this offer. I signed up on the spot and was scheduled to depart the following week. I had no commitment to the Air Force and could renege on entry into the service even though I passed all the tests. Now came the hard part: telling my parents and friends what I was about to do. My Dad thought it was a good idea, but my mother burst into tears and said something about not wanting me to go. I boarded the 400 train in Menomonie and rode it to Chicago. It was my first train ride, and I was thrilled. The Air Force rep met me at the station and took me to the Armed Forces Entry Center in the city.

I spent the next few days taking written tests and, finally, a full medical exam. The last thing I had to pass was the weight requirement. I was about 6 feet tall and skinny. I believe I weighed in at 117 pounds, and the minimum for acceptance was 120. The sergeant at the scale told me to go next door to the commissary and buy a bunch of bananas, eat as many as I could, and then drink as much water as I could hold, and come back to get on the scale. Thirty minutes later, I weighed in at 121 pounds and passed the exam. It is possible that that fine sergeant put his foot on the scale – we will never know.

I had passed the Aviation Cadet entry tests and went back to Menomonie via the train. The recruiter told me I would be given a class entry date some months later. I was so excited about the thought of entering the Air Force that I asked him if I could not go in immediately. He said I could enlist now, go through basic training, and when I graduated from Basic Training, they would immediately assign me a Cadet Class, and I would start training at that time. I signed the papers that day, was told to get my affairs in order, and was to report to Hudson on May 4, 1954 (Dad's Birthday) to be sworn into the Air Force. I had only a few days to tell everyone goodbye.

My final week as a civilian was spent living at the farm and tying up loose ends. I had recently received a letter from the draft board telling me to plan on going into the Army in a few months. The Korean War had just ended, but the draft was still going at full speed, and my draft number had been drawn. I was now very motivated to get on with my new life.

Chapter Six

The Air Force Training Years Off We Go into

The Wild Blue.........

It was May 4, 1954, my dad's 57th birthday. Early that morning, he and Mother had driven me two miles from the farm to the bus depot in Wilson (Joe Carl's tavern).

The bus ride from Wilson to Hudson was uneventful and about one hour long. I was processed by the county at the St. Croix County Wisconsin Courthouse and put on another bus, which took me to the Armed Forces Processing Center in Minneapolis, MN. There, I raised my right hand and was sworn into the United States Air Force as an enlistee and given a flight to San Antonio, TX, and then taken to Lackland AFB, where I started Air Force Basic Training.

A Life Lesson

While awaiting my flight from Minneapolis, I had another life experience. I observed a Black man seated in the terminal. I had never seen a Black person before, and my curiosity overcame me. And I went over and sat by him and introduced myself. I do not recall his name, but he told me he was a porter on the railroad. We chatted for a few minutes, and I savored a new experience. One of many to come. I did not realize it at the time, but the U. S. Air Force had integrated about seven years earlier, and I was about to meet many blacker and browner-skinned men as we lived and trained together in Basic Training.

My first order, Letter Order No. 188, dated 4 May 1954, was issued from Headquarters Minneapolis Recruiting Main Station Detachment #9 5115 ASU Military Personnel Procurement Group, Minneapolis 1, Minnesota. I received my first airline ride that evening on Northwest Air Lines.

LACKLAND AFB

I landed at San Antonio International Airport in the early evening of May 4th and was met by an airman and transported by bus to the Lackland AFB Basic Training area. I was assigned to the 3700th Military Training Wing.

The old WWII two-story open bay barracks were to be my new home. I was bunked down for the night and, the next morning, met my Training Instructor, Airman Intelhouse. Over the next weeks, he taught us everything military, from making our beds to marching.

There were different races of men in our Flight, including Black people and Hispanics. We had men from all over the U.S., and I started to make friends. Some of these friends would be mine for the rest of my life. I remember two recruits with whom I formed a fast bond, Arthur Himple and Harold H. Harder. On our first off-base pass, we went into San Antonio and had a few beers. We then found a tattoo parlor and had a tat of wings and propeller with USAF on top and our first name on the bottom inked onto our left forearms.

The only remarkable thing about that idea was that we did not put any old girlfriends' names with it. As I write this seventy-plus years later, I look at the blob of faded color on my arm. Tattoos were legal in the Air Force during my tenure, but in the 1980s, they became illegal. Now, as I am writing this, in 2023, they have again become legal if they are not visible while in uniform. My tat now is barely recognizable. In 1954, we could have been court-martialed if it had become infected, but things worked out well.

I found basic training relatively easy. I was taught new things like military marching, setting up a uniform, doing kitchen patrol (KP), firing the M-1 rifle on a firing range, and qualifying by using bullseye targets, first aid, swimming, as well as basic academics. We took many aptitude tests, and I found that I could qualify for many fields such as mechanics, electronics, etc., but nothing would count as I was destined to go to Aviation Cadet Pilot Training as soon as I graduated from Basic.

My First USAF Graduation – One Stripe

That switch occurred on 30 July 1954. Most of us graduated from Air Force Basic Training with the rank of Airman Third Class (one stripe). I was told not to sew mine on my uniform as Aviation Cadets would wear their rank on their shoulder boards, and I was not to ruin my newly issued uniforms. On the fateful day that I graduated from basic training, I packed all my belongings into a duffle bag and walked across Lackland to the 3741st Training Squadron Aviation Cadet area. I had been selected for an assignment to Aviation Cadet Class 56-D.

LACKLAND AFB- AVIATION CADETS

In June of 1950, the North Koreans invaded South Korea. The US backed the government of South Korea and answered the call for help from South Korea. By the summer of 1951, it was apparent that the US was in for a long, tough war. It was also apparent that providing close air support to the ground troops was essential to the success of the ground war. That meant control of the skies over the battlefields. But the Air Force, after WWII, our country had allowed the service to degrade to a shadow of its former self, and it was not capable of providing this support without a crash program of pilot training and aircraft production.

The Aviation Cadet Program had started during WWII under the U.S. Army Air Corps and was again increasing in size as the USAF continued to produce pilots for this build-up in 1954. As an Aviation Cadet, I was going to be a part of this effort.

Aviation Cadet Class 56-D

The Lackland AFB Aviation Cadet area buildings were newer – again, two-story barracks but made of cement block with outside areas that were sharp and clean, and the grounds were decorated with colored rock patterns. I was now in USAF Pilot Training Class 56-D as an Aviation Cadet underclassman (an enlisted man paid at the rate of an airman first class – 3 stripes) and would have a lot of upperclassmen yelling at me and putting me in a physical brace with my arms tight against my side, my fists clenched, my chin on my Adam's apple with eyes locked forward. There were lots of "Yes Sir," "No Sir," and "No Excuse Sir" in the short answers I would give.

We, again, lived in open bay barracks. Our upper class taught us more military procedures, such as reporting to the water fountain with a salute saying, "Aviation Cadet Hanson reporting as ordered, Sir." I must admit that I did use that knowledge many times throughout my Air Force career when reporting to senior officers.

During cadet training, I met and became friends with an Air Force Sergeant from my hometown of Wilson by the name of Robert Shultz who was stationed there at Lackland. One weekend, he and his wife Liz brought me to their home in San Antonio for dinner. At that dinner, I was talking about the hazing I was experiencing, and he advised me to look at the hazing during my training as a game. I did, it was, and I got through it.

I was now in the Pre Flight part of Aviation Cadets and was retaught most of the same things that I had just learned in AF Basic with a few differences, like using a 45-caliber pistol instead of an M-1 rifle for weapons qualification. Due to my exposure to guns as a lad, I easily qualified as an Expert on both weapons. After six weeks of training as the underclass, a new group of Cadets arrived on 27 September 1954 – 56-G class.

We were now the upper class and got to do the yelling and hollering. This was teaching us to become leaders. As the saying goes – "To become a great leader, you must first learn how to follow."

As an Aviation Cadet in Pilot Training Class 56-D, I was scheduled to get my commission and wings on 18 November 1955. The weeks of training went fast, and at the end, about 40% of my class had flunked out or quit in the form of SIE (Self- Initiated Elimination), where you just had had enough of the hazing and other BS. These troops were sent back into the enlisted Air Force and fulfilled their four-year commitment to doing something other than flying airplanes.

I do not remember much fun during the Lackland days. We were kept terribly busy and had only a few passes to go into the city. No more tattoos as they were for the enlisted troops, and we were training to be commissioned officers – leaders.

Most new USAF pilots in the 1950s came from the ranks of Aviation Cadets. The remainder were college graduates from ROTC units and military schools such as the Military Academy (Army) and the Naval Academy. The Air Force Academy was just forming during this time period. I would not have qualified to become a member of that group due to the timing of my enlistment. I would meet these student officers in my next phase of training – Primary Flight School.

Graduation from Lackland AFB

After 26 weeks of two separate basic training courses, on 27 October 1954, I was given a short leave and went back home to Wilson, Wisconsin, to relax and visit. While there, I borrowed money from my dad to purchase a used 1952 Chevrolet 4-door sedan. It was dark green in color and had the standard Chevy six-cylinder engine, standard column shift, and a heater. On my way to my next assignment, Spence AFB, I stopped in Waukesha to pick up Aviation Cadet classmate Bob Cherwink and in Chicago to pick up Bob Hunt. They were both cadets who had served with me at Lackland AFB in the Preflight part of Pilot Training Class 56-D. We drove non-stop to our next assignment.

Chapter Seven
Flight Training SPENCE AB T-34

I got to my Primary Pilot Training Base, Spence Air Base, in Moultrie, GA, on 4 November 1954. Spence was a small civilian contract base located in the farmland of southeast Georgia. Lots of cotton, tobacco, and peanut fields and some wood but flat fields. It was called Spence Field in the WWII days, and the locals still name it after its past.

The base was constructed by the government in 1941 and used during WWII as a training base for single-engine Army Air Corps Advanced training. (P-40 aircraft). This training was discontinued by the Army Air Force in 1945, and the base was reopened in May of 1951 as a Primary Flight training base using the PA-18 (Piper Super Cub) and the North American T-6G. Both aircraft had tail wheels (tail draggers).

The base was a contract base operated by the Hawthorne School of Aeronautics with Bevo Howard, a well-known acrobatic show pilot, as the president. The instructors were civilians, and the check pilots were military officers. The support part of the base was civilian, including our dining facility and cadet club.

We lived again in the old WWII two-story barracks with two-man rooms and bunk beds. We marched to class, the flight line, and any other place we would go to as a group.

This was my first exposure to Southern living. The first time we marched over to chow at the dining hall, Mrs. Beulah Kilgore, Director of Food Service, briefed us Yankees on Southern food such as grits, collard greens, and black-eyed peas and how to properly eat them. The food was excellent but a bit foreign to this Wisconsin farm boy's palate.

Music

Our lives at Spence were now going to be more relaxed. Flying was now the major focus, and we were even going to have a regular day schedule with most weekends off. We now had time for extracurricular activities.

Throughout my young life, music kept popping up. I had been in the Drum and Bugle Corps at Lackland as a Bugler. One day, soon after my arrival at Spence, one of our Flight Instructors announced that he was forming a Cadet Marching Band for parade ceremonies and a dance band to play dances at our Cadet Club. I asked my parents to send me the coronet my cousin Morris Peterson gave me, and we got our band going. I remember playing Cadet dances and honor ceremonies when President Eisenhower arrived in Air Force One (a Super Constellation) en route to meetings and golf at an estate close to nearby Moultrie.

I recall performing (playing and marching in formation) for a graduation ceremony class when the base commander flew a T-33 exceptionally low overhead as we marched down the parade field. I now only remember my classmate Terry Crain playing trumpet with me in that band.

Recently, while doing research for this book, I had a phone conversation with Lloyd Stucke, who was also in the 56-G class and was the Cadet Band Captain of our group. I found his picture and many other cadet pictures in the 56-D and 56-G class books. Cadets with the white rope on their shoulders indicated they were in the band. There were 25 musicians in the marching band and 8-10 in the dance band. The band, without any professional players, may not have sounded the best, but what we lacked in talent, we made up for in enthusiasm.

Spence AB operations

The first weeks of training at Spence AB were academics. We studied flying regulations, weather, maps, flight instruments, navigation aids, and the mechanical workings of the Beech T-34 aircraft, which we were about to start flying.

Spence was transitioning to modern aircraft with nose wheels, and we were the first class to fly the T-34 Mentor aircraft. It was brand new and based on the popular Beechcraft Bonanza civil aircraft. We were issued the aircraft operating manual known as the Dash One. On the front cover was a picture of three T-34s flying in tight formation, climbing straight up. We were impressed! That impression would come back to haunt some of us later in the course.

We were assigned our instructor on our first day on the flight line. Mine was a civilian by the name of William High. He was also working as the safety leader for my squadron – Squadron One. Four students were assigned to each instructor. My fellow students were Aviation Cadet James Wood of Traverse City, MI; 2nd/Lt William Bargmann of Charleston, SC; and 2nd/Lt Charles Smith of Lake Charles, LA. These student officers had been commissioned through ROTC and had been on active duty for about six months.

None of us knew much about flying an airplane. We started the day by all sitting around a table in the briefing room and discussing what maneuvers we would be performing that day. Then, we would all go out to our assigned T-34 aircraft and preflight together.

The First Flight

Mr. High would then pick one of us to get in the front cockpit and go and fly for an hour or so. When they returned, the next student would jump in and do the same thing until all four had flown that mission.

I recall when my turn came, I got in, and the instructor taxied out and took off with me, lightly following along on the controls. We climbed out into the training area, and I was taught to clear the aircraft by looking all around for other airplanes. I was then given control of the bird and sat there, afraid to do anything. In a moment, my instructor told me to move the stick around to get a feel for flying, which I did. It was great! He taught me how to maintain a level flight by picturing the nose against the horizon. We then made turns, hopefully staying level. Then, a stall was demonstrated which was exciting as the aircraft went into a steep diving spin after it stalled, and I was taught how to recover. We then did some aerobatic maneuvers such as loops and rolls. Then, back to the field for a demonstrated landing pattern and landing. I was thrilled with my first Air Force flight and was now Gung–Ho, an official Junior Birdman.

The following weeks were spent continuing academics and flying. Each Flight was now mine to control. I did all the radio talking and flying unless the instructor felt I needed correction or something new was to be demonstrated.

Solo Flight

After twelve hours of dual instruction, the day came when we took off, did some air work, and came back into the traffic pattern and landed. That day, we had been bussed out to the Tifton, GA, auxiliary field about twenty miles from Moultrie. This was normal because with the whole squadron flying at the same time, the traffic pattern would get too crowded.

After the landing, I was told to stop on the taxiway, and Mr. High got out, secured his cockpit, and told me to go out, fly the pattern, make three landings, and then stop and pick him up. I soloed! It was a great feeling, and the plane seemed to fly easier without the guy in the back.

Being alone as the Pilot was a thrill. I was elated! And again, I knew that my friend Jesus was right beside me. It was a custom for the newly soloed Pilot to be thrown in the swimming pool, and that custom was conducted that day.

As the weeks rolled by, flying got to be more routine, with most of my flights being solo. One thing that was practiced repeatedly with the instructor was emergency landing procedures – engine failure forcing a landing after gliding without power. The steps were memorized and would be done without much thought – check the fuel tank, switch to the fullest tank, check outside for a suitable landing area, and start setting up an approach to the area. Retract the landing gear. If it is evident that the landing was not going to be on a runway, glide it down using the correct airspeed and make a normal landing. We practiced this over and over.

I always knew that flying was a dangerous occupation. Earlier in this book, I described witnessing an Army Air Corps B-25 crash and burn near our farm. It was my first experience with death. I still remember seeing the pilots' bodies strapped to their seats, smoldering from the fiery crash.

A classmate dies.

On February 21, 1955, I experienced a classmate's death at Spence AB. Aviation Cadet Howard Street, class 56-G, my under classmate, had recently soloed in the T-34 and was flying one of his first solo missions near the base when the engine seized, and the propeller broke off his aircraft. Oil from the front of the engine blew back over the windshield, and Howard, not being able to see very well, glided the aircraft toward the runway but was too far from the airport and could not make it to the runway. He tried to stretch his glide, stalled the aircraft, and it spun into the ground and burned.

One of my classmates, Bob Smith, Howard's roommate, and his instructor, Joe Poole, were stopped just short of the runway and witnessed the whole event. Howard had less than 15 flying hours and had not been trained to manage this type of emergency. A more experienced pilot may have bailed out of the aircraft or stuck his head out of the cockpit and glided to a crash landing outside the airport. I again realized that our emergency training was the most valuable training we were given, and aircraft accidents were part of life. I was tied to this situation as, in a week or so, I was to have my own crash landing.

Overconfident?

I had amassed around 40 hours of flying time in the T-34 and was starting to feel confident in my flying skills. I particularly enjoyed aerobatics, where you could do some wild flying. I remembered that picture in the front of our flying manual showing the T-34 climbing vertically, so I decided to try it on one of my solo missions. I cleared my area and went into a dive to gain airspeed as I would do starting the loop maneuver. I allowed the aircraft to climb straight up instead of pulling up and over the top as in a loop. I soon found out that even at full power, the engine was not powerful enough to keep climbing. After climbing about a thousand feet, it fell backward, went into a stall, and fell sideways into a spin. I was terribly busy for the next few moments recovering from the spin. I got reorientated and flew back to the base. I was still shaking when I crawled out of the bird after making a shaky but safe landing at home base.

It was quite a while before I shared that experience with any of my classmates, and I never told my instructor, although I should have been indebted to him for teaching me to spin recovery. I mentioned this experience to my fellow student pilots while at the bar one evening just before we graduated from Spence. A few of them said: "Wow, you tried it too?" I guess we all had the same curious minds and were not afraid to experiment with our new toys.

The twelve weeks of training in the T-34 had gone smoothly, and I was looking forward to starting training in the next aircraft, the T-28. On January 27, 1955, t*he day of my final Flight in the T-34, my world changed again. I needed a total of 40 flying* hours in the T-34 before entering the next phase of primary flight training in the new, larger fighter-type aircraft, the North American T-28 Trojan.

The Accident

I was flying solo out of one of the auxiliary airports - Tifton Field in T-34, tail number 53-3345 - logging my fortieth flying hour practicing aerobatics and other basic maneuvers. This would be my final Flight in the T-34.

Approaching the airport for my final landing, I was on a 45-degree entry to the traffic pattern at Tifton Field and had just lowered my landing gear when all hell broke loose.

The engine blew up, and I lost all power. The prop was still turning slowly, so I lowered the nose to maintain airspeed and looked for a place to make a crash landing. I was losing altitude rapidly as the landing gear was extended. When I started through the engine failure checklist, which I had memorized, I almost heard my instructor, Mr. High, telling me what to do. I raised the landing gear and turned toward the airport, but it was obvious that I was too low to make the runway, so I made a smooth landing straight ahead in a cotton field with the landing gear retracted. I slid through a barbwire fence that was the airport boundary and came to a quick stop just inside the airport boundaries. After turning off all the switches, I got out of the plane and was standing by the nose when the fire trucks arrived. Since there was no fire, there was little for the firefighters to do, so they had me pose for pictures.

A Bent Airplane

The wing was dented when I took out a fence post, and the tail was damaged by the barbed wire that was part of the fence. The prop was bent back. There were some scratches from the wire fence, and the engine had come apart with pieces laying on the top of the engine.

The safety director gave me a ride to the operations building, and I got to ride the bus back to Spence. The end of a remarkably interesting day!

End of my career

The Air Force required an accident investigation, so I was now going to be given several medical exams to see if my physical condition had caused the accident. This took me to Moody AFB, a major USAF base near Valdosta, GA, about fifty miles away. Eye exams, hearing exams, and many other exams were the order of the day.

An accident evaluation board was convened, and all of this took time. I had completed the T-34 part of Primary training and should have started the T-28 training right away, but it did not happen. The Air Force did not wash me out because the engine had failed, and it was not my fault. The accident board did find that if I had raised the landing gear as soon as the engine failed, I might have been able to land within the confines of the airport, but that was speculation, and I had only 40 hours of flying time.

I was commended for making a successful gear-up landing and washed back to my underclass, 56-G. Ironically, I was assigned to fill the vacancy on Civilian Flight Instructor Joe Pool's group that Aviation Cadet Howard Street had left vacant when he was killed.

The Rule of Three

It is said that aircraft accidents happen in groups of three. Spence AB had its third on 6 April 1955. Mr. Norman Joy, a civilian flight instructor with my old class 56-D, crashed on a night training mission. The T-28 he was flying caught on fire, and he ordered his student to bail out. The student survived, but Mr. Joy stayed with the aircraft until it crashed and burned, taking Norman Joy's life. Those three accidents occurred within a month's time while I was stationed at Spence. Two had fatalities, and the third was mine – not even a scratch!

T-28 SPENCE- Link Trainer

As we started training in the T-28 aircraft, we also started learning how to fly on instruments. We had many hours of ground school instrument flying theory, and now it was time to put it to use. The first step was flying the Link Trainer, a box that simulated an airplane with controls and instruments. The machine was mounted on a hydraulic system that caused it to twist, turn, and spin around. We got our first taste of vertigo and motion sickness and never left the ground.

It was a basic flight simulator that was developed during WWII. It concentrated on flying blind (on instruments) and using radio navigation aids to fly point to point and make approaches to the airport. These machines had been around since the forties and did a remarkable job of preparing a student to step into a real aircraft and actually fly it on instruments.

My T-28 group.

My new flying group was made up of 2/Lt Herschel Alpwein, A/C Art Himpele (now my roommate), and A/C Ed Sheldon and Joe Poole as the Flight Instructor.

The T-28 was much larger than the T-34 and had a seven-cylinder radial engine made by the Maytag Company. The Maytag

Company started out in the 1930s manufacturing washing machines with little 2-cycle gasoline engines. (My clothes were washed in a Maytag gasoline-powered washing machine as I grew up since we had no electricity on the farm.) The Maytag engine caused the Air Force version of the T-28 to be considered underpowered and not very reliable. The Navy had the same aircraft but with a larger engine and a three-bladed propeller. They used it for training pilots to fly on and off aircraft carriers.

I continued to have no problems with my flying but had a couple of maintenance problems. The first occurred on one of my first dual missions with my instructor, Mr. Poole. We came into the landing pattern, and the landing gear lever would not go to the down position. It was mechanically jammed in the UP position. After trying several things to loosen it, Mr. Poole told me to get out of my parachute harness, climb up on the top of the instrument panel, and jump on the handle. He said if we were going to land gear up, at least we would have tried everything we could to get the handle to go down. I did that while he flew the airplane, and the handle went down, and we landed safely.

Carbon Monoxide

Some weeks later, while I was solo on a cross-country trip, I began to feel dizzy and ill. I radioed an instructor who was orbiting one of our checkpoints, and he told me to open the canopy and put my head into the slipstream to breathe fresh air. I did and immediately began to feel better, which allowed me to finish my trip and return to Spence. After I had landed, the maintenance folks came over and discovered a baggage door that was under and behind the exhaust of the aircraft had lost its gasket and was allowing carbon monoxide to enter the cockpit. Had we not taken the actions we did, I would have died on that flight. God was again with me.

The T-28 had an unusual spin. It would be spinning, and when recovery was initiated, it would tighten its spiral for three more turns before it would break and recover. That and its Maytag heritage made it a good transition platform for advancing to single-engine jet aircraft.

The remaining time I spent at Spence was honing my skills and finally taking and passing a check ride with one of our Military Pilot Evaluators. Most of us student pilots wanted to go on to the T-33 jet in our next phase. The check ride given by the military evaluators rated you as qualified for single-engine jets, and I was one of the pilots who qualified. I, however, had been thinking about eventually becoming an airline pilot and opted to go to multi-engine training. So, on July 23, 1955, I graduated from Primary flight school at Spence AB and moved on to Basic flight school at Vance AFB north of Oklahoma City, arriving there on 2 August 1955.

Spence Field in my rearview mirror

What were my experiences at Spence? We continued our military training by living in barracks with bunk beds, room inspections, and the odd open ranks personal inspection. We found out that the military is concerned about you spiritually. We were encouraged to take part in chapel programs, including ushering at Sunday services. Chaplain Miller was a friend to us all and helped us transition to more mature thinking and, in my case, expanding my personal relationship with God. I was raised a child of God, and now my belief was greatly strengthened. On the less spiritual side, I grew closer in my relationships with my classmates. We were all going through a trying time in our lives and were experiencing shared trials and tribulations.

We had opportunities to travel together to Florida beaches on weekends and got a firsthand introduction to beach parties. I got introduced to "moonshine" liquor by a couple of my Buds who were from this part of the country where stills were operated at large. I found that "White Lightning" needed to be taken in small sips and greatly respected. I had a lot of experience with beer back in college and found that it was a much better choice for me.

Our Cadet Club, where we could legally buy beer, got us into socializing with the young ladies of the area who were trolling for husbands. Even though I normally played in the dance band, I met some local girls. Two sisters who had a father who was the mayor of Moultrie. They had interesting southern names – Hopesie and

Hulaine. I was invited, along with a couple of classmates, to parties at their apartment in downtown Moultrie. These were classy events that demonstrated true southern hospitality. I was impressed. I never had a serious relationship as I aimed to get my wings and commission, and there was no time or money for a serious girlfriend. I enjoyed the Southern culture and style of living as I found the locals very friendly and inviting. Overall, Spence was a beautiful introduction to the USAF and opened a window to my future.

Chapter Eight
Advanced Pilot Training VANCE AFB – North American B-25

I drove my green Chevy to Vance AFB in June 1955. This was the final six-month part of pilot training, which was called Basic Multi-Engine Pilot Training.

Vance AFB has a long history of flight training. As I write this in 2023, Vance is still an active pilot training base as it has been since 1941. The base website says that Vance has now issued pilot wings to over 35,000 military officers. The base is fifty-five miles north of Oklahoma City, next to the town of Enid.

The B-25 Bomber

I was assigned there to learn how to fly a multi-engine aircraft, the North American B-25 Mitchel bomber. The B-25 was the aircraft that Lt. Col. Jimmy Doolittle placed on the Navy aircraft carrier Hornet after the December 7, 1941, Japanese attack on Pearl Harbor to retaliate by attacking the Japanese mainland. The aircraft performed well, and most of the bombers bombed Japan.

After WWII, this aircraft was used to train us fledgling aviators how to fly a two-engine aircraft. It had been stripped of its machine guns and bomb equipment, so it was light and powerful, and it was the same type of aircraft that had crashed and burned near our farm when I was about 10 years old.

Vance AFB

The base was modern compared to Spence, and we were assigned to 2-man rooms. Freddie Pennel was my roommate. We first started academic training to learn B-25 operating systems and now would learn advanced instrument flying along with the 60-4 Air Force Flying Regulations. We would also learn how to fly close formation flying.

As Aviation Cadets, we still marched to classes in formation, but things were a bit more relaxed. We still had the upper/lower class supervising system, but we had relief such as cars and the Cadet Club, which gave us more freedom to enjoy ourselves while not flying or going to academics.

My Flight Group

My flying group was made up of a military flight instructor, Lt. Bruce Rauhe, myself, and three other cadets -John (Spike) Helmers, Jerry Hoppe, and Bob Hunt. First, we each got checked out as aircraft commanders in the aircraft flying in the left seat. After that, Lt Rauhe would fly dual with one of us, and the other two would fly formation in a separate plane, trading off as the left seat pilot in command.

Flying the beast

I think the hardest thing to learn about the B-25 was how to taxi and maneuver it on the ground. It had a free pivoting nose wheel, and one had to use split engine power and individual wheel brakes to make it go where you wanted it. It was quite amusing to see the new class trying to get to the runway for takeoff. A lot of arm waving and cussing in the cockpit caused the plane to drunkenly zigzag down the taxiway.

In the air, with both engines running, the bird flew quite well; however, the loss of an engine would cause the beast to turn into a dead engine, which had to be immediately counteracted by the application of lots of opposite rudders. We then had to learn how to identify the bad engine and shut it down by feathering the propeller. Shutting down the wrong engine would turn the craft into a glider and cause more arm waving and cussing. We learned to stall and spin the aircraft, but no aerobatics. The goal was to fly straight and level and land and take off without too many deviations. The most fun we had was close formation flying, where we would tuck a wing into a position about 15 feet from the other aircraft. We got surprisingly good at it, and I remember flying copilot for Jerry when he got too close and seeing Lt Rauhe's eyes get really big when he saw us about 3 feet away in a tight jet-like formation. Again, arm waving and cussing, this time over the radio. I can still see Jerry sitting there grinning and thinking how sh** hot a pilot he was.

We did not have too many other interesting events during the

B-25 training at Vance. We flew a lot without the instructor - I'm sure it started giving us confidence that we truly were pilots and that we could get ourselves out and about and back home without any major problems. The B-25 was a good old aircraft – older than we were, and I never heard of an engine failure. We did, however, have one of our classmates land while forgetting to put down the landing gear and, one night, when we were about to finish the course, we had a bad windstorm come up while we were out practicing night flying, and the whole area went to very poor visibility. We had to use our instrument flying ability and lots of luck to find the base and get on the ground. Again, no mishaps but lots of anxious moments, which simply added to our confidence to show that we were getting to be seasoned pilots.

A DRY State

We had more free time now and found more time to sit around the Cadet Club or wander downtown and even go to Oklahoma City (OKC) for an evening. Oklahoma was a dry (no alcohol) state, and most of us were partial to a beer or two now and then.

I remember getting to OKC one afternoon and checking into a hotel for the weekend. We needed some beer and were told that if we asked a policeman where to get some, he would help. We did, and he pointed out an old brick building near our motel. We knocked on the door and, lo and behold, we bought beer. You just never know.

Women

I was now dating occasionally and had met this young lady at the Club one evening. Edna Smith was the daughter of the Enid postmaster, had recently graduated from high school, and was obviously looking for a husband. The Cadet Clubs were a great feeding ground for the eligible girls in the local area. We had a few dates, but I was not ready to settle down just yet. My idea had always been to have an excellent job before marriage and a family. Edna must have wondered about my intentions as she fixed me up with her younger sister for a date. None of this worked out for them, although Edna pinned my wings at graduation.

Pilot Training Graduation

Most of my classmates were on board for the long haul by this time in our training. My roommate, Fred Pennel, had a hearing problem from the noisy prop spinning just outside the window on the B-25. The exhaust manifold on the B-25 engine was made up of short pipes coming directly out of the cylinders and produced a very intense noise. We were wearing WWII headphones, which did little to attenuate the sound, and Freddie's ears could not take it. He was grounded until things settled down, and he started wearing better ear coverings. He graduated with me on January 19, 1956.

Now my life has really changed. Many of the goals I set some years ago have been met. I have now been in the USAF for nearly 2 years, using my one year of college, albeit a shaky one, to qualify for the program I have just completed. That is - I was a commissioned 2nd Lieutenant and awarded my coveted USAF pilot wings.

I own a new car, my 1956 Olds 88, and I have managed to stay single. I just turned 21 years old!

1956 – A GREAT YEAR

The year 1956 will stick in my mind forever. It was a historical year. It started out big but was going to get much more interesting with many milestones. Air Training Command is over. I am going to fly multi-engine aircraft in the Strategic Air Command - SAC - and my next aircraft is the B-29 at Randolph AFB – THE REAL AIR FORCE.

Chapter Nine

The Real Air Force

It seemed to be a tradition, although possibly a dumb one, that newly commissioned officers needed new automobiles. I had been driving my 1952 green four-door Chevy since I graduated from Basic Training and Preflight at Lackland, and to me, it was a Wisconsin farmer's family car – not cool. Many of my classmates had made some good deals with the General Motors Oldsmobile dealer in Woodward, Oklahoma, about 35 miles west of Enid. I lost my mind and took my Chevy down and came back with a spanking brand new 1956 blue and white Oldsmobile 88 two-door hard top. I had been impressed with the Oldsmobile since one whizzed by me one night in Wisconsin while I was driving my 1940 Chevy at a high rate of speed (70mph?) near Knapp, WI, on US Highway 12. The Rocket 88 engine came out in 1952, and it was a powerful V-8 compared to my little Chevy 6-cylinder. I was unable to catch it.

I now own one, along with car payments of about $50/month for 36 months. Trading in my old Chevy took care of the down payment, and the Valley National Bank of Tucson was very willing to lend a new USAF Second Lieutenant the needed funds. I was in tall clover. Free, white, single, and 21 (I had my 21st birthday 12 days prior to my commissioning) and now was ready to take on the world.

Prior to taking on the next Air Force hurdle, I had earned a long leave. At the urging of my parents, my classmate Freddie Pennel and I drove my new Olds down to Houston, TX, to visit with my cousin Genevieve Turner and her family. Genevieve was related through the Hanson side of the family; my Dad's Aunt Bertha had married A.M. Johnson and Genevieve was their daughter. She and her parents had always kept close touch with my mom and dad and were probably responsible for changing my middle name from Linden (a tree) to Lyndon (a Texas congressman and future president). My parents had always said that the Texas relatives named me.

On the way to Houston, we stopped in New Orleans to enjoy Mardi Gras. My cadet classmates Fred Pennel, Spike Helmer, and one who was from that area - Russ Krogsgard - met us there, and we attended a parade or two drank some beer, and then Fred and I departed to Houston and finally to Randolph AFB, arriving there on 14 February 1956.

RANDOLPH AFB B-29

My first operational assignment was to be a KC-97 Tanker pilot in the Strategic Air Command (SAC). Scuttlebutt had me going to a new base - Limestone AFB Maine (later to be called Loring AFB)- to be part of a new SAC Wing of B-47 bombers and KC-97 tankers. It was to be the closest SAC base to the USSR, which would be in our cross hairs if a nuclear war ever broke out. This would be my entry into the "Cold War." More on this later.

I did not have official orders at this time, so my final assignment was a moot point. Now, I had to complete Advanced Training, which found me at San Antonio and the historic Randolph AFB. I would learn 4 engine flying using the Boeing B-29 Bomber, the same type that dropped the atom bombs on Japan to end WWII.

I was pleased with this assignment because the airlines used four- engine airplanes, and I would soon be a qualified multi-engine pilot; in fact, I had already received my Commercial CAA Pilots License, giving me the ability to fly multi-engine airplanes on instruments and be paid for the job. The date of my first Civil Aviation Administration (CAA) license was 4-5-1956.

Operations

I, and many of my past classmates, arrived at Randolph AFB and immediately started ground school and check outs in the B-29. Another 56-G grad, Chuck Templin, and I became close friends at Vance AFB, and we now hung out together. Chuck, like me, had recently purchased a new car. His was a 1955 red and white Chevy two-door hardtop. It was a chick magnet.

Chuck Templin was assigned to a different training crew than me and took a flight on April 3rd-1956 that proved to be memorable to all of us young B-29 pilots. These training flights were designed to familiarize us with the problems of flying a large four-engine aircraft. These crews were made up of three pilots, an instructor, and two students, plus a flight engineer and two scanners. The sole purpose of these flights was to demonstrate the intricacies of flying large machines and the emergency procedures, such as flying with an engine shutdown or engine failure or fire in flight.

B-29 Crash

On April 3rd, 1956, Chuck and his crew were flying low around San Antonio, and all three pilots were experiencing flying on three engines (they had the throttle on an outboard engine back in the idle position simulating a failed engine) and were busy in the cockpit and not paying much attention to where the plane was headed or the altitude. They allowed the aircraft to descend so low that they hit radio station WOAI's transmission tower (which stood about four hundred feet above the ground). The impact was taken head-on with the number three engine and forced the B-29 to crash straight ahead and, of course, knocked the tower down. Fortunately, there were no houses or people on the ground in the impact zone. The plane hit the ground, bounced back into the air, and then came down and slid about one thousand feet before catching on fire. The pilots were wearing parachutes and managed to exit through the front windows, jump to the ground, and run from the aircraft.

Chuck, who was sitting in the jump seat (a small seat

between the pilots) when they hit the tower, jumped up and had the engineer lower the nose gear in preparation for a bailout. He lifted the floor hatch, which was behind the nose gear, looked outside, and determined they were too low to bail out. A moment later, the aircraft struck the ground and slid along the field with its loose dirt, which came billowing up through the open entry hatch and covered Chuck and the cockpit with thick dust. As soon as the airplane slid to a stop, Chuck followed the co-pilot through the right sliding window. This window was only about 18" square, and Chuck, who was 6'4' tall and weighed in at 200 plus pounds, got through it with a parachute on his back. Unfortunately, one of the crew members in the back of the airplane decided to jump out on the first impact and was killed when he hit the ground while the aircraft was still in the air. The aircraft burned after the impact, and WOAI was off the air for some time after the accident (see newspaper story). The lesson we pilots learned was to assign one pilot to fly the aircraft while the others worked on the emergency.

Chuck, Me and Two Girls

Chuck and I had another interesting situation (a life-changing event for me!) occur during our assignment to Randolph Field. Just outside the main gate of the base was a drive-in BBQ diner called the Bun and Barrel Restaurant. One day, Chuck and I had gone to the B&B in his Chevy to get a sandwich. As we sat in the car eating, two young ladies pulled in beside us, and, of course, we started a conversation. After some time of chatting, Chuck decided we had places to go, so we bid our new friends goodbye and proceeded down the road. A mile or so down the road, I recognized this old Plymouth coming up behind us and told Chuck that we had better pull over as our new-found lady friends, Leah and Betty, still wanted to chat. About 30 minutes later, Chuck and I had arranged to meet the girls at Betty's boarding house (Mrs. Anthony's home) the next day for a date night.

At the appointed day and time, Chuck and I arrived at Mrs. Anthony's house and were invited in to meet Betty's landlady. After 20 minutes of pleasantries, it was time to go, so Leah, Betty's Jewish friend who was a good-looking gal about five feet eight, and I went out the door and crawled into the backseat of Chuck's car, and Betty – a five-foot-four cute little brunette - got in the right front seat. Chuck – six feet four, came along and looked in the car and remarked that we were mismatched and suggested that Betty get in the back with me and Leah upfront. So, we proceeded out that evening in that manner.

Betty and I hit it right off, particularly when we found that we were both from Wisconsin (born about 100 miles apart) and that we were both of the Lutheran persuasion. After that evening, Betty (real name Elizabeth Ann) and I started frequent dating. She obviously was impressed with my being an Air Force pilot and my sharp blue and white Oldsmobile two-door hard top. I was impressed that she was cute, out on her own, had a well-paying job, and certainly was an independent person. (Funny Fact: I had to borrow $20 from her on our first solo date – it must have been just before payday, and I had a car payment! I did the honorable thing, of course, and paid her right back). The weeks flew by, and as I was progressing with my B-29 training, Betty and I were getting to be close friends but had not addressed marriage.

One day in late April, Betty told me about her sister Joanne and her family, who lived in the small town of Alpine in West Texas on the Mexican border. Joanne had invited us to come over for the following weekend so I could meet them. Joanne's husband, Charlie, was an FBI agent, and they had two young daughters, Chris and Candy. Not having anything better to do and looking for a chance to take a trip in the Olds, I said OKAY. Little did I imagine what skullduggery Betty and her sister were up to.

Alpine, Texas

We arrived in Alpine late in the afternoon, around dinner time. We were just getting out of the car when Joanne, Charlie, and their two young girls came rushing out of the house, telling us that they had an engagement they had to attend but for us to go on in, and there was food and drink for us to enjoy, and they would be back later in the evening.

They left, and we went inside to discover a cozy fire and a great meal and wine. Even then, I did not realize what was happening – I was being led down the long path to matrimony – just like a lamb - and I was one happy fellow. My life was coming together, and my future was very bright. When the Hess family got back from their "engagement," they were the first to know that Betty and I had just put together an engagement of our own.

Speed Trap

The trip back to San Antonio from Alpine also had an interesting twist. It was dark as we crossed the desolate West Texas desert, and the Olds was cruising effortlessly at the speed limit of 65 mph. A car came up on us from the rear and started to pass and then held parallel, matching our speed, and then accelerated rapidly away. That got my goat, and I immediately accelerated and caught up and tried to pass. I suppose we were doing 80 or 90 when he let me go by. He followed me a short way and then turned on his red and blue police lights. Betty thought that we were being hijacked, but I knew that we had fallen into a Texas speed trap. We were the only cars on this isolated stretch of highway for many miles. I stopped, and a smiling West Texas Sherriff checked out my license and wrote me a ticket. He then told me to follow him to the next town and the Justice of the Peace. We stopped in Sanderson, Texas, and I went into this small office to find some good ole boys sitting around a warm, potbellied wood stove. One of them, the Justice of the Peace, was sitting with his feet propped up on the old stove. He told me what my fine was to be - $78.00 - and I told him I did not have that much cash. He said not to worry since I was an Air Force Officer, and he trusted me to send it to him when I got back to my base. That put a damper on Betty's and my exuberance, but we made it back in one piece.

Ass Chewing

The next week, my Squadron Commander called me into his office and told me that we both had a meeting with the Commanding General on the subject of my speeding ticket. The General was not happy (or was pretending that he was unhappy), and I was scared. This was my very first meeting with a two-star (Major General), and he acted like a nasty bugger. I think he chewed on my Squadron Commander more than me, but it may have been a set up for my benefit. Who knows? I survived the ass-chewing from the two-star and got back flying the B-29. Betty and I were together as much as possible- NO, we did not co-habitat or sleep together. This was against the mores of this period of American history. We were "almost" prudish!

Get Married?

I went downtown San Antonio and bought Betty's engagement ring, which I gave her at a park in San Antonio the next week, and now we were officially engaged. Betty flashed that ring at anyone who might be in eyesight, and we started planning our life together.

We first set the wedding date – June 16, 1956, and the church would be Betty's home church in Superior, WI - Pilgrim Lutheran. We knew that I had, after this B-29 school, a KC-97 orientation school in West Palm Beach, Fl, to get under my belt before we headed to our assignment, but the dates lined up, and the wedding would fit right in the schedule. I gave myself about a week from the end of school in Florida to drive to Superior and make the wedding date.

I also received my permanent assignment. Not the cold Limestone AFB but Kindley AFB on the island of Bermuda. Bermuda is straight East of South Carolina, about 800 miles. It has a balmy climate, i.e., no snow!

Palm Beach & South Range

I completed B-29 training on March 21. April 1 was Easter Sunday, and the two of us attended a Lutheran church in downtown San Antonio. A few days later, I left San Antonio for West Palm Beach to start KC-97 school. Betty, who was working as the head Secretary for the Fox Photo Finishing Company, quit work and took the Greyhound bus to her parents' home south of Superior, Wisconsin. She lived with her folks there and found a part-time job while planning the wedding.

KC-97 Tanker

I started KC-97 transition school at West Palm Beach AFB, Florida, on April 11, 1956. My school was interesting, and I found it easy. We flew again with three pilots, including an instructor, and simply learned how to manage a heavy, slow-reacting large aircraft. Some of our aircraft were C-97s without a boom for air refueling, and we were told that the KC-97 tanker would fly just like the cargo version and that we would have no trouble becoming tanker pilots once we got to our permanent assignments. We also attended ground school on the KC-97 systems. The KC-97 airplane had four Pratt and Whitney R- 4360, 3500 horsepower radial engines, the most powerful made. Its wingspan was 141 feet, and it could transfer 8500 gallons of jet fuel to a B-47 bomber. The maximum weight was 175,000 lbs.

A flight engineer was part of the crew, and his job was to watch all the engine instruments such as oil pressure, fuel pressure and quantity, cylinder head temperatures, propeller RPM etc. He also had his own set of throttles and propeller controls, and his seat was directly behind those of the pilots. Managing these engines was more than two pilots could be expected to do and still fly the airplane.

The normal KC-97 tanker crew was 2 pilots, 1 navigator, 1

flight engineer, 1 boom operator and a radio operator. The boom operator and radio operator would act as scanners when they were not doing their assigned duties. The KC-97 had a flying boom on the back of the fuselage where the Boom Operator would lie on a board and fly the boom with controls on each side of the board. He could see the bomber through a window and talk to the bomber via a UHF radio.

The bomber had to fly a close formation with the tanker and was, for the bomber, flying slow at about three hundred mph. The 97 was flying as fast as it would go and sometimes had to go into a descent to increase the speed so the bomber would not stall. It took a lot of skill for both flight crews to complete a safe midair refueling.

The KC-97 airplane was based on the Boing B-29 but had a larger fuselage and more powerful engines. It started flying in 1948 and was used (C-97) in Korea as a medical evacuation aircraft. Boeing built 811 KC-97 tankers during the period 1948 – 1958.

I thought it was a great Boeing airplane.

A change of plans

I found out during the first week of class that I had an additional Boom school at Hunter AFB in Georgia to attend after completing this one. This put a big crimp in the wedding plans as I would be in this school on June 16th.

Being young and naïve, I called Betty and told her of the problem and stupidly said that I would not be there for the wedding, thinking, I guess, that it (the wedding) could easily be moved back a week or so. WELL, that did not go over particularly well in Superior, WI. Agnes, Betty's mom, said, "He probably doesn't want to get married", and that set off a terrible kerfuffle. One of Ag's friends suggested she call the American Red Cross and see if they could intervene and have the Air Force send me home on emergency leave. So, she did.

Embarrassing

I was sitting in class the next day with all my fellow student pilots around me when this young airman walked into the classroom and asked if there was a Lieutenant Hanson there and when I raised my hand, he said, (in front of the whole class), "The Red Cross called to say that you have to go home and get married"! Well, you can imagine the uproar in that classroom. I think there was laughing and snickering going on for the rest of the day. Well, the Air Force had a solution.

Marriage June 16, 1956

I completed the KC-97 school at West Palm Beach on June 9, 1956, and immediately drove to Hunter AFB and started the Boom school. I went on emergency leave on June 14 and flew to Minneapolis and was met by Betty and her parents, Waino and

Agnes Juntti. We drove to their farm south of Superior, Wisconsin, and I spent the next two days getting to know my soon-to-be in-laws.

My future father-in-law was Waino William Juntti. He was 58 years old and sailed the Great Lakes for the Pittsburg Steel Company, serving as a crewmember on an ore boat that transported iron ore from the Mesabi Iron Range in northern Minnesota to the various steel mills located on all the Great Lakes. Waino was a Finlander, born and grew up on a farm near Brule, Wisconsin, and had two brothers and three sisters from that area. Both of his parents immigrated from Finland. Waino loved coffee and cigarettes and was quite bald but had a good sense of humor. My new mother-in-law was Agnes Marie Anderson Juntti. Her parents had also immigrated from Finland and had settled in Superior, Wisconsin, and eventually on a forty-acre farm in South Range. Ag had two sisters and two brothers. She had become a teacher early in her life using a "one-year rural certificate" and taught school in Washington State during WWII when Waino worked at the shipyards in Bremerton, WA. After many years of raising a family, teaching school, and taking courses, she finished her bachelor's degree at Superior State College (now the University of Wisconsin Superior) in the Summer of our marriage in 1956. She finished her teaching career in Maple, Wisconsin, where she taught first and second grade for many years. In her earlier teaching career, she had taught Richard Bong, the WWII P-38 fighter ace, when he was in elementary school in Poplar, WI.

The Juntti's had three girls, Joanne, Betty and Mary. Betty was the last to marry and that made this marriage a major event. Note that the Richard Bong mentioned in this past paragraph was the same Richard Bong who put on the airshow with the P-38 that day in Spring Valley and got me all hot to be an Air Force pilot – small world.

The wedding was attended by my parents and many of Betty's relatives. It was in Betty's home church, Pilgrim Lutheran, a beautiful church in downtown Superior. My groomsmen and I wore formal white jackets and dark trousers. Since I was an only child, I asked my best friend Dewey Wienke to be my best man and Betty's sister Mary's husband Jerry Bourassa to be the groomsman. Betty's bridesmaid was her friend Pauline Gustafson and Betty's sister, Mary, the Matron of Honor. Betty wore the same dress that Mary had worn eight months prior.

The wedding party was small. The service was simple and short, but as part of the ceremony, I had to repeat my vows orally, and I was scared shitless. I had never done any speaking in public, and this was a tense situation. I guess Dewey and Jerry kept me calm, but I was very nervous.

Wedding Day, June 16th, 1956

The day had started early, with me having to leave the Juntti house and go to the Bourassa's to bathe and dress. I had not slept well on the couch at Juntti's house and had not been part of any of the planning, so everything was new and strange.

During the ceremony, I managed to croak out the right words, and with the support of my groomsmen, I survived.

There was a reception in the church basement after the service, and I got to meet a lot of new people that suddenly were my relatives. I do remember one of Betty's uncles asking me when he found out we were going to live in Bermuda if we were going to drive!

We did not have a car in Superior as I had left our Oldsmobile with Whitney Sullivan in Florida. So, we had to hitch a ride wherever we went. I do remember that my new in-laws, Ag and Waino, threw a party at their home in the country south of Superior and that the wind started blowing off Lake Superior, and the temperature dropped many degrees to the point that it was very cool- notice I said cool- you save the description of cold for the winter season when it can go many degrees below zero. Now, for a couple who had just lived for a couple of years in the South, the temperature was damned cold!

Wedding night

Betty and I had failed to plan for a place to spend our wedding night, so we borrowed her parents' car and drove 10 miles to downtown Duluth and checked in to the Hotel Duluth. This was an old dirty building that had seen better days. We were given a room with twin beds, but that made no difference. It was our first night together, and we were blissful.

Honeymoon?

The next day, June 17, was Father's Day, and we had to rush back to "the farm", Ag and Waino's home, where we visited the site of last night's party. Waino said they drank up everything but the Clorox, so it must have been a great time. We spent the next couple of days visiting friends and relatives and then flew from Duluth to Miami on June 19th to pick up our Oldsmobile. A new friend, Captain Whitney Sullivan, and his family were also being assigned to the 303rd Air Refueling Squadron in Bermuda and had volunteered to drive our car to Miami as they were going on leave in Florida.

Back to Duty, June 19th, 1956

We stayed overnight in Miami at the Fontainebleau Hotel and drove the next day to Savannah, GA, and signed in again on June 20 at Hunter AFB to complete the Boom school. While at Hunter AFB, Betty became an official Air Force wife by completing a lot of paperwork which involved producing our new marriage license and then receiving her official dependents Military Identification Card. We stayed on base and dined at the officer's club for the three days that covered the school and left Hunter AFB for Wisconsin on June 23, 1956. On our way back to Wisconsin, we stopped in Chicago to visit with my cousin Youland and her husband, Ed Gueruink. She and Ed had adopted three lovely children and, as Ed was a stockbroker, had done quite well. They had a beautiful home.

We believe that it was after a nice dinner and drinks with them that we conceived our son Steven.

Back to Wilson, my old home

Another day's drive found us in Wilson, staying with my parents. This was a bit like camping as the folks never had running water in the house, so we had to use the outdoor toilet, the outhouse, which was housed in the woodshed back of the house. We had to drive ten miles to Aunt Pearl's in Baldwin to bathe.

We were given a wedding shower at the Wilson Lutheran Church (my church) across the road from the farm, and our friends even gave us a charivari, a noisy party celebrating our marriage. This was hosted by one of my school friends, Jeannine Kuhn, who was Dewey's cousin, at her parents' farm about a mile away from my parents' farm.

Our First Military Separation

Shortly after returning to Wisconsin, I learned that Betty

could join me in Bermuda only after I arrived on the island and obtained living quarters. We also found out that we could not take our Oldsmobile since it was too large for the island.

I had only a week to get to New Jersey and had all my baggage to take with me. Dewey came up with the idea that he, my dad, and our friend Harry MaGee should drive me in the Oldsmobile to Manhattan Beach AFS in Brooklyn, NY, since they all wanted to see New York City and its surrounds. I agreed, and the planning was complete.

Troy leaves for Bermuda

Since Betty would have to wait until I could rent an apartment in Bermuda, she decided to go to her parents' home. She had never driven a car and did not have a driver's license, so leaving the Olds with her would not help, so I decided to leave it with my dad for the three years that we would be in Bermuda.

We four guys then drove to New York City, where I was met by a 56-G classmate, John Kaczynski, who lived in New York and was also going to Bermuda with his new wife, Marie.

Wisconsin Farmers in the Big Apple

The story about my dad, Dewey and Harry driving the Olds around in the Big Apple will never really be told, but I know that they were led out of the city by one of NY's finest, who was a motorcycle cop.

When I recovered the Olds some three years later, it had no dents or scratches, so Dewey must have been a great driver. Anyway, I shipped out of Manhattan Beach AFS to McGuire AFB, flying to Bermuda on July 24, 1956, while Betty waited at her parents' home for orders to join me in Bermuda.

Chapter Ten
July 24, 1956 – June 8, 1959

303rd Air Refueling Squadron,

308th Bomb Wing M. Strategic Air Command 38th Air Division

Kindley AFB, Bermuda

Lt. Col. Rufus Ward, Squadron Commander

Bermuda is an island group about 21 miles long and one mile wide. Its history dates to 1609, when British colonists landed on shore when their ship was wrecked on a nearby reef. It is a self-governing colony and is well known for its tourism and pink beaches.

Kindley AFB, on the Southern end of the island, shared the runways with the international airport. A long causeway connected the airport and base to the main island. The city of Hamilton is the capital, and the island's population in 1956 was about 41,000. The country lived on banking and tourism and, consequently, was an expensive place to live. The tour of duty was to be three years, and those three years were going to be life-changing and eventful as Betty and I started to raise our family. We made lifelong friends and formed a bond for our marriage that would last over 67 years.

A staff car met me on the civilian side of Kindley right after I arrived on a BOAC Viscount airliner. I was transported about a mile to the BOQ (Batchelor Officer Quarters) on the base proper and found several of my new Squadron mates already living in the Q.

The Mission

The 303rd Air Refueling Squadron had, for several years, been stationed at Davis Monthan AFB near Tucson, AZ. The B-47 Bomber was just coming into service in the Strategic Air Command, and that bomber needed the KC-97 tanker to extend its range. The B-47, the newest Cold War weapon, was about to start standing nuclear alert in the Azores, and SAC needed a tanker unit out in the Atlantic to assist the bombers in flying non-stop between the USA and Lajes Field in the Azores, Portugal, where the bombers stood nuclear alert. Bermuda, being about 1,000 miles east of the US, was an ideal location to have a squadron of tankers to rendezvous with the bombers as they flew both East and West to their temporary alert location and their home bases in the US.

The 303rd was chosen to be part of the Cold War and fill this role. The squadron had now moved en mass from Arizona to Bermuda five months before I joined them.

The Squadron

I was the youngest pilot assigned and was flying with pilots in their thirties who had just been recalled after being released from active duty when the Korean war ended.

I was quickly assimilated into the squadron and assigned to a crew headed up by a seasoned Aircraft Commander, Joe Hildebrand, Captain USAF.

My first crew and Aircraft Commander (AC)

My first Aircraft Commander (AC), Captain Joe Hildebrand (nick name is Moose), was a stocky fellow with a handlebar mustache and had been a plumber prior to being recalled. He was married to Edie, and they had younger children.

Our Navigator was a Texan, 1st Lieutenant Jimmy Ford, who was also married with children. The enlisted members of the crew were M/Sgt Dale VanVorce, Flight Engineer, T/Sgt Frank Willsey, Boom Operator, and Airman Larry Bergdahl, Radio Operator.

I was a 2nd Lieutenant Co-Pilot at age 21 and the youngest officer in the Squadron. A few other 2nd/Lt's arrived about the same time – Charlie Jensen, John Kaczynski and others but they were at least a year older than me.

I started flying immediately, and our crew was "combat ready" (ready to fly a war time mission) in only a few short weeks. Joe was a good pilot, Jimmy a great Navigator, and the enlisted crew were highly qualified. I was trained by the best.

Our Squadron Commander was Lt. Col. Rufus Ward, Operations Officer Major Art Ray, and Assistant Ops officer Major Elmer Powell. This command section was older – in their 40s, and most had seen service at the end of WWII. The 303rd was a proud unit and performed well. I was lucky to be assigned there.

Life on the Island

After processing, my first concern was transportation. My AC Joe had a Triumph Motorcycle. I needed transportation but already had a car payment on the Olds, so I looked for something cheaper. I purchased a new BSA 125cc motorcycle. The speed limit was only 15mph on the island, and the tourists were renting Mopeds, which were smaller and had less power. I figured that ~~Betty~~Betty, and I could ride the BSA bike until the baby came, and then we would figure something else out.

The First Apartment

After the motorcycle purchase, I needed to rent a temporary apartment so Betty could join me. One was recommended near the Church of England Cathedral in the center of the main city of Hamilton.

It was a third-story unit that had no entry door. One would

climb the stairs past the second-floor unit, and the top of the stairs came directly into the living room, which contained, among normal furniture, the refrigerator. Also, the only window in the bathroom opened directly into the kitchen. The kitchen stove was an ancient old electric with thick metal plates over the burners.

The advantage of renting this unit was that the military had already inspected it, and it was an authorized apartment that would allow the Air Force to publish official orders to allow Betty to immediately come over.

Lt. John Kaczynski, one of my classmates at Vance, had also been assigned to the 303rd and was renting this apartment when he found a better one. I took the lease over from him and got Betty on her way about August 15, 1956. I signed the lease for this downtown apartment in the building called Vista Marina, Devonshire, at the cost of 30 Pounds Bermuda- $90.00 US. Our lease started in mid-August 1956, and we moved in on August 21st. We would stay there only a brief time as I had also found a cozy apartment on the North shore owned by Mrs. Outterbridge that was being vacated by a 303rd pilot, Bill Warwick and his wife Marsha, who was about to give birth to twins.

A new Air Force Wife gets her first military orders.

After I rented the downtown apartment, Betty got orders to join me at Kindley AFB Bermuda. She then had to have our possessions packed into two shipments, one hold baggage which was shipped priority to be in Bermuda when Betty got there and then the rest of our stuff in a regular overseas shipment.

Betty came to Bermuda in August 1956

It was mid-August 1956 when Betty boarded a steam-powered train one evening in Superior to embark on her first Air Force move. She remembers the train going by the farm in South Range that evening, and she was crying. 20 years old, newly married, and pregnant, and she was scared starting out by herself in her railcar compartment. The next morning, she arrived in Chicago and had to change trains. She had been worried that she would sleep through and miss her next train, but things worked out fine and after another overnight on the train, she found herself at the Depot in Ocean Port, New Jersey. Betty took a cab from the depot to Fort Monmouth and then flew to Bermuda that afternoon on a propeller aircraft (probably a Lockheed Constellation). She remembers the Bermuda Governor being on board that flight.

Betty Arrives

My aircraft commander, Joe and his wife Edie and I were at the civilian side of Kindley Field to meet Betty. Joe and Edie in their car and me on our new motorcycle. We then went to their place for drinks and dinner and then to our apartment in Hamilton for our first night together in our temporary apartment.

We did not live long in this apartment. Our new one on North Shore, Vista View, would soon be available, and our hold baggage had arrived. We moved to our first home, the duplex vacated by Bill and Marsha Warwick, on the first of October.

Our First Home - Vista View on North Shore

We were now used to riding tandem on the motorcycle and depending on friends or taxis to move larger items. The duplex on North Shore was owned by an older widowed lady, Mrs. Outerbridge. It was pink in color, which is not an unusual color for houses in Bermuda and had one bedroom and one bath plus a kitchen and living room. It was fully furnished and had the typical mildew smell from the high humidity. The house was across the road from the rugged Bermuda North Shore. We would later go down to the shore and get mussels which we would prepare and eat for dinner. A neat place to live with a view.

There was a bus stop on the road in front of the building, and Betty, who was used to riding busses in San Antonio, took them to the base and into Hamilton. The ride to work only took a few minutes as our new home was close to the causeway to the base. We were also close to the famous "Swizzle Inn," which was a tourist hangout and had a lot of tipsy tourists crashing their Mopeds after a couple of delicious rum swizzles served by the friendly staff of the Swizzle Inn.

Mrs. Outerbridge was a great landlady, and we enjoyed living next to her in our very first home. Our new landlady had a long-time boarder who was a German immigrant. I think his name was George, and I remember that he was employed by the Bermuda Postal Service. George told us that during WWII, German U Boats would surface off the North Shore, not far from where we lived and would bring mail ashore to be sent to their families in Germany. I tended to believe that story as the main channel into Hamilton Harbor was less than a mile offshore, directly East of our house. We would watch the cruise ships navigating the channel every day.

The Church of England

We tried to fit into Bermuda's society by attending a local church. There were no Lutheran churches on the island, so we attended the Anglican Church of England cathedral in downtown Hamilton. Our first service started with the hymn, which had a melody we knew as "My Country Tis of Thee." We were thrilled that they recognized us as visitors; however, the words were different, and we were soon to discover that it was the British national anthem known as "God Save The Queen". Welcome to foreign service!

Fun Living on The Island

We, like the rest of our squadron mates, did not have much money to live on. I believe my Second Lieutenant pay was

$222/month, and I received an additional $100 in-flight pay and $47 in a housing allowance. We could buy a bottle of Beef Eaters Gin for $.99 at our duty-free base store, while a quart of reconstituted milk cost over $1.00. We used the commissary and BX and managed to survive. We did have a lot of parties at our homes and really got to know our fellow 303rd members. Lt. Charlie Jensen, who came to the 303rd at the same time as Kaczynski and me, was the bachelor in our group. He hung with us and had a sailboat and was part owner, with me and some other squadron mates, of a power boat that I bought prior to Betty's arrival. Charlie was a good friend and would take our wives to dinner when Kelly and I were gone TDY. He was the mussel picker at our place on North Shore. The remainder of our time at the Outerbridge apartment was routine, with me flying regularly and regular duties on non-flying days.

I do remember our first marital discord. I had been on a long flight and came home at supper time. When I asked Betty what we were having for dinner, she produced a tuna fish casserole. I had a major brain fart and said, "I fly all day and get this crap for dinner!" The meal got pitched out the front door, and I went hungry that evening. I started learning that one should never let his mouth overload his ass.

I had my first sailboat experience with our friend Kelly on Charlie's sailboat. Kelly and I took the boat out into the bay one windy afternoon and ended up becalmed and, since we did not have an outboard motor aboard, had to wait for the wind to pick up to get back to shore. Betty was visiting Kelly's wife, Marie, and they got very worried when we did not get back until after dark. We had no radio or cell phones, so we just had to make do. I didn't know it then, but that was to be the first of some very interesting sailing that I would do in the far future.

U-2 - Spy plane of the Cold War

Early in our assignment, we had a unique experience when a U-2 super-secret spy plane had to make an emergency landing at Kindley. It was a single-engine aircraft that could fly at extremely high altitudes and carried cameras that had extremely high resolution.

Designed to gather intelligence on foreign countries, it apparently had engine failure and glided to the runway at Kindley and was parked by one of the 303rd hangers. We were told not to photograph the aircraft, but that did not keep us from looking at it from a distance. Betty even had a chance to view the aircraft. It was on the ground for several days and was launched at night to avoid publicity. Few people had ever heard of this aircraft in 1956.

Lantana

We were expecting our first child sometime in March 1957. To have room for our new arrival, Betty and I moved from Vista

View into a house named "Lantana" on January 15, 1957. The rent now went to 45 pounds ($135.00/month). I was due to be promoted to First Lieutenant in July, so we felt we could afford the new rent as my pay would now be $478.00 per month. It was a nice house with 2br, 1b, living room, dining room, kitchen and garage. It even had a patio. The home was on Middle Road, not too far from Kindley AFB. But then, since the island was a mile wide and 21 miles long, nothing was far away.

While at Lantana, I met a British fellow who was an amateur radio operator. Brian Bush, call sign VP9IVM, had the radio equipment but no place to set it up. I volunteered our living room since we had a large yard to put up an antenna and plenty of space for the Heath Kit radio and receiver. I got a chance to get on the air and operate using Brian's call sign. I began my career as a Ham when I got my first license in California in 1963 (WN6AJD).

Brian married another Brit – Elizabeth, while he was stationed as a Bermuda policeman and, near the end of our tour, loaned us his Morris Minor convertible to use while he and Elizabeth were back in England on vacation. A fine friend.

Steven William, March 22, 1957

Our first child, Steven William, decided to come into the world on March 22, 1957. We only had the motorcycle for transportation, so our friend and squadron mate, John Kaczynski, the 303rd pilot I had met in New York City, again came to our rescue and drove us to the hospital. I planned on being with Betty for the birth but was told that regulations did not permit the husband to be in the delivery room. I checked in at the BOQ, and Betty was alone in her childbirth misery. She stayed in the hospital for about six days, and then we all went home to our home in Paget.

When Betty and our new son Stevie checked out of the Kindley AFB Hospital, the total bill was for subsistence and was $10.50. Payday was near, and we had to write a hot check to cover the bill. Our bank was Valley National in Tucson and was very understanding with Air Force Officers and did not return or fine for overdrawn checking accounts. An interesting note. Steve was born on Bermuda soil. He had the option to become a Bermuda citizen. Bermuda gave him that option until he was eighteen. We had to naturalize Steve through the U.S. government, which we did when he was about five years old. I don't think Steve regretted our decision.

A visitor for Steven

Steve was healthy and grew rapidly. Betty's sister Joanne came from San Juan, Puerto Rico, where she and her husband Charlie were stationed with the FBI, to visit in April, and she and I toured the island on our motorcycle while Betty stayed home to tend to our new baby. Betty did not think much of that arrangement.

The Only Child and His Brothers

The Bermuda "Hangman" (who rarely performed his duties as crime on the island was low) lived next door to us. When Steve was christened at age 3 months, this fellow crossed Steve's palm with a silver Bermuda shilling – an English custom to bring Good Luck. We had Steven baptized at the base chapel by a traveling Lutheran chaplain. Steve had developed a "cradle cap' so he was pretty well covered up during the ceremony.

A new officer, Lt. Walter Inge, arrived at the squadron just prior to Steve's birth. He and his wife Jane were southerners from Mobile, Alabama. They were frequently at our house for parties, and we became close friends.

We all liked the island cocktail rum and ginger ale, and we have pictures of Jane and Betty, both quite pregnant, holding cigarettes and drinks. No one had told us that was bad for the unborn child. Neither Steve nor their girl, Gracia, seemed to be affected.

Steve's first Christmas was memorable as his Grandmother Ag flew in to spend time with him. We toured Ag throughout the island and even got her an airplane ride in the base aero club Aeronca with our Squadron mate Charlie Jensen at the controls. At the end of her stay with us, Ag continued her tour by flying to Puerto Rico for a visit with Betty's sister Joanne and her family. Ag tried to get Betty's Dad, Waino, to come along, but he didn't like to fly.

Bermuda Drinking Water

Water wells cannot be dug in Bermuda because the Island stands on legs in the ocean, and all one would find drilling in the ground would be salt water. Therefore, the white roofs one sees on Bermuda houses collect rainwater which drains into a cistern under the house. This water is the whole household supply for cooking, bathing and flushing. The cistern at Lantana was cracked, and our water supply would leak away. Because of this, we had to move after only four months.

Normar

We decided that we needed a larger place and found a small house called "Normar Cottage" on White Sands Road. The rent was about $150.00 /month, but the location was better than any of our previous places. The house was next to Captain Stanley Burns, Royal Navy retired, and his wife, Ruby. Stanley was the Bermuda Harbor Master, and Stanley and Ruby were Steve's stand in grandparents. The Bermudians were great hosts to their American military guests, and Ruby and Stanley were super neighbors. Stanley had his daily glass of Stout every afternoon, and many days, our son Steve would go over and sit on a small stool with Stanley and would be given his own libation by Ruby. Then the two would raise their glasses and shout, "Cheers!" Years later, when Steve was a Midshipman and skipper of a boat in the Newport/Bermuda Yacht Race, he visited Ruby (Stanley had died a few years prior to this visit).

Stanley gave me his Wembley 44 caliber Royal Navy pistol as a remembrance when we left the island. I later gave it to Steve with the idea that he would return it to the Bermuda Museum. I am uncertain that that event ever happened.

Better Transportation

Upon moving into Normar in May 1957, it became evident that the motorcycle was not going to transport the family. Sergeant Ron Shane, a Boom Operator in the squadron, had an early 1950s very rusty Ford Anglia 2-door Saloon for sale. It was advertised by the Ford Motor Company as "All that anyone could ask for in a light car". I paid $50 for the vehicle and kept it until just before we returned to the states.

Betty remembers infant Steve lying in the back seat during a rainstorm and being noticeably quiet. She looked back to see rain dripping on his forehead through the leaky canvas roof.

The salt water and air had rusted the fenders, and they were held on by many layers of masking tape, which was painted to make them waterproof. The car ran well as it had exceptionally low mileage and had been driven at 15 mph. It provided safe transport for us until I took it to the Kindley dump a few months before we rotated back to the states, and that is when we borrowed our British policeman's convertible, which we drove for the rest of our tour.

Steve's Saltwater Baptism

I gave our young son Steve an experience that may have affected his life. One sunny afternoon I had a small errand to do on base. Steve was now approaching his second birthday and was a true boy – very active. I put him in front of me on the motorcycle and proceeded out to the base. The wind was quite strong, and as we drove across the causeway to Kindley, the spray from the ocean was blowing on us. Steve was delighted and was giggling and breathing in that salt air. As Steve grew up, only a few years later, we found that he was in love with boats and water and, later, sail boats. This love of the sea is still with him today. Could it be an early Bermuda life experience that formed him?? Of course, the genes he received from his Irish, Finlander and Norwegian ancestors may have had an effect too.

More Money - more flying

July brought my promotion to 1st Lieutenant and the much-needed raise.

I now have been flying many missions, including flights to Hunter AFB in Savanah, GA, to wash the aircraft. Our KC-97s were parked remarkably close to the water, which was really the actual Atlantic Ocean. Salt spray getting on the aluminum causes corrosion which is bad for aluminum-covered aircraft. The KC-97s needed to be washed monthly to prevent corrosion. This was done at Hunter AFB near Savannah, Georgia. My first trip to Hunter was with my first crew, with Joe Hildebrand as the aircraft commander. Joe and I both brought our motorcycles along and rode around Savannah, going to restaurants and bars. Only in the 303rd could you take your airplane on a trip and bring your ground transportation with you.

Hunter AFB-Sears Roebuck

Our squadron had a special arrangement with the Savanna, Georgia, Sears Roebuck store where the squadron families could special order from Sears. Sears would bring a truck to the airplane and help load merchandise on to the KC-97 just before we returned to the island. Since we were in the military, the customs people did not get involved when we arrived back in Bermuda.

The 303rd brought back many 12-inch black and white television sets as we had an Armed Forces Radio and Television station on the base. The signal was broadcast over the island, so most of us had one channel of TV. Not much different than when I was working for Meyer Music in Eau Claire.

Moving Along

I have now been assigned to a new crew. As copilots gain experience, they are evaluated on their ability to take command of the aircraft if the aircraft commander should become incapacitated. Apparently, I was doing a good job as a pilot, and I was placed on a crew that was just formed with a pilot who had been a copilot and was now upgraded to aircraft commander. My new aircraft commander was Captain Carl Johnson, who had early in his career been an Air Force navigator. He was a great guy, and his wife, Vanice, was a very amusing person. They had a family of four children.

I had a number of TDY trips to the USA for assorted reasons, from washing airplanes to escaping hurricanes. Betty remembers the hurricane trip where my crew had to, on short notice, take an airplane to the states as Bermuda was in the path of a hurricane. She and little Steve had to shelter in our house, which had only shutters to close over the windows for protection against flying objects. I had flown to McDill AFB in Florida well out of the hurricane's path. Fortunately, the hurricane missed Bermuda, and the neighbors helped the family through this experience.

Vacations (leave)

During our time in Bermuda, I took leave only two times. In September 1957, my Great Uncle Les Hansen, Grampa Louie's brother, came to Bermuda on a cruise ship for a few days, and we showed him around the island. Our big vacation occurred on March 18, 1958. Betty, Steve, and I flew to Minneapolis on a trip paid for by my parents. We took 30 days' leave and spent it between Wilson and Superior visiting relatives and using our 1956 Oldsmobile, which was stored at the Wilson farm.

Flying the Airlines

We traveled from Bermuda to New York with BOAC on their Viscount turboprop aircraft and from New York to Minneapolis on Northwest on their luxurious Boeing 337 (civilian copy of the KC/C-97).

When we left Minneapolis to return to Bermuda, the air was very rough, and a tornado touched down a mile North of our farm South of Wilson, killing the farmer who we knew – George Peterson. This was the same farm where I received my first airplane ride with Roger Litchfield in 1946, flying off George Peterson's hay field.

During this vacation, Stevie got to meet his grandparents and relatives on both sides of the family and his Great Grandpa Louie Hansen. When I got back to the 303rd, I was on yet another crew.

Different Crews

My next crew was with Captain Harry Cutlip as the aircraft commander. Harry was a little guy who struggled to fly the KC-97. Our crew was an interesting conglomeration. 1st Lt. Rod Wheeler was the navigator, and he was inexperienced as a crew member.

T/Sgt. Sam Boyer was the flight engineer, and he, too, was a low timer. I think the radio operator and boom operator had previous crew experience. I had to use my limited flying experience to help Harry keep from having a major accident.

Harry was a great guy, and Betty and I stood up for him and Nora when they were married at Kindley AFB.

Outside of some very interesting landings where I flew the ailerons while Harry pumped the elevators and rudder, I only remember one funny event. One moonless night we were flying somewhere between the US and Bermuda with Rod, our navigator, practicing a navigation leg using celestial (by the stars) procedures. We were droning along on what ~~Harry~~Harry, and I thought was a heading that would take us back to Bermuda. The airplane was on autopilot, and I think Harry was napping. I noticed Rod come up and say something to Harry which caused him to quickly sit up and tell Rod, "You can't just quit!" Harry then told me, "You have the aircraft". He got out of his seat, and he and Rod went into the back of the airplane to have a serious conversation. I started trying to find the Bermuda navigation radio station by tuning around the low-frequency navigation radio dial and listening for the Morse Code identifier B-D-A. I finally found the station, and the cockpit pointer was pointing out in front of us, indicating that we were in fact headed toward the island.

After a few minutes, Harry and Rod returned to the cockpit. Apparently, Rod had messed up his navigation procedures and was frustrated and lost. Harry had talked him into finding our location and taking us home. It was a remarkably interesting flight.

Later that month, Harry was assigned to the command post as a controller, and Lt. Ralph Chadwick took over the crew. I only flew with Ralph a few times because I was slated to be the co-pilot on a crew that would be going to train stateside in the new KC-135 Strato jet tanker. This was a premium assignment coveted by all the returning flight crews.

Captain Leonard Dixon was the aircraft commander, and 1st Lt. Mike Katz was the Navigator. We would fly together in the final months of our 303rd assignment. Then the three of us would move to the 916th Air Refueling Squadron at Travis AFB near Fairfield, California.

A Clemson Grad is my Aircraft Commander

The new crew was a lot of fun. Leonard did not take himself too seriously and had a profound sense of humor. I remember one of my last flights in the 303rd was a night refueling/navigation mission that was similar to the one I had with Harry Cutlip and Rod Wheeler.

An Amusing Lesson

Our radio operator was a young Black airman by the name of Prior. His job was to transmit our position to Air Traffic Control each hour via morse code on our High-Frequency radio. The job was boring, and Prior took to sitting in the cockpit latrine and reading comic books and forgetting to do his job. Leonard had talked to him about his lack of responsibility a number of times, and now the time had come for action.

KC-97 aircrews all had the capacity to bail out of the airplane if there was an emergency. We would put on our parachutes, remove the over-wing hatch and jump onto the wing to escape. Each crew member had his parachute hanging on the wall near the over-wing hatches. If the situation required abandoning the airplane, the alarm bell system could alert everyone on board as there were bells throughout the cabin. The control switch for the bells was above the copilot's seat. The signal was three short rings to prepare to bail out and one long ring to jump.

It was nighttime, and we were out over the Atlantic Ocean, droning along while our Navigator was practicing his navigation trade. The cockpit area was bathed in red light, which allowed the crew to better see outside in the dark. Airman Prior, the Radio Operator, had gone into the latrine and closed the door so he could turn on white lights to read his comics. Leonard told me to slip down in my seat so it would appear that no one was in the cockpit and wait a few minutes while the engineer, boom operator and Leonard and

Mike went to the very back of the aircraft and hid in the boom pod. They partially blocked the door to the latrine as they left. I then rang the alarm bell three times, waited, and gave it one final long ring. I could hear Prior banging on the door, trying to get out, and when he finally got it open, he looked up front, and no one was there, so he opened the door to the main cabin and did not see anyone and panicked. The crew had to stop him from putting on his parachute and bailing out. It was the last time that he goofed off during a flight. Leonard's discipline worked. I later flew with Leonard and Mike for three years in the KC-135 and participated in many pranks, mostly thought up by Captain Dixon.

Water Survival

Operating out of Bermuda, we flew all our missions over the water of the Atlantic Ocean. It occurred to our trainers that we should have some water survival training, so they came up with a scenario that would put about 15 of the crew members in a 20-man life raft in Hamilton harbor. They would tow the raft and occupants out about a mile and leave us out there to practice making drinking water and other survival tactics, which included fishing for our food.

The raft was not large – about fifteen feet across, and with 15 survivors aboard, it was crowded. Leonard, Mike and I were among the trainees, and after a few hours of bobbing around, we got bored. Mike had made some drinking water using the sun to evaporate sea water, and we all were snacking on C rations which were minimally tasty.

After darkness had set in, one of the other crewmembers decided to try fishing. He used some meat from the C rations and threw out a line. The waters around Bermuda are filled with fish, and some are sharks and barracuda. The barracuda are vicious fish with teeth that go all the way down their throats and protrude out of their mouths. They are flat ugly. Things had settled down, and some folks were trying to get some sleep when our fisherman shouted that he had a large fish on the line. He fought it in the darkness and finally hauled it on board. It was a large fish, and it was jumping around, and you could hear it snapping when someone finally shined a light on it. It was a two-foot barracuda. There was major scrambling among the crew members that ended up with 15 guys on one side of the raft and one barracuda on the other. The fish was jumping and snapping. There was yelling and screaming, Cuda! Cuda!!! There were only a few flashlights on board, no one really knew what was happening. The fisherman finally kicked the fish back into the ocean and cut the line. So much for water survival at the 303rd Air Refueling Squadron.

Sandra Lynne, March 8, 1959

The last big Bermuda event occurred on March 8, 1959, when our daughter Sandra Lynne was born at the Kindley AFB

Hospital. The event was a bit different than Steve's birth in that we were driving a new Morris Minor convertible car loaned to us by our police officer friend Brian Bush, the Bermudian cop with the Ham license. He and his wife Elizabeth had gone to England on an extended vacation and allowed us to drive the car at the end of our Bermuda assignment. Steve, now two years old, stayed alone in the car while I picked up Betty and Sandy at the base hospital about a week after her birth. We now had a complete family with a boy and a girl. Times were great. As I mentioned about Sandy's brother, Sandy was also born on Bermuda soil, even though it was a US Air Force Base. She, too, had the option to become a Bermudian if she chose by age eighteen. We had her naturalized around age three.

Our first official transfer, June 5, 1959

I was at the end of my three-year assignment to the 303rd ARS in Bermuda. During my years there, I was offered and accepted a route to a regular commission which would mean that I would make a career in the Air Force. I was rewarded for this choice by a new assignment to Travis AFB in California to fly the new KC-135 tanker in a newly formed squadron, the 916th Air Refueling Squadron. My orders stated that I must report to the squadron by July 21, 1959. We packed up and flew out of Bermuda on a Pan American Strato Cruiser on June 5, 1959, to New York and then Northwest Airlines Boeing 337 to Minneapolis, where we were met by Betty's Mom, Ag, and brought to Wilson to pick up our now paid for 1956 Oldsmobile and start visits with all of the relatives showing off our kids. We had over 30 days to visit our families and drive the 2,000 miles to our new assignment and home in Fairfield, California. Neither Betty nor I had ever been to the state of California, and we were looking forward to palm trees and great weather. We enjoyed our visits and showing off our kids to all the relatives. Our first shipment of personal goods arrived at the Juntti farm soon after we did, and now, we had to load the Oldsmobile with our "hold baggage" and kids and start the long, very warm drive. Our new Olds did not have air conditioning, so it was going to be miserable driving across the Western US in July.

Chapter Eleven

June 9, 1959 – July 12, 1962

916th Air Refueling Squadron,

5th Bomb Wing H, Strategic Air Command Travis AFB

Fairfield, California

Lt. Col. John Martin, Squadron Commander

We left the Juntti farm around the 4th of July and had our first problem when we were south of Minneapolis and reached the east-west highway that would take us toward California. I was driving and prepared to make a right turn, i.e., west onto the highway, when Betty insisted on us turning left! Well, we sat there and had a lengthy discussion about our need to go west to get to California. Betty was convinced that turning left, i.e., East, would get us there. We finally turned right, and after passing through some towns that were on our map, my young wife was now satisfied that we were going the right way. Betty had not learned how to drive until we got back to the U.S after our Bermuda assignment. I put her in our Olds and taught her how to drive on the same roads and in the area where I had learned to drive ten years earlier. She went to Baldwin and met the St. Croix County Sheriff, who administered the driving test, which included parallel parking. She was now sporting a fresh Wisconsin driver's license and would share the load on our new adventure.

California Here We Come

We went first to Ellsworth AFB in South Dakota where my old Aircraft Commander, Harry Cutlip, and his wife, Nora, and their kids lived. I believe Harry was in the SAC command post there. We stayed on base at their home and had a brief visit before we pressed on toward Sacramento where we were going to stay with Betty's Uncle Art and his wife, Helen. We got to Sacramento after a number of hot days on the road and found Art Anderson's little house. Art, Helen, their kids, Richard and Karen, and Art's mother, Betty's Grandmother Hilda, were living in the home, so it was crowded before we ever walked in. Over the next week, we stayed there and left the kids there while we drove the 40 miles South to Fairfield to find our next home.

House Hunting

The city of Fairfield was about 3 miles southwest of Travis AFB. Travis was one of the largest Air Force Bases on the West Coast of the US. It was the main base for military cargo and passenger aircraft for service to the Far East. When we arrived, there were C-124, C-97, C-141, C-133 and B-52 (5th Bomb Wing) aircraft stationed there. I signed into the 5th Bomb Wing around July 21, 1959, and was now the Co-Pilot on Captain Leonard Dixon's KC-135 crew in the 916th Air Refueling Squadron.

My KC-135 Crew

The crew was made up of Leonard, the Aircraft Commander; Mike Katz, the Navigator; and Gary Jones, the Boom Operator. This was a much smaller crew than I was used to when I flew the KC97. Now the pilots have taken responsibility for engine management, High-Frequency Radio communications, fuel management and performance data calculations. The Boom Operator was now also the Loadmaster and did the weight and balance calculations. It was going to be a more challenging flight situation.

The KC-135

The KC-135 was a Boeing airplane. The Boeing Aircraft Corp. had a great reputation for building fine airplanes. They started in 1916 and, in later years, manufactured the B-17, B-29, B-47, B-52, KC-97 and now the tanker I would be flying.

In 1954 they rolled out the first four-engine jetliner, the Boeing 707. The 707 was picked up by most of the major airlines throughout the world. The KC-135 was taken from the 721 model, which was similar to the 707. It rolled 803 tankers off production lines between 1955 through 1965.

The tanker had 4 turbojet engines that produced 12000 lbs. of thrust on a standard day. It had a water injection system that cooled the air going into the engine to allow it to maintain its thrust rating on a hot day. Once activated on the takeoff roll, the water would last for 4 minutes, enough time to take off, raise the landing gear, climb 500 feet and retract the flaps. There was a noticeable loss of power when the water ran out on a heavy-weight takeoff on a warm day. The use of water would allow you to lift an extra 10,000# of fuel. This would be critical for an Emergency War operation, i.e., taking off very heavy at 320000 lbs. This would only happen under a nuclear war scenario. The aircraft could refuel any aircraft capable of receiving fuel in the Air Force/Navy inventory. It was fully equipped to start up without external ground support and was very reliable. By the time I got into the program, the first aircraft off the production line was 7 years old. I was very much looking forward to checking out as an Aircraft Commander as I could then leave the Air Force and go to work for an airline.

My new squadron, the 916th Air Refueling Squadron, would bring in about 12 new KC-135 aircraft, and we would join the 5th Bomb Wing, a SAC unit on a MATS base. My unit was just starting to form, and the flight crews still had to go to the 4017th CCTS at Castle AFB, about 120 miles south of Travis, to get checked out in the KC-135 tanker. The crew and I were to report to Castle AFB on September 15, 1959. In the meantime, we would get our flying time in base aircraft such as the U-3, C-47, C-45 and T-33.

California housing

Our house hunting proved to be difficult as there were not many homes to rent in Fairfield. One of the better options was to purchase a house since I was now a Veteran and qualified for a Veterans Administration loan which we could get without a down payment. We found a new home in a subdivision on the south side of the city. We were not sure we could afford the $111.00 monthly payment that came with the $17,000 purchase. I was not to be promoted to Captain for another year, but the $111.00 monthly payment was less expensive than the $150 plus monthly rent for a home of comparable size. We purchased 1700 sq. ft. pink colored, 4 bedrooms, 2 1/2 bath, 2 car garage home at 1336 McKinley Street in Fairfield and moved in within a week.

Our household goods were awaiting us at Travis. We had used the 303rd/Sears Roebuck delivery system during our final year in Bermuda and had purchased a Kenmore refrigerator, gas stove, gas dryer and washing machine. There was also a 12-inch black and white TV set that was used on the island. While in Bermuda, we hooked up the washer and dryer, and that helped with the diaper load that we had been taking to the base each week. These appliances were in our household goods shipment, but we did not have any furniture to put in our 1,700-square-foot home, so we went to a large furniture store in Vallejo and made a large purchase. We were now living pretty well, and all we needed to do was make that $111/month house payment. The family was healthy, and California at that time was a delightful place to live. To make it even better, John Kaczynski and his family, our squadron mates in Bermuda, purchased an identical house next to us so our kids had playmates.

Training at Castle AFB

The KC-135 Training at Castle AFB went without any problems. We left our families in Fairfield and would drive back to Fairfield for the weekends. The academics, simulator and flying formed us into a solid crew.

After completing the training at Castle's 93rd training squadron, we flew in a Travis AFB MATS C47 to Moses Lake AFB and picked up a brand-new KC-135 and brought it down to Travis AFB for the 916th ARS. We made this trip a few more times, and soon, we had our new squadron fully manned with brand-new aircraft. We started weekly training flights as a crew, and in the Spring of 1960, my crew and new squadron were declared combat ready.

Ending a Nasty Habit

Transitioning to flying jet aircraft had me changing some habits. I had been a cigarette smoker since I first started college at Stout Institute. The Air Force had no restrictions on smoking in the cockpit once the bird was airborne, so I had no motivation to stop. Flying the KC-135 was different. We had to wear our parachutes while flying and a jet pilot flight helmet with an oxygen mask. One pilot always had to breathe normal oxygen. When one pilot decided to have a cigarette, he had to be sure that the other pilot had on his oxygen mask and was breathing normal oxygen. Then the would-be smoker had a procedure to turn off his oxygen supply, take three breaths from his mask to use up the oxygen in the system and then wait for three minutes before lighting up. If there was a flight examiner on board evaluating the crew, he would carefully note these steps, and if a step was missed, it would fail the crewmember.

One did not want to fail a flight check in the Strategic Air Command. Doing so would possibly end your career. So, I decided that I had enough fallibilities and one day threw my cigarettes away and simply quit smoking.

I did not find it difficult to do since I was motivated to advance my military career. I don't think I have had a cigarette since that day in 1960. Betty was also a smoker and used to think she was sneaking smoking from me, but she forgot how smokers smell with the smoke on their clothing etc. She finally quit a few years later.

Nuclear Alert on the ground

Now things fell into a routine. We would stand on nuclear alert with our B-52 crew at the SAC alert facility for one week and then have a week of flying and then back to alert. Our alert facility was off the end of the main runway, and there would be three bombers and three tankers fully loaded with fuel and the B-52s with nuclear bombs. We were on what we called the Christmas tree parking area, so if we were called to taxi for takeoff, the tanker would roll first, followed by a bomber, followed by the next tanker bomber combination. The tankers would take off, followed immediately by the other bombers and tankers in a minimum interval takeoff operation that would have 6 aircraft rolling for takeoff on the same runway simultaneously. The whole operation was frightening as we were so heavily loaded that the failure of one engine during the initial roll and lift-off could cause the airplane to crash. It was possible that the following aircraft would be involved in the accident too.

We did practice these types of takeoffs, but they were not loaded as heavily, and the bombers were not loaded with nuclear weapons. It was still a tense operation as your aircraft was so close to the one in front that the wake turbulence would cause your aircraft to shake violently and try to roll over. This became our way of life. We would be away from home for a week living and eating at the alert facility and would do ground training during our ground time at the facility. Our families could come out to visit in the parking lot, or we could drive our alert four-door truck over to the base proper to visit. On one Thanksgiving, we had dinner in the alert facility parking lot.

I had been promoted to the rank of Captain, so things were looking a bit brighter. However, alert duty and not much flying were beginning to bother me. I had not logged enough flying time to be upgraded to Aircraft Commander, and I did not have quite enough time to get out of the Air Force and get a job with an airline. I started looking for a new job.

Airborne Alert

We did have some interesting flying from time to time. My crew flew to Eielson AFB in Alaska in the late winter of 1962 to support a Cold War mission that had a fully nuclear war-loaded B-52 in the air constantly. We would fly from Eielson toward Thule Greenland and refuel the bomber when he passed through. Then we would orbit within sight of Thule and watch for an attack that would shut down the monitoring sites on the ground near Thule and watch for the lights to go out or them to radio us that they were under attack. This would be a sign that the United States was coming under attack by the Soviets, and we would radio the Strategic Air Command to warn them so they could launch our bombers and missiles. This operation was called Thule Monitor, and we did this during January and February, so it was dark and minus 70 degrees on the ground most of the time. The runway at Eielson was snow packed to the point that one tanker took off with its brakes locked and never knew it. The tires acted like a sled, and the temperatures were minus 60 -70 degrees, so the engines put out lots of power. It was so cold that portable heaters had to be blowing on the struts of the aircraft when we were on the ground, or they would collapse, and the aircraft would become useless. While there, all we did was fly and sleep. We built up a lot of flying time, and it was mostly boring except for one night when we were refueling the nuclear-loaded B-52 when he under ran us and almost knocked us out of the sky.

A Near Miss

I heard the boom operator call, "Break Away – Break Away!" and we went to full power straight ahead. I was in the right seat and looked out to see the bomber under our right wing flying up into us. I rolled the aircraft to the left, and the B-52 just missed us. We recovered and advised the bomber that we would not refuel him as he was dangerous. This forced him to go back and land somewhere, which created a major problem as the USA did not have another nuclear bomber airborne. We later found out that a Wing Commander was flying the bomber and was not proficient in night air refueling. We never found out what base they were from, but we did not get in trouble.

A Nuclear War - MAD

The United States and the Soviet Union engaged in a concept called Mutual Assured Destruction (MAD) as part of the Cold War during the 1960s and 70s. It meant that we watched each other, and if we detected that one side was attacking, the other would launch its nuclear force, and both countries would be blown to bits (see

Cold War- MAD). Our population was schooled on what to do if we were attacked - like crawling into a bomb shelter if you had one in your basement or the kids at school crawling under their desks. It was not a happy time in the world as the countries were always testing each other, and political tensions were high.

TOP- SECRET?

This next story is going to be written vaguely as I have been unable to determine if the Top-Secret classification has been lifted. I think it was one of the most interesting flights I ever participated in during my whole career.

Our crew was selected to participate in a very interesting exercise called "Dusty Beard." The war mission of a tanker, if launched while on alert, was to take off first and, since we were going to war, turn toward the bomber's target in the Soviet Union. The bomber took off immediately behind us, and we flew entrail to a point where the bomber would be refueled, and he would continue to strike his target.

We in the tanker then had little fuel left, so we would turn back toward our home air base and try to find a base where we could land and possibly refuel and take off again to meet the returning bomber and give him more fuel.

The main problem with this concept was finding a surviving runway that could handle a large aircraft and one that might have fuel to give us.

Strategic Air Command came up with an exercise to test a possible solution to this problem. It involved the KC-135 and a B-52 landing on a non-runway (dirt).

Dusty Beard was a secret operation that tested the ability of a B-52 and KC-135 to land and takeoff on a dry lakebed. The assumption was that, after a nuclear strike, the major military and civilian airports would have been demolished by the Soviet attack and would not be available for our strike force's recovery. For this operation, it was assumed that the tanker still had fuel to transfer to the returning bomber.

After both the bomber and tanker had landed on the lakebed, a hose from the tanker's boom would refuel the bomber so it could fly to a surviving base to be loaded with bombs and used to strike again. The problem was to find a lakebed that would support the weight of a large aircraft without it breaking through the crust and becoming permanently attached to the earth. Operation Dusty Beard was designed to observe the feasibility of this type of mission.

Dusty Beard

My crew was selected to fly the KC-135 test aircraft in the Dusty Beard Operation. I don't know if we were selected because of my unhappiness with my lack of flying or the luck of the draw, but I was excited about the mission.

It was in the Spring of 1962, and the lakebed selected cannot be named due to possible classification. Air Force engineers had tested the load-bearing lakebed to be sure that a heavy aircraft would not break through the surface. We were briefed that we would land, taxi to the front of the waiting B-52 and hook a special hose that we had on board to the bomber and transfer a small amount of fuel. We would then spend a few days sitting on the lakebed with the bomber before taking off and returning to our home at Travis AFB.

The flight crews would live aboard our aircraft, and we would use our on-board APU for electrical power for our tanker. For this test, a support group of security police and aircraft ground crews would also be in place.

Spring weather in the desert is generally warm and dry. We took off from Travis and flew for about an hour. Looking down at the lake, you could see the outline of the landing area, and we saw that the B-52 had arrived and was parked just off the side of the marked landing area. The engineers had tested and graded the lakebed runway, so we had about 4 or 5 miles of area (think runway) on which to operate. The weather was clear, and we estimated little wind, so we set up a visual downwind, base and final approach in an Eastern direction. Leonard made the landing, and when we touched down, the landing gear sunk about a foot into the lakebed runway. We slowed down quickly and needed a lot of power to taxi to the front of the B-52.

The bomber and ground crews greeted us as soon as we shut down our engines, and a loading stand was pushed up to our cargo door for easy access to our tanker.

The first order of business was to hook the hose to our boom and to the bomber and prove that we could transfer fuel. We had to start one of our engines as the fuel pumps ran on hydraulic pressure from a pump driven by the jet engine. After that, I turned on the HF radio and called the SAC command post to report that we had accomplished the ground refueling.

As part of the exercise, a C-47 cargo airplane from Castle AFB flew in later, bringing some food and other supplies in to support the exercise. Unfortunately, the old bird broke down with a bad starter.

Now we had three aircraft down on a dry lakebed. To make things more interesting, the B-52 was sinking into the lakebed, and it was becoming obvious that the aircraft would not be able to move under its own power. By the time it was noticed, it was already a couple of feet in the sand. Now the sun was setting, and there was not much that could be done with the equipment we had on hand, so we had some C rations for dinner and settled down for the night.

The next morning, we got going, and the B-52 ground crew decided to dig a long sloping trench to the front wheels of the bomber with the idea that it could, under its own power, roll forward and up to the surface and then taxi for a takeoff. The next couple of days were spent shoveling out the bomber. During those days, we had yet another aircraft land. A U-3 light twin airplane from Castle brought in a starter for the C-47 along with a mechanic to change the unit. Later in the day, the C-47 and U-3 both took off, leaving the two large aircraft on the lakebed. One was still stuck.

Around dusk on the third day, we observed a light aircraft flying overhead and circling. We were in a military restricted flight area and no unauthorized flights were allowed. Much to our amazement, it came in and landed near our group. We had an armed security detail guarding us, and they drove to the little airplane and met the man and woman who were flying it and immediately put them face down in the sand. This was a Top-Secret operation, and we were not to take pictures or tell anyone what we were doing. After an hour or so, a very frightened couple got into their little airplane and flew away. I never found out who they were, but I am sure that they were told that they did not see anything on that lakebed, and I bet that they believed it.

After a couple of days and nights sitting on this ancient lake, it was time for us to leave and go back to Travis AFB. The bomber was still stuck, and the crew said that they would start their engines after we left and see if they could come out of the hole they were in and fly home. We got our engines started, using lots of power and raising a huge cloud of dust. We taxied to the landing area, and after an exceedingly long and dusty takeoff run, we got into the air and flew home.

We later learned that it took two Army Sherman tanks to pull the bomber out of its hole, but they did manage to recover the B-52, which ended a remarkably interesting Dusty Beard Exercise.

Back to the old routine

Upon our return to Travis AFB, we again were put into a cycle of one week on nuclear war alert, then one week flying a training mission, then back to alert, etc. I was gone from home about half the time and did not feel that I had much future in the USAF. However, family life had been and was doing very well as California was a model for fine life in the 1950s and 60s.

California Family life

Betty and the kids were living in our new house in a good neighborhood in Fairfield. Steve and Sandy were growing up, and living in Fairfield, California was great. We were close enough to Sacramento to visit Betty's Grandmother, Hilda, who lived with Betty's Uncle Art and Aunt Helen Anderson, and their two children, Richard and Karen. Betty also had Aunt Esty and other cousins in the Sacramento area, so we had some large family gatherings at the Andersons. Betty's sister, Mary, and her husband, Jerry Bourassa, were also in the Air Force at a radar site in Prince George B.C. Mary and her daughter, Denise, stayed with us when Mary was about to have her second child, Jannette, and was using the hospital at Travis AFB.

My parents, Everett and Letty, took their first jet flight and came to stay for a couple of weeks. Betty and I gave them the master bedroom, and we tried the spare room. Steve, at age 5 in 1962, started kindergarten. California schools were excellent in Fairfield.

The neighborhood around our Fairfield house was a tract with houses looking alike on each block. We had an Italian family a couple of doors from us that were constantly getting lost and going to houses that looked like theirs.

Steve and Denise could play on the driveway and sidewalk without supervision as the world was a safe place. In fact, Steve, while still in diapers, wandered away one day and, after some frantic searching, found a blook away playing with another kid. Later he and Denise would ride around the block on his tricycle. Life was good.

A New Job

Alert duty and limited flying continued as a sad but normal way of life. However, one day an ad appeared in our military daily bulletin paper stating that Castle AFB had an opening for a KC-135 Simulator Instructor pilot.

Castle AFB, in Merced, California, was about 160 miles south of Travis and was the base where I took my training to upgrade to the KC-135. I had been talking to a real estate company that was looking for a pilot for their corporate aircraft and was strongly thinking of leaving the Air Force. I, instead, applied for the position at Castle and, after a couple of telephone interviews, found myself transferred.

Chapter Twelve
July 13, 1962– August 1, 1969

4017th Combat Crew Training Squadron

93rd Bomb Wing Strategic Air Command

Castle AFB

Merced, California

Lt. Col. Troy Drew, Squadron Commander

I began my new assignment on July 13, 1962, at Castle in the 4017th Combat Crew Training Squadron as a KC-135 aircraft simulator Instructor Pilot. This unit was the same unit that Leonard Dixon and I had trained in during September 1959. They were the same simulators, designated M-260 KC-135 models, that Leonard and I had flown during our training; however, I was assigned to a new mobile simulator group that was about to activate using the M-26 simulators mounted on railroad cars. These simulator units would now visit the SAC bases to give refresher training to the combat-ready B-52 and KC-135 crews - a new concept.

I was immediately sent to Hill AFB in Utah to pick up the first KC-135 railroad simulator. When I got to Hill, I found the simulator in a long railroad car sitting on a siding, ready for my inspection. The operator was an enlisted guy who had preceded me and was trained in the operation and maintenance of the unit. He maintained the unit and was in the back running the electronics that made the thing fly. These simulators did not physically move up and down, nor did they bank or roll like their modern airline counterparts, but they still worked well for normal and emergency procedure training. The pilots sat in a fixed seat, and the instruments and controls were actuated electronically.

The Air Force did not spend money as the airlines did for fancy equipment. However, one could start the engines, hear the sound, go down the runway and fly and crash if procedures were not followed. The simulator instructor pilot could fail engines and systems and put the flight crew in critical situations to see how they would perform under stress, and they would cause the simulator to crash and burn if they did not properly apply the corrective actions.

We simulator instructor pilots had many situations to grade the crews on and if they failed, we simply went back and practiced until they were proficient.

The Mobile KC-135 Simulator

After accepting the simulator unit for the Air Force, I left Hill AFB for my first class at Ellsworth AFB. A new railroad siding had been built at Ellsworth AFB which included a high-power electrical line that the simulator would plug in for operating power. There was also a B-52 simulator mounted on a railroad car that went from base to base performing the same training as I was doing. We were never on the same base together as the base would have only one railroad siding to support the simulators. I would meet the crews at the train and the operator, and I would put them through the curriculum to refresh them in flight emergencies.

Almost a Nuclear War

That is where I was when the Cold War caused America almost to go to nuclear war on October 27, 1962. Here is the story.

The Cuban Missile Crisis

After we were transferred to Castle AFB in July, Betty, being a great military wife, stayed back in Fairfield to sell our first home. It took some months to get it sold, and during that time, I was on the road with the simulator and/or living in the BOQ at Castle while Betty and the kids stayed in the Fairfield house.

The Cuban missile crisis started in May 1962. Tensions

increased over many months, and then Cuba shot down our U-2 spy plane, and SAC went to a DEFCON (Defense Condition) TWO on October 27, 1962. When that occurred, all the nuclear bombers and tankers alert crews in the USA ran from their alert building, started their engines, and taxied to the end of the runway and prepared to launch. I watched from my mobile flight simulator, which was near the runway at Ellsworth AFB.

Only a month before, I could have been in my own KC-135 at the end of the runway at Travis AFB, facing a major challenge. Now, I was feeling helpless and worried about my family at Travis thinking they must be afraid.

Military Families Face a Terrifying Situation.

The families around the bases were told to stock up on survival rations and prepare to evacuate. They were not, however, told where to go. Betty was in a panic. She found the commissary out of food, and since the highways were already jammed, she packed the downstairs bathroom with food and sheltered in place. I was TDY with my mobile simulator at Ellsworth AFB and sat helplessly watching the alert force sitting on the runway, ready to go to war.

The aircraft sat at the end of the runway for at least 30 minutes with their engines running, waiting for the signal to take off. Finally, the Soviets said they would dismantle the missiles they had put in place in Cuba and turn the ships around that were carrying more missiles to Cuba.

We were at a shaky peace again.

A Close Call

The United States Air Force's Strategic Air Command motto was "Peace is our Profession." That day, we lived up to the motto. I later found out that the 303rd ARS tankers in Bermuda located the Russian missile cargo ships on their way to Cuba. The US Navy would have destroyed these vessels had Russia not stopped the aggression. The 303rd tankers were from my old SAC outfit I had flown with some years prior.

A New Way of Life at Castle AFB

Our Fairfield house was finally sold in November of 1962, and our family experienced their first full military move. After the packers came and loaded up all our belongings, Betty loaded the kids in our blue 1961 Oldsmobile 4-door and drove to Merced. There, using Wainwright Realty, she found a nice rental house at 456 Iroquois Street. We had Maynard, his wife, and his daughter as neighbors on one side and John and Joanna Talbot on the other side. Maynard was known to stand in his back yard at night playing the bagpipe. Eerie! Maynard also had a quality 1953 Chevrolet,

"Woody," which I was later able to purchase to use as a second car. I wish I had that car today. I would be rich!

My best Assignment

The assignment at Castle AFB would turn out to be the highlight of our Air Force career. We were to be there for nearly seven years, allowing our children to go through grade school in one location.

In the Spring of 1963, we had a custom home built at 2120 Almondwood Lane in East Merced, close to Bear Creek. We moved into our new home in August of 1963 and lived there for the rest of our tour at Castle AFB, selling it in August of 1969. The house had three bedrooms and two baths with a see-through fireplace between the family room and living room. It was a California ranch home that gave the whole family lifelong memories and gave us lifelong friends. We bought the lot from John Wainwright and his real estate company.

Almondwood Lane

Almondwood Lane was a cul de sac formed in an old almond orchard. We were told that if we kept enough trees on our property, we could produce enough almonds to pay the taxes. Well, it was a stretch, but we did get the experience of knocking almonds from the trees, bagging them, and taking them to the almond exchange, where we sold them or took our earnings in whole almonds which Betty would roast in the oven, so we had healthy snacks. We never got nearly enough almonds to pay the taxes, but the kids got a lesson in getting very dirty from trying to knock the almonds out of the trees using long poles. Lots of dirt and insects, such as spiders, would come raining down with the nuts, and one got the brunt of it while standing under the tree. Most of the trees left on our lot died during the years we lived there, but our street was aptly named.

I spent my first year at Castle teaching student crews normal and emergency procedures in the mobile and base KC-135 simulators. These students would go to ground school classes during the day and then start their simulator sessions in the late afternoon, which meant that I would be working into the late evening.

Heavy Fog

In the winter, the San Joaquin Valley would be filled with a very heavy fog in the late afternoon and evening. We lived east of town, and Olive Avenue, the road from the base to a mile north of our house, was about three miles long. I would use my odometer starting when I left the main gate and follow the white line until I had driven 3.5 miles and then would slow down and look for my right turn onto McKee Road that led to Almondwood Lane which was just 70 feet short of the Bear Creek Road stop sign. I could then find my turn into our cul de sac and our house. I had cars sometimes follow me right to our driveway as they were lost in the fog. I never had an accident or even a close call during that period as we drove slowly and cautiously. It reminded me of flying in a cloud but without instruments to guide you to your destination.

Flying the KC-135 Simulator

Teaching in the simulator was fun. I would sit in the jump seat between the two pilots and direct the simulator operator behind me to fail the different systems, and then I would observe the crew handle the emergencies. It was simple to correct them on the spot, and they learned quickly. I had done a lot of mobile simulator traveling duty starting as soon as I arrived on base in July of 1962 and had logged over 2,000 hours of KC-135 simulator Instructor pilot time. I now came off the road and settled into the on-base teaching after the family arrived in the Fall of 1962.

Building our first house

We started construction of our new Almondwood Lane home after Betty and the kids arrived and moved in about four months later. By July of 1963, I had been recruited to teach KC-135 academics. I started in a new field which I found challenging and fulfilling.

Now a School Teacher

I started to train as a teacher back in 1952 when I enrolled in the Industrial Arts course at Stout Institute in Menomonie, Wisconsin. At that point, I had never thought about standing in front of a class and imparting knowledge. Now I was expected to teach very technical classes of eager USAF-rated pilots. It was going to be a demanding task.

I had very little public speaking training and was uncomfortable in so doing. I remember repeating my marriage vows in front of a friendly congregation that left me "spit less". My new boss, Major Roy Spoutz, suggested that I enroll in the Toastmasters organization, which turned out to be a life saver. My presentations improved to the point that I received top ratings on my teaching abilities. I advanced in the academic field to the point that I was teaching the most difficult courses to foreign students and high-ranking officers, and I was enjoying all of it.

I was teaching KC-135 and B-52 students for the remainder of my next six years at Castle AFB. Flying now was an important part of my job. I had a lot of experience in the right pilot's seat of the KC-135. As an instructor in the simulators, my knowledge of procedures was valuable to the staff pilots who were rusty when it was time for their evaluation flight checks. I volunteered to fly as their copilot and tried to keep them out of trouble. I never had anyone fail their flight checks while I was their copilot.

TDY to the Vietnam War

During my second year at Castle, I was finally able to check out as an aircraft commander, and then during the remaining years, I flew two extended trips to Southeast Asia named "Operation Young Tiger."

The first of these was two months long and was busy. I had a crew from the 924th Air Refueling Squadron on Castle AFB. We left Castle on January 29, 1967, and flew to Kadena AB, Okinawa, stopping in Hawaii and Guam on the way. We led and refueled six Air Force F-4 fighter/bombers as far as Hawaii. Then a few days later flew to Guam refueling a B-52 on the way. Guam was busy with B-52s flying missions bombing North Vietnam. After a day there, we flew to Kadena AB on the island of Okinawa, where we stayed and flew a number of missions refueling fighter/bomber aircraft, which were flying into North Vietnam, destroying missile and radar sites.

While at Kadena, I had the privilege of dining with my old 303rd Aircraft Commander, Carl Johnson. Carl was stationed at Kadena and had his wife, Vanice, and the kids with him. I remember him complaining that he had been passed over for a promotion to Lieutenant Colonel and was not very happy. I also started meeting a number of KC-135 pilots I had known from Travis and other bases. Many were my students when they were upgrading at Castle AFB. All were participating in the Vietnam War. Small world.

I had my first introduction to the Vietnam War when we left Kadena to travel to Utapao AB in Thailand with stops at Clark AFB in the Philippines and Danang AB, which was just south of the DMZ in South Vietnam.

My First Vietnam On-The-Ground Mission

We picked up a B-52 maintenance crew in the Philippines that was going to replace the vertical fin (tail) of a B-52 that had made an emergency landing at Danang AB after experiencing a midair collision with a fighter aircraft coming back from a bomb run in North Vietnam.

Danang AB was historical in that it was the first United States military installation to bring the USA into the Vietnam Conflict. 25,000 U S Marines arrived at this base in March of 1965, two years prior to my crew arriving, to guard the base against attack from the North Vietnamese. The war heated up and expanded from that point, and that is why we found the base heavily involved in war activities. The base had been under constant attack ever since that time. It was a great introduction to a shooting war for me.

When we arrived at Danang, we found the base very crowded and busy, with fighter aircraft landing and taking off every few seconds and some landing all shot up. We were taxied directly behind the damaged B-52 and told to shut down. I asked the ground crew how I was going to back up to leave as there was no room to put a tow bar and tug on my aircraft. They smiled and said don't sweat it, as they would get a bunch of GIs to push us back by hand! Welcome to Vietnam- the job gets done but sometimes in an unusual way.

A Rush to Get Airborne and Away from Danang AB

The arrival of our big tanker aircraft alerted the North Vietnamese to a potential target to destroy, and that is why we were only on the ground at Danang for a couple of hours. We off- loaded the B-52 repair team and their equipment, got our manpower push back, started engines, and taxied out for takeoff.

We were warned that there was ground fighting going on all around the base and to climb quickly and avoid certain areas on departure. As we broke ground on takeoff, all the instruments in our #4 engine dropped to zero. I thought at first that the engine had failed because of a bullet or missile in the engine, but it was still running and looked fine, so we kept going and turned South toward Ban U Tapao AB in Thailand.

We were now "in country" and flying in hostile territory, supporting the bombers and fighters which would fly into North Vietnam.

Later in the TDY, I even had to fly north of the DMZ into

North Vietnam one time to pick up a shot-up F-4 that was leaking fuel badly. He would not have made it back home without refueling and a tow that we did while he was locked on to our boom. We, and many others who did something similar, were forbidden from flying North of the DMZ because we would be within range of the North Vietnamese surface-to-air missiles that the North Vietnamese had to defend their country. To my knowledge, none of our tankers were ever hit, and we saved many aircraft.

During my two trips, I flew out of first, Tahkli RTAFB and the second trip, Utapao RTAFB, both in Thailand. I was awarded the Air Medal for these flights. I logged 132 combat hours in the KC-135 and never took a hit.

Worldwide flying

I also had a couple of long trips to England, flying out of Upper Heyford AB and to Spain, flying out of Torreon AB. These trips were in support of US fighter aircraft operating in Europe. We had many aircraft and crews stationed on foreign soil, and they all needed air refueling training.

I brought back many souvenirs from all those trips which you see today around our house. I was upgraded to Instructor Pilot in the KC-135 aircraft in 1967 and had amassed about 3,000 flying hours by the time I moved on to March AFB in 1969.

A Lifelong Family Memory

The family had many great years living in Merced. We had a great neighborhood with Ruth and Maurie Crawford, a math instructor at the new Merced College, living on one side of us and Carl and Peggy Morgan on the other side. Carl was a KC-135 Instructor pilot. We also had another KC135 Instructor, Art Goodwin and his wife, Cindy, living down the block. We had Bud Johnson and his wife Dot across the street. Bud was a B-52 Instructor pilot, and next door to him, a Ph.D. at the college Earl Fry and his wife, Patsy. Patsy was the organist at our church, Shepherd of the Valley Lutheran, where I served on the council. A Mormon family, the O'Brien's, lived at the end of the street and the Kennedys across from them. We had the naughty teenage boy, Andy Speziali, who drove extremely fast on the street and caused Maurie and me to try to discipline him when his parents failed to do the job. The kids played throughout the neighborhood and generally had a great time. Bradley and Tracy Crawford, Cammy Morgan and Karen Goodwin were our kids' playmates. Life was good. Steve had some memories there: The block behind us also had several school-age children. Steve was putting up with a bully who rode the school bus with him. Betty's brother-in-law, Charlie Hess, an FBI agent, found out about it and bought Steve a punching bag and taught Steve how to use it. One morning, while waiting for the school bus, Steve and the bully got into it, and Steve punched him in the nose and broke his glasses.

That ended the bullying and cost us a pair of glasses. Steve also had a more serious problem when he and another friend were pretending to burn Viet Cong straw villages by pouring gasoline on the hut and throwing a match at it. Fumes got on Steve's ragged shorts, and he had to jump into a fishpond to extinguish them but not before his leg was badly burned. Dot Johnson, our across-the-street neighbor, heard the commotion and popped Steve in the bathtub to avoid shock. When Betty was taking him to the hospital at the base, Steve asked if his dad was going to meet them, and Betty said "no." Steve said that was the best thing that happened to him that day.

Hard Nosed Dad

I guess I had a bad reputation as a disciplinarian. We had lots of fun things too. Steve got to build a tree house in one of our almond trees. He and his buddy built a submarine out of barrels and wanted Betty to take them out to lake Merced so they could submerge it to test it out.

Camping in Yosemite National Park

We bought a partially finished two-wheel camping trailer from a friend, finished it, and took it up to Yosemite national park for many office camping trips. Our first campout in Yosemite was in an old canvas army tent. In the middle of the night, a bear stuck his nose under the tent by Betty's head. That was why we got the camping trailer.

Steve had another experience on an office camp out when he and some other kids were sleeping on the ground in the center of the campsite. He was near the McBride's trailer. Major John McBride was my office mate. His family had left some food outside and a bear came along and stepped on Steve as he got the food. The next morning, we asked Steve if that scared him, and he said, "No, but my heart sure hurt."

We had good times in Yosemite on the days when it was not crowded, and it was only an hour's drive from the house. Another special happening was Steve's kindergarten teacher being a college acquaintance of his Grandmother Ag, Betty's mom. Small world.

My Folks Come to California

My parents, Everett and Letty, expanded their lives by flying out for two winters and living in a rented apartment. They and the kids got to know each other, which finally formed the grandparent relationships all children need.

Everett would go on walks and had always had sharp eyes for things on the ground. He found a very small $10 California gold piece one day. It was fair value as a collector piece, and I believe Steve has it today in his coin collection. Everett found it shining in the grass near his apartment.

Light Plane Flying

Betty got to do some flying during our years in Merced. I started flying at the Aero Club at the municipal airport and checked out in their Cessna 172-7705T aircraft.

All our family would pile into the 172 and fly to Sacramento for family affairs, and the kids enjoyed it. I got to thinking that it would be a great idea if Betty would take the co-pilot course offered by the club which would allow her to land the aircraft if I became incapacitated. She passed the course, became a light plane co-pilot and has some of her own flying tales to tell.

Small Plane Flying Across the West.

We did take the 172 aircraft # 7705T on June 15th, 1963, from Merced to Superior, Wisconsin, and landed at many airports such as Elko, NV; Ogden, UT; Evanston, WY; Lander, WY; Rapid City, SD; Redwood Falls, MN; and Baldwin WI enroute.

We landed at Baldwin and gave each of my parents a ride. When we flew to Superior, we gave Ag and Waino a ride and then took the plane to Betty's uncle Harold Bysted's hay field near Brule and gave rides there too.

We experienced all the situations of flying light airplanes across the county such as bad weather, muddy runways, bad turbulence over the desert, and even losing the propeller spinner. No one in our family ever cried or even got airsick.

My Dad causes a minor problem on takeoff. When I gave my dad his ride out of Baldwin, he got excited and, as we were on takeoff roll, threw his cap in the back and pushed in the right rudder pedal just as we broke ground. I finally got him to relax and look around to find the Hansen homestead, and then he really enjoyed it.

My mother, who was in her 70s at that time, was very relaxed and helped me find the farm she grew up on near Baldwin.

The whole trip was a wonderful experience, and Betty was a great co-pilot.

I had another 172 experiences on December 26, 1964, while flying for the aero club with the Castle AFB Base Commander, Colonel George Fuller. He and I were out with the aircraft this winter afternoon, and he was giving me my annual check pilot ride. The fog moved in before we could get back to the airport, and we did not have much fuel, so we called Castle AFB approach and had them give us a GCA (radar-guided approach) to the base. I flew the aircraft, and GCA took us to touchdown on the long runway. Neither of us pilots ever saw the runway. We just felt the aircraft hit the runway, and I took off the power and let it roll to a stop. The whole thing was probably illegal, but we saved ourselves and the airplane, and since one of the pilots, Colonel George Fuller, Castle AFB Base Commander, owned the base, nothing was said.

I did some 172 flying in April of 1964 for the Air Force when a renowned scientist, Professor Karl Hausmann from Livermore National Laboratories, a nuclear weapons government-funded organization in Livermore, CA, was invited to speak at a base function. I flew the 172 over and picked him up and brought him back after the speech. Very interesting.

Highlights of Castle AFB

We were stationed at Castle from 1962 to 1969. It was the longest assignment we had and probably the most fruitful career-wise. I served as a project officer for two airshows, representing the base on the United Fund drive. I taught a special course for French KC-135 pilots and a special senior officers tanker course. I received praise from one of the general officers in the course. He stated that it was the best course he had ever attended in his career. I did not know it then, but I would be working directly for this officer two years later.

I also had two "Young Tiger" Southeast Asia Temporary Duty deployments as well as a special TDY to England and Spain to support fighter aircraft deployments. I also attended the Boeing Aircraft Company Performance Engineers 707 course in Seattle, WA, and became a certified aircraft performance engineer.

During these years, I earned an AA degree from Merced College which set me in line for my bachelor's degree from Chapman University some years later.

I was fortunate enough to be sent to the USAF Instrument Pilot Instructor School at Randolph AFB. I got to fly the North American T-39 aircraft at that school which would come in handy a few years later. I worked hard and graduated as a Distinguished Graduate. When I returned to Castle, I took over the Base Instrument Flying Course and had a great time teaching pilots how to improve their critical instrument flying skills.

During my time in Merced, I attended the new Merced College and graduated with a degree in Psychology and History. It was a busy but fun time. I did a lot of teaching and flight instruction. One of my last evaluations stated that I was the most knowledgeable KC-135 pilot at Castle AFB. I was pleased with that OER, and it helped me get promoted to the rank of Major.

Master Mason

I was also introduced to Masonry by my fellow officers in the 4017th. I became a Master Mason and Shriner during this assignment. I am, to this day, active in Masonic and Shrine work.

My Turn to Go to War.

I went to work one morning and was greeted by a call from personnel. I had been selected to go to Vietnam as an RF-4 pilot! This was a major shock as I had never been a fighter pilot and wondered if I would be able to handle that type of aircraft. Betty thought that I was too old to be a fighter pilot and that I would probably be killed flying the thing – she was probably right.

A few days later, I was sitting at the bar in the Castle Officers club when the fellow next to me told me that he had volunteered many times to go to Vietnam and fly the RF-4 but had always been refused because SAC needed him to fly the KC-135. I had an idea. The next day the two of us went over to personnel assignments, and when we came out, the other fellow was happily going to fly F-4Cs, and I was staying at Castle as a KC-135 pilot. Betty was pleased. However, Vietnam was beckoning.

Another Move

I had a feeling that it was again time to move on in my career. I had, in 1968, applied for an Air Attaché position but had not been selected. Now I felt that a job change was necessary, and I realized that my promotion potential was reduced by staying at a Wing level. I needed to go to a Numbered Air Force position to be promoted to the rank of Colonel which was my retirement goal.

I noticed that the 15th Air Force Headquarters at Riverside, California, was looking for an Aide for the Vice Commander. They wanted a Major who qualified to be an instructor pilot in the T- 39 Sabreliner. It was now time to move on, and with the blessings of the family, I applied for the position. I did not realize it at that time, but the Vice Commander I was going to aid was the same general who had attended one of my classes for senior officers and was the one who had written the glowing commendation I referred to earlier - Major General Burl Mac Laughlin. After a telephone interview with General Mac, I got the job.

We were now faced with another move and decided we would sell the house. Betty, again the outstanding Air Force wife, stayed behind with the kids and put the house on the market. I went on ahead to March AFB as the job was urgent, and I had a lot of work to do to be able to fill the position.

On September 24, 1969, an Air Force Officer by the name of Russel Hansen (no relative) bought our Merced home, and my family immediately came to March AFB and moved into our on-base quarters. It was the first time in our family life that we were assigned a base house.

Chapter Thirteenth
August 3, 1969 – 22 April 1972

15th Air Force Headquarters,

SAC March AFB California

15th Air Force Headquarters

Lieutenant General Paul Carlton, Commander

I was somewhat apprehensive about approaching this new position as I had no staff experience, but I figured that it would all work out. I again left Betty and the kids to sell our Merced home, and I moved to 15th AF Headquarters at March AFB near Riverside, CA, about 325 miles south of Merced.

I found that my job required me to live on the base, and I was assigned Qtrs. 133, (133 Adams Ave), which was in the original March AFB housing area, built by the Civilian Conservation Corps CCC during the great depression. It was about a block from the officer's club.

I reported for duty in the Command Section of 15th Air Force Headquarters, about a block from our new quarters, on August 3, 1969. Ms. Dottie Hunter, long-time secretary to the Vice Commander, would be my trainer for my position as Aide de Camp to Major General Burl McLaughlin, Vice Commander 15th Air

Force. This was going to be an interesting assignment.

My desk was just outside Gen. Mac's office door. All he needed to do was call out, and I would be his Executive Assistant, ready to do whatever, which included taking notes of a meeting, writing speeches, arranging inspection tours of the many 15th Air Force bases, coordinating special events, driving he and his staff car to meetings on or off base, picking up laundry, running errands for his lovely wife, Betty, and standing in for Major Tom Tobin, Lt General Paul Carlton's Aide.

General Carlton was the top general in the 15th AF as its commander. Serving the 15th Air Force Command was a demanding 24-hour a day job but a fun one.

Another Instructor Pilot Job

My most responsible job was to start immediately and would require me to be trained as an instructor pilot in the North American Sabre Liner, the T-39 I had flown at the IPIS course at Randolph AFB a few years earlier. It was the primary USAF executive transport aircraft.

I had never checked out in the T-39 but had flown it for about forty hours when I attended the Air Force Instructor pilot instrument school at Randolph AFB a few years earlier. Major Ed Sheppard, the March AFB T-39 Standardization Instructor Pilot, was tasked to get me checked out in a minimum amount of time. My first flight was on August 12, 1969, and by the end of September, I was flying as a personal Instructor Pilot and Aide for the Generals at 15th AF Headquarters.

I had my first flight with General Mac heading off to Offutt AFB. The General was to fly as an airborne Nuclear Commander on an aircraft called "Looking Glass," which was a 24-hour-a-day airborne command post that could command a nuclear war if the underground command facilities were to be destroyed in a nuclear attack or sabotage.

We were still fighting the "Cold War" with the Soviet Union, and after our experience with the Cuban Missile Crisis were on constant alert as I was at Travis AFB in 1960.

The T-39 Sabre Liner

The T-39 was a fast executive five-passenger twin-engine jet aircraft. It had a fuel range of about 1500 miles and would cruise at 35,000 feet at 450 kts true airspeed. I called it the Model "T" of passenger jets as it was very maneuverable, being built on the F-86 fighter aircraft air frame. And was reasonably forgiving with its flight characteristics. It resembled a fighter-type aircraft as it had no auto pilot and had to be hand flown all the time. It was very stable, so the workload was reasonable for a single-pilot aircraft. I seldom had another qualified T-39 pilot with me, so I had to perform most as a solo pilot.

My job was to mentor the Generals so they could maintain their proficiency as pilots. The Air Force would not allow a General to be in command of an aircraft as they had more important things to think about than flying airplanes, but they had to maintain their flying knowledge since they commanded many aircraft and crews within the Strategic Air Command. When I was not flying, I was remarkably busy acting in the position of an Aide for the General Officers. I wore many hats and had an exciting time.

I flew this airplane for the next five years of my career and logged nearly 4000 flying hours, with most of them acting as an instructor/evaluator pilot. I believe I had more flying hours in this aircraft than any other pilot in the whole Air Force when I stopped flying in 1973.

The second year of assignment to the 15th AF saw a dual job situation. I could no longer simply be an aide but had to have a "real" staff job. My work at Castle AFB gave me an interest in working in the "Plans" division. I continued to support General Mac as his aide and pilot when he needed me and worked under Colonel Roy Watkins, the Director of Plans for the 15th Air Force. I worked directly for a Finlander from Ishpeming, Michigan, Lt. Col. George Johnson. The work was mainly classified but interesting, and the two jobs kept me very busy. I also had started completing my bachelor's degree with Chapman College there on base and was also the March AFB Boy Scout Troop scout master.

The family was still living on base with Steve and Sandy enrolled in the Allesandro Middle school just off base. My last Travis AFB KC-135 Aircraft Commander, Leonard Dixon, had also been assigned to the headquarters and lived near us, not far from the Officer's club. His wife, Betty Deane, was teaching school at the kids' school, and she had Steve as a student.

Steve's next school was as a freshman at Moreno Valley High. Steve then started earning money by providing a lawn mowing service for the senior officers who lived around us on base. He put in long dusty, hot days and was well-accepted by our high-ranking neighbors.

The last five months of our 15th AF assignment saw me again serving as an Aide De Camp to General Mac's replacement, Major General Richard Reinbold.

My first introduction to my new boss was when he and his wife walked into his office for the first time with Dottie and me standing by. Mrs. Reinbold walked behind the General's desk and attempted to pick up the red telephone. Finding it firmly attached to the desk, she looked at the General and said, "Well, Dick, you're not going to be able to throw this one through the window!".

That was the beginning of a rather rocky time in the Command Section. General Reinbold, a Military Academy grad, (West Point) would hold Open Ranks inspections of the Colonels and Lt Colonels in our headquarters, gigging these senior officers' bad haircuts, sloppy uniforms, poor shaves and unpolished shoes. I was required to make a gig list as the General went from person to person so he could call them in separately and severely reprimand them. I had never seen my fellow officers cry, and many of them left the office in tears.

I found this unsettling and started wondering if I really wanted to be associated with this type of organization. I flew the General many times and had an enjoyable time with him, but he could turn on his staff and leave them in tatters. His time, however, had come.

In March of 1971, I was called into his office and was told that he was about to retire. He asked me what I wanted to do now that my job was ending. I had been working hard on my degree at Chapman College and asked him if I could finish it on "BootStrap," where you are allowed to become a fulltime student. I reminded him that I could not get another promotion without a degree.

He took my request into consideration, and I was told the next day that he would put me into a six-month program at Chapman which would culminate in my getting a bachelor's degree in psychology with a history minor. There was a catch - immediately upon graduation, I would go to Vietnam for one year. I agreed, and we went our ways.

Off To Vietnam

We were allowed to remain in our quarters on base while I attended school, but the family would move into town when I left for Vietnam. Betty had started working as an administrative assistant to the Director of the Chapman campus about a year into our tour in March.

Son Steve took advantage of this and gave up his lawn mowing, and he and a buddy started selling coffee during the class break in the evenings at the College. I did manage to have most weekends off, so we were able to take the kids and pull our 21-foot travel trailer to the fishing village of San Felipe in Baja Mexico for a couple of vacations along with my scouting and Betty helping Betty Mc L with her Girl Scout troop of which our Sandy was a member.

Lt. Col. George Johnson, his wife Martha and their family lived across the street from us. I worked on some psychological exercises with their daughter while I was attending college. She said I had helped her, so I guess some of that stuff stuck.

Overall, our years at March AFB worked out well. We had good AF friends, and the 15th AF staff were telling me that I should come back after Vietnam and pick up my career in the Strategic Air Command. I thought that I probably would do that.

I graduated in April of 1972 and immediately moved off base

into a suburb of Riverside called Sunnymead to a lovely home that we purchased for the family to live in while I went off to war.

I didn't know it at the time, but this ended my long career with the Strategic Air Command. I had always thought that SAC was a quality by the rule's organization. General Curtis Lemay had a major hand in forming it from its inception. I was honored to know General Lemay as I got to fly him around after he had retired. I also found that General Curtis Lemay, the founder of SAC, was a Free Mason! My big boss, General Carlton, had been an Aide to Lemay as he had come up through the ranks. At that time, I was hoping that after Vietnam, I would be back at 15th again working for General Carlton. One just never knows what fate has in store.

Chapter Fourteen
August 5, 1972 – 12 January 1973

377th Air Base Wing

7th Air Force PACAF

Tan Son Nhut Air Base Republic of Vietnam

My Vietnam assignment was to be flying the T-39 in a small unit called Scat Back. The unit was part of the 7th Air Force, which was located at Tan Son Nhut AB in Saigon, Vietnam. I needed some survival training prior to arriving in Saigon.

I immediately went to McDill AFB in Florida for a water survival course. This one was different than the one I had taken years ago in Bermuda. I got into my flying suit with all of my gear attached as though I was going to bail out of a fighter-type aircraft. An open parachute was attached to my harness, and I was towed (para sailed) by a power boat to the middle of Tampa Bay, where I was released to float down a few hundred feet or so and splash into the water. I then released the chute, inflated my raft and floated around for a few hours, trying out the radio and other gear. A helicopter then flew out and picked me out of the water, giving me a fun day with lots of excitement.

I flew back to March AFB after that training and then left for Vietnam via Travis AFB and Clark AB in the Philippines.

I flew commercially to Travis and stayed with Betty's niece, Candess, and her husband, Steve Vought, and then off to Clark, AB, for Jungle survival. I spent a few days at Clark attending the Jungle school, spent one wet night under a tree in the Jungle and was judged trained.

A T-39 from my new unit came to pick me up, and I was in the country on 5 August 1972. My one-year tour had started.

SCATBACK

Scatback was a small, close-knit group of about 30 Pilots and Flight Mechanics who flew about 12 T-39 aircraft. It was operated like a small courier airline with seven flights each day covering the major flying bases in Vietnam and Thailand. The first flight left early morning and stopped at Danang AB near the Gulf of Tonkin and just South of the DMZ (the closest land flying base to Hanoi). I had flown a KC-135 there while stationed at Castle AFB in the 1960s with a repair crew to replace the vertical fin(tail) of a B-52. The huge bomber that had met a fighter aircraft head-on lost the fin during flight and managed to land safely at Danang. This base was still known to come under attack from time to time, and the bad guys (VC) were close most of the time.

We would carry people, combat strike film, aircraft parts and any other small high-priority classified material as we made our way on each flight. Our call signs were "Scatback Alpha" for the first run of the day up to Scatback Golf for the seventh flight of the day, which flew at night, leaving Saigon around midnight and returning at sunrise. We had other special flights to cover each day as well. In fact, Scatback was called the CIA airline, and I was to fly many missions for them.

On 6 September 1972, about a month after my arrival, I had a special flight that few US Air Force pilots will ever have. I was in Scatback operations that morning when Navy Lieutenant Commander, Peter Blades, walked in and looked around at the other pilots in the area. He spotted me (I was the oldest pilot in the room) and asked me if I had any reciprocating (propeller) time, and I told him I had a lot. He said that he was a pilot on a Navy Admiral's COD aircraft (a twin reciprocating engine propeller aircraft called the C-1) stationed here, and his copilot was sick. The Admiral wanted to fly out to the USS America aircraft carrier that was stationed in the Gulf of Tonkin, a hundred miles or so from Hanoi. Peter wanted me to go along as the copilot, saying that I would bring the COD back to Saigon if he became incapacitated. I figured I could handle that as the COD was about the size of a B-25 and had two engines like the B-25, and I had lots of B-25 time back in primary. I asked my boss if I could do that, and he said GO, so I did.

Fly Navy

I met my new crew at the COD parked not far from our

Scatback operation at about noon and noted that about 12 nurses were on board. I did not see the Admiral, but he may have been there too.

I got into the right seat and noted that the controls were much like the B-25, but the throttles were hanging down from the ceiling. I was shown where the landing gear and flap levers were located and told to use 120 knots (air speed) on the final. I guess that's all I needed to know to recover the aircraft on a long land runway. We took off and, about 45 minutes later, were circling the armada, which included this aircraft carrier.

My first Aircraft Carrier Landing

I noted that there were aircraft parked on both sides of the landing area, and I asked Peter, my pilot, if they would be cleared off before we landed (I didn't think we would fit between the rows of planes). He laughed and said we would fit. He then told me there would be three cables spaced about ten feet apart stretched across the deck. We would try to hook the middle one, but any one of them could stop the aircraft.

I imagine my eyes are big by now. We proceeded to fly a pattern that got us lined up with the carrier. It was a beautiful day, and we were making a smooth approach, but the landing area looked awfully small. I was told to put my hand atop the pilot's hand on the throttles, and when we hit the deck, and he pulled the throttles back and dropped his hand, I was to then push them to full power in case we missed the cables so we would then simply fly away to try again.

The landing was hard, and I pushed the throttles to full power. Then Peter reached up and pulled them to idle. We had caught the middle cable, or wire, as the Navy calls them. We immediately made a hard right turn, and I looked out my window to see a Navy F-4 touching down only feet away from us. He hooked the wire and stopped before he ran over us. Exciting!

I elected to skip lunch on board and instead went up to an observation deck where I could watch the action of the carrier launching a strike force of F-4 aircraft.

It seemed like mass confusion with people jumping around running aircraft, bombs being armed, and finally, the launching of a number of fighter/bombers. I still can't comprehend the confusion I thought I saw on the flight deck. It amazed me that they didn't have accidents, explosions, and fires. I was impressed.

Our pilot, Peter, arranged a catapult launch (I'm sure to impress me). We taxied into position, got hooked up and then, with the engines screaming at full power, got shot down the flight deck. I was holding the throttles at full power, and Peter was pumping the control wheel back and forth until he felt we were flying. He raised the gear and flaps, and we were on our way back to Saigon. (My eyes still were big). Upon our arrival, I was presented with an honorary Tail Hook card to keep as I was now a member of a special society of Naval aviators. This was a flying experience I will never forget.

Scatback Approach

The Scatback flights over Vietnam, Cambodia, and Laos were always exposed to ground fire approaching and departing the airfields. We would climb as fast as we could after takeoff until we reached 10,000 feet and came down in the same manner. We had a maneuver that amazed me the first time it was demonstrated and scared our passengers when we used it, particularly at night. We called it the Scatback approach. I had heard that the other types of jet aircraft, including airliners, used a form of it as well to avoid a long low approach to these war zone bases. We did not have to use it for the Thailand bases as they did not have hostile forces surrounding them.

The Scatback approach worked like this: We would line up on the runway about five miles out at 10,000 feet and be slowed to approach speed. At night we would turn off all lights except the pilot instrument lights. When we were about a mile off the end of the runway, we would power down to idle, drop the landing gear, extend the flaps and speed brake and go into a dive. Dropping at over 4,000 feet per minute, we would drop to about 1,000 feet from the ground and bring power up on one engine and continue descent and land.

This maneuver got us to approach an altitude about a mile from the runway, and that was considered a safe area. Most of the time at night, you could look outside and see tracers coming toward the aircraft meaning someone was shooting at you with a rifle or small machine gun.

Scatback never had a plane hit during their whole time in Nam. Performing this approach at the war zone bases was one of the reasons for this fact. The approach was only comfortable if you were the pilot flying the aircraft, even the other pilot was hanging on.

I had, one night, picked up a passenger in Da Nang and as we were coming down at Saigon, he started screaming as he had not been awake to clear his ears. I had to stop the descent, clean up the gear, flaps, and speed brake and climb back up to allow his ears to clear and then circle back and repeat the approach. I felt the fellow had been drinking and did not hear the Flight Mech briefing which told the passengers to keep their ears clear and try to keep them calm during the Scatback approach. After my initial concern, I had fun flying it. We never got shot.

I personally flew many special flights such as transporting CIA personnel into Cambodia and Laos and Ambassador Ellsworth Bunker and his wife Carol Laise to Nepal and Bangkok. We flew almost daily.

When I arrived at the unit on 6 August 1972, they, due to

early rotations out of Vietnam, were truly short on pilots so I got checked out the second day in country and flew combat missions the very next day. The lack of normal training caused me a small amount of concern, but I realized that my background made up for any shortcomings in preparation. I could fall back on my experiences assisting weak pilots with complex situations and international flying in many parts of the primitive world.

The long flights into India and Nepal were handled by the experienced senior pilots and a recently arrived pilot normally flew the first time with one of those pilots who had gone on the route previously. I got to fly on my first trip without any experienced pilot to guide me as they had all left at the end of their tour. My SAC tanker experience came in handy as I had to navigate myself in primitive countries such as Burma and Bangladesh where there were limited radio navigation aids, so you had to navigate through the country visually. Our aircraft were fitted with an old technology low frequency directional radio, but we did have radar and a high frequency radio and, of course, the modern VHF/UHF radios. A fun challenge, similar to Amelia Earhart?

I remember my first trip into Katmandu Nepal with Ambassador Carol Laise and her staff on board. We were winding our way around high Himalayan mountains visually to find the airport. I had had, about an hour earlier in the flight, an embarrassing encounter with her when I came out of the cockpit to stretch and found her sitting on the head with her pants down. The toilet (head) was under the Flight Mechanic/Crew Chief seat in the open area just behind the cockpit and had no privacy from the cockpit and only a curtain between the passenger and cockpit section. I quickly returned to my seat, and she did not seem to be upset. Anyway, she now was suddenly standing behind me as we looked for the airport and offered her guidance. I was told to bear left as we passed this mountain and then I would see the first part of the runway which was a concrete strip that had its beginning about 2,000 feet on top of a hill. To the uneducated it would appear that the runway was only 2,000 feet long – not enough for our aircraft. She assured me that if I touched down near the approach end, I would then roll over the hill and would have an additional 4000 feet in which to stop. I had been told this in my pre-trip brief, but it was reassuring to have an experienced set of eyes backing me up.

We made an uneventful landing and taxied into a large group of Nepalese civilians who swarmed the aircraft as soon as we shut down. It was obvious that Carol Laise was loved by the natives. I later found that she had brought them all the treats.

While the Ambassador tended to her duties in Katmandu, the crew and I stayed at a downtown hotel. It was strange to walk the streets where there was a marijuana stand on each corner which also sold stronger drugs. I did some shopping and brought back the Prayer Wheel lamps that we have in our home today. We had a couple of down days in the city and then a morning departure back to Bangkok.

The T-39 was an excellent choice of aircraft for this type of mission as it was fully self- supporting and did not need any external power units to get it started. Since the airport at Katmandu had no support for a modern airplane, we simply got in the bird, fired it up and took off. We again had to stop in New Delhi, India, to refuel prior to going back to Bangkok. There we would get a weather briefing and then about a four-hour flight home.

I flew this mission two times during my tour and on the last mission, Ambassador Laise asked me if a Nepalese/American citizen could be on board on the way back to Thailand. The Ambassador's request was my command. Therefore, we had a famous Catholic Priest come back with us. Fr. Marshall Denis Moran, a Jesuit Priest who started St. Xavier School near Kathmandu in 1951 was our special passenger. He was a licensed Ham Radio Operator, 9N1MM, and his radio contacts were in demand throughout the world. I had never talked to him using amateur radio but recognized that I had a celebrity on board.

As we cruised back to Bangkok at 37,000 feet, I put him in the pilot's seat and let him have what he said was the experience of his life as he actually flew the aircraft.

War Stories

I had some other "firsts" while serving with Scatback.

I had a special VIP mission one afternoon where I was to fly to a radio fix near the DMZ and fly a heading and descend and look for and land on a runway cut out of the jungle. The passengers turned out to be four Air Force General Officers, one of which was my 15th Air Force boss, P.K. Carlton. He greeted me and chatted, telling me that his group would be inspecting a secret base that was monitoring North Vietnam and assisting the bombers and fighter aircraft. He told me they would be gone for a couple of hours, and when they returned, we would fly them back to Saigon. The weather was clear, and we flew as directed and found the runway and landed, pulled onto a taxiway on the edge of the jungle, parked and shutdown. A staff car then arrived and drove away with our group.

We were parked at the edge of trees and noticed deeper in the jungle some Marine F-4 aircraft. They were parked, and we did not see any human activity. The runway and taxiway were primitive and not level. As we sat there waiting without the engines running, the fuel started draining from the tanks in high wing to the low wing tanks, and there was nothing we could do to stop it.

After a couple of hours of waiting, we had about a 600-pound fuel weight difference between the left and right-wing. The flight manual warns that take-offs should not be made with more than a 400-pound difference. So, we sweated out having to wait and have the difference really large. I decided that we would add a lot of speed before taking off and prepare for the heavy wing to drop as we rotated to become airborne.

The group came back about 4 hours later, and we fired up as we started to roll down the runway. I noted that we had a 1,000-pound difference, with the right-wing being heavier than the left. I cocked the flight control wheel to the left and rotated about 20 knots above our normal rotating speed, and the bird came right off the ground and was controllable. The T-39 was a great airplane. I often called it the Model T of jets as it was simple and reliable.

When General Carlton deplaned in Saigon, I should have asked him for a job at the end of my tour. I probably would have gone to the Pentagon, and I did not want to do that.

After I got back to the States, a letter arrived that had been addressed to me in Vietnam. It was a letter of appreciation for this flight signed by a four-star general, General Glen Martin, Vice Chief USAF, He was on the flight with General Carlton, and I didn't realize it!

I was called to Scatback operations one afternoon in early January (9th?) and was told that a special mission had just been sent to us by the 7th Air Force Commander. President Nixon was arriving that coming night at Tan Son Nhut AB, and the commander was genuinely concerned about his safety while on the ground. Sitting on the ground at the Tan Son Nhut airport, even at night, would make Air Force 1 a missile magnet.

I was to take a T-39 to the end of a taxi strip which was near the main part of the base and wait with the door open while Nixon visited. If the Viet Cong attacked while he was on the ground, Air Force One, a large 4-engine aircraft, would not be able to react quickly enough to get into the air and save the president. If the attack occurred, I would be told to start my engines, and the President would be brought on board quickly. We were then to immediately roll down the taxi way and get airborne, and then we would be told via radio where to take the President. I was told that they would literally throw the President through the door and shut the door immediately and takeoff. They said he would be scared shitless, and there would be a lot of yelling and swearing, but not to worry, as his people would be with him. An exciting assignment.

We sat on the taxi strip in the dark for a couple of hours, and nothing happened, so we were finally told to go home. SIGH!!! I never saw Nixon's aircraft and am not sure he ever came to Viet Nam. A few weeks later, I had another remarkably interesting flight that actually did occur.

Kissinger

On January 23, 1973, President Nixon announced that the war was ending and that the documents were to be signed in Paris on January

27, 1973. I was called to Scatback Operations on the evening of January 25 and told that I would pick up a VIP within the hour and take off as soon as he was on board take off and check in on a special radio frequency, and we would be told where to go.

Nixon's Secretary of State, Henry Kissinger, appeared at the airplane, got on board and did not say anything to anyone including the crew. I took off and was told to first fly to Phnom Pen, Cambodia, where he was met by a black car. He came back about an hour later and again got on board without saying anything, so we took off and called in on the special radio frequency and were told to take him to Vientiane, Laos. We left there well after midnight and flew to Bangkok, where we dropped the Secretary off. He did not speak to the crew, except maybe to the crew chief, who was acting as a flight attendant. I wish that we had had a picture taken as this was a historic flight.

The United States was now withdrawing from the Vietnam war. That would mean that our unit would soon be leaving Saigon. We continued flying our courier flights from Tan Son Nhut AB but not as frequently as before. On the first of February, our unit received orders to move to Nakhon Phenom AB Thailand (NKP).

In Country Move

56th Combat Support Group

Nakhon Phenom AB Thailand

March 1, 1973 – July 10, 1973

We were now attached to the 56th CSG, which had top-secret aircraft flying intelligence-gathering missions. NKP was only a few miles from the Laotian border, so these flights were close to the action of the NVR supply routes. The aircraft we joined were the EC-47 (I found my past 303rd Navigator from Joe Hildebrand's crew, Jimmy Ford, serving there as a C-47 Navigator. Vietnam is a small world for USAF people). He was flying in an old WWII airplane called a Goony Bird that flew unarmed at night over the thick jungles listening for enemy radio transmissions.

Also, the C-130 gunships with their long cannons sticking out the side. They, too, flew night missions. A special C-130 that I never really found out what they were doing, but the mission was top secret. That aircraft was painted Black! We also had the odd fighter aircraft land generally when they had maintenance problems or had been shot up attacking the North Vietnamese supply vehicles. By the time I arrived there, the war was winding down, and the base was not terribly busy. The timing was right for me to take my 2-week rest and recreation vacation. R&R.

Betty Comes to Southeast Asia.

Betty and I had been planning on her coming to Saigon for the R&R, and I had gotten clearance for her to come into Vietnam. R&R stands for rest and recreation. Many of our militaries, when finishing their yearlong tour in Vietnam, qualified for a two-week vacation at special locations in SEA. Since things were quieting down, I thought Betty could join me – at her expense, and I thought that Saigon would be neat without a war, so we had planned it for mid-March. Now I was advised that we should have her come to Bangkok since the North and South Vietnamese were not honoring the peace settlement and were still fighting.

Scatback was still flying the courier missions into the various bases that we had previously flown to, but things had changed when we flew into Saigon. We wore civilian clothes and were met at the airplane by North Vietnamese Viet Cong soldiers. On one trip, they asked me if they could see the inside, and I saw no reason not to, so they crawled in and simply looked. I thought that it probably was a good idea that Betty did not come "into the country."

Betty's R&R

Betty arrived at Bangkok airport on the evening of March 22, 1973. Earlier in the day, I, along with Sgt. Derry Loftus, a T-39 Flight Mechanic whose wife was coming in on the same flight as Betty, had hitched a ride into Bangkok on one of our Scatback T-

39s. We checked into the Indra hotel that the USAF flight crews used in downtown Bangkok and waited for our wives to arrive. We had brought champagne and other consumables for the welcome party. The plane was late arriving, so Flight Mech and I decided to start the party early. When the ladies arrived at the airport, neither of the Scatbackers were feeling much pain. This caused a kerfuffle when Thai Customs asked Betty to find out the name of her hotel from me. I was standing on the other side of a fence separating the arriving passengers from the awaiting crowd, so Betty came over to ask me the question, and I gave some stupid answer like, "Don't sweat it!"

The Thai's finally let Betty into the country, and we went to our hotel and started a busy two weeks of travel around Thailand, which included a trip to the Bridge Over the River Kwai, a Bangkok River cruise, where we saw the locals bathing, crapping, peeing, and cooking in or on the river. The smell of the water and the streets where the streets were used as sewers was unforgettable. The smell was throughout Southeast Asia. Betty will never forget it.

We spent part of the time at Pattaya Beach, which was a couple of miles South of the new Utapao AB, where the B-52s and KC-135s striking North Vietnam where based. I flew a tanker out of that base on a Young Tiger deployment while I was stationed at Castle AFB back in the late 1960s. Pattaya Beach was an R&R facility for the US military who would spend their two weeks of mandatory rest and recreation during their yearlong Southeast Asia assignment. We found it nearly empty since the war was over for the USA, and most of the troops were on their way home. We took advantage of the water and went water skiing. Betty got brave and parasailed, and we cruised the islands with our own boat crew, fished and had the fish cooked for us at Alice's Restaurant somewhere in the jungle beach area South of Pattaya. (I think I got some kind of a bug from the unsanitary conditions at Alice's which caused me stomach problems for a year or so after I returned from Vietnam).

We had one interesting experience while we stayed at the lodge in Pattaya. Our group had run out of beer one evening, and Betty and I hired a Hop Tac (a motorcycle with wide rear wheels where passengers sat on a bench facing backward). We drove to the small village of Pattaya and purchased a case of Singha beer. We placed the case between us and rode back to the lodge and were met by our thirsty friends. As I lifted the beer case from the motorcycle bench, I noticed a small snake under the case. I identified it as a "One Stepper" (a very deadly snake where, if you were bitten, the bite would cause immediate paralysis and death). Excitement reigned supreme as the Security Police came rushing up, and someone was yelling, "Get the Raid". The police took the snake, and that was the last we saw of our "One Stepper". I don't know what would have happened if it had crawled out while we were riding down the road. I know that Betty was impressed.

Our super R&R ended on March 30th with Betty and Derry's wife flying back to the states and Derry and me hitching another ride from Bangkok to NKP to finish our Southeast Asia tour.

My last flights for Scatback took me to interesting places such as historic Hue, where the 5,000-foot runway was, according to the book, too short for the airplane. It was a flight for the CIA, so we thought we would give it a try and got in and out without a problem. The runway was covered in shrapnel, and I was sure we would blow a tire during that operation. I brought some shrapnel home. It is nasty stuff.

I also flew into Pleiku and made more trips to Phnom Phen. These unusual trips were mainly supporting the CIA in their hush-hush war.

At the end of my flying in Nam, I had flown 167 combat missions and was awarded an Air Medal and Cluster. I had, including Castle AFB during the 1960s, flown over 100 combat support sorties from Thailand into Vietnam and was awarded an Air Medal for those flights too.

I had one fun flight to Hong Kong and had to fly around the Huge "Barber Pole" to get lined up with the runway. When we left Hong Kong, I had to fly a reverse ILS which was a rare aeronautical procedure that one learned how to do by actually doing it.

FINAL FLIGHT

My final flight for Scatback and, as it turned out, for the USAF, was flown on June 24, 1973, with a call sign of "Scatback Bravo" from Nakhon Phanom to Udorn RTAFB, Tahkli RTAFB, Korat RTAFB and finally to Tan Son Nhut Intl. The airport in what was to shortly become Ho Chi Mihn City (Saigon), Vietnam.

Lt Col. Jack Wimer, the new Scatback Operations Officer, was the Co-pilot. My friend and fellow R&R mate, Derry Loftus, was the Flight Mechanic. I think the flight was to give the new Ops Officer a close look at the bases that Scatback had been flying to during the Vietnam War.

I logged nearly 1,000 flying hours and 300 combat sorties during my Vietnam War experience. My aircraft was never hit by enemy fire, nor did I experience any emergencies. I had received a promotion to Lieutenant Colonel as well, so things were looking up (Thank You, Strategic Air Command!) I greatly enjoyed the flying that I was allowed to do, but now I was ready for a new assignment.

Back to the States

I left for the United States the day after the June 24th historic (to me) flight by traveling to Clark AB in the Philippines and then to Travis AFB in California.

The Vietnam War had become very unpopular with the

American public. Many riots had taken place, and the returning military was sometimes spat on and called "Baby Killers". We were advised to wear civilian clothes when traveling on nonmilitary aircraft.

I did not do that. I flew an airliner from Travis AFB to Los Angeles International Airport (LAX), where Betty picked me up and took me to our temporary apartment in Riverside. She had sold the house at Pico Vista Way in Sunnymead, again showing her great ability to run the family and her own life without me there to boss her around! Thank you, my love. You didn't know what you were getting into when you chased those young flyboys down the road back in 1956 in San Antonio, did you?

We now were to start on the rest of our careers and more.

Why was I now leaving the Strategic Air Command? Well, I had been told by the 15th Air Force Director of Operations before I left for Vietnam that I would be returning to the Headquarters in March AFB when my tour was up. Betty and I had some conversations about the poor schools outside of March AFB and that the kids were afraid to use the bathrooms for fear of being assaulted. She felt we had to move.

A month prior to the end of my Vietnam tour, I was called by Air Force Personnel and told that I would now be going to a non-flying job as they needed the younger pilots to get flying experience.

Besides that, I had been stationed in the state of California now for fourteen years straight. It was time to see another geography. I was given a concise list of possible assignments, and after hearing "Colorado Springs" mentioned, I chose it. I felt that this choice would please our family. We visited Colorado Springs in the 1960s and found it lovely.

A day or so after accepting the Colorado assignment, I was called by the 15th Air Force Director of Operations and told that he would request me to come back in March. I had a long talk with him and told him that I had to move my family out of Southern California, and he understood. I may have given up a different career and promotion path, but I felt that God was telling me where I should go. So… Onward to Colorado. I would no longer be flying for the military, and I would not be working around aviators and the like, so now we will see what the "ground-pounding" side of the Air Force looks like. I know I will be challenged, and I hope I get to do important things.

Chapter Fifteen

ENT AFB

USAF Air Defense Command & NORAD Colorado Springs, CO

June 26, 1973, to January 31, 1979

To Colorado Springs

We left Riverside in the last week of June 1973, driving two vehicles. Betty and me in the 1967 International Travel- All pulling our 21-foot self-contained travel trailer with Steve, Sandy, and the dog following in our 1967 Mercury Cougar.

Steve had turned sixteen a few months before in March and was inexperienced in driving, but Betty and high school driver training had taught him well, and we had confidence in his driving abilities. We did not realize the stress he would be put through during this long trip.

We had a number of overnights, but the most memorable was in Las Vegas, NV. We camped in a major casino campground right downtown, and it was a new experience for all of us. We only stayed one night and found ourselves, the next day, on the road again. The next experience was driving into Old Town in Santa Fe, NM. The further we got to the center of town, the narrower the streets were until I thought I would have to back out. Steve was right on our back bumper, and we finally found a way out, much to the relief of us all.

We arrived in Colorado Springs around July 1ˢᵗ and went to the Monument, Colorado, campground at the small lake in the town of Monument, where we stayed while we looked for a house to purchase. We finally found one at 4855 Windward Circle, which was, at that time, the far Eastern edge of the city of Colorado Springs.

The home was under construction when we bought it, so we continued to camp out in Monument. The four of us and a dog were cramped in that small trailer. I was still on leave, so we picked up and took a trailer trip to visit the folks in Wisconsin. It was an interesting time with the family, having to get used to me and vice versa.

New House

Our new house was a four-level on a large lot in the Village Seven subdivision. The subdivision was the latest platted in a city that was now starting to grow rapidly. The close neighbors were middle-class folks with some other active-duty military.

Steve got his own room in the basement, and Sandy had a room on the upper level near Betty and my master suite. The house had two- and one-half baths cand a two-car garage. We were able to park our trailer next to the garage, and we had a patio on the West side of the house. We were to live there for about five years. During that time, Steve graduated from Wasson High School and went off to the Naval Academy, and Sandy completed middle school at Washington Irving and graduated from Wasson High School. We made some close friends on that street, including Bob and Barbara White, Hank and Kay Hankins, Harold and Janis Stoltenberg and across the street Sid and Faye Brockman. Barbara White, now a widow, still lives in the same house as of this writing in 2023.

Now a Public Information Officer

It was now time for me to do my first ground pounder job in the Air Force. I was assigned to the Air Defense Command Office of Public Information and was informed that I would be the Director of Community Relations for ADC/NORAD. I was soon to find out that ADC was the Air Force arm of NORAD, the North American Air Defense Command, which is a joint country command with Canada and the United States. I knew nothing about public information, but since I had volunteered in this field, I knew I had to give it my best, and I did.

My office was located on Ent AFB, which was a base on the East side of downtown Colorado Springs on the corner of Union and Boulder. A small area that also included ARADCOM Headquarters, which was the Army's surface-to-air missile defense. In earlier days, these missiles were located around major cities in the US and Canada as a defense against Soviet Bombers, which were the threat prior to the invention of intercontinental ballistic missiles. Ent AFB was in the process of being shut down, with the land being given to the City of Colorado Springs. It housed the original NORAD facility, which included the command center, which used the inputs of various radar sites around the coasts and on top of the world in Greenland and the North Pole to warn of an incoming attack. Later in the mid-fifties, the underground command in Cheyenne Mountain, which is a few miles south of Colorado Springs, took the place of the Ent command center.

The new office

I was well-received at the office. They did not seem to be concerned about my lack of public affairs experience. My boss, Colonel Jim Sunderman, had been a glider pilot in WWII but did not talk about that experience. I don't know if he ever saw combat. Al Cochran was the deputy with a wealth of military public information experience, and he had a few years rank on me as a Lt. Col but was a great mentor as he had been in the Information Field most of his career. I found that, among other things under my purview, I had the 56-piece NORAD band. It was a great bunch of musicians, both from the USA and Canada. I supervised their budget and approved their travel as they entertained bringing the NORAD story to folks in both countries. Mel Huwett and John Nalezny were the band commanders while I was there. Both were exceptionally fine musicians and band leaders. I later regretted not sitting in the band with my euphonium to be able to say that I had played with the NORAD band. The band had some subunits, such as the jazz unit, the NORAD Commanders, and a country western group as well.

I had a variety of other projects, such as being the command representative for the Pikes Peak Street breakfast, which saw horseback riders, the Pikes Peak Range Riders, off on their weeklong adventure advertising the Pikes Peak Rodeo. My office increased the number of tourists that got tours into the Cheyenne Mountain Command Center by advertising the tours in the local newspapers and taking the tourists in military busses from our headquarters, the Chidlaw Building, to the entrance of the tunnel leading to the complex. We would then walk the group through the blast doors and into a briefing room where we would present the NORAD story, answer their questions and then walk them to the command center and the space center. NORAD received much positive publicity because of the efforts of the Community Relations Division. I had a staff of folks such as Lt Glen Brady and Sgt Waymon (Bud) Benssinger, who were invaluable in supporting our projects. Army Major Don Stephens, who came from the Army missile command, joined the office as my deputy during my second year on the job. That was the U.S. Bicentennial year, and a four-star general by the name of Chappy James had taken over as CINCNORAD. General James had the honor to be the first Black four-star General in the US military and was a hot shot fighter pilot. I was called to his office soon after his arrival, and he told me that he wished to turn the historic civilian air passenger terminal at Peterson into an ADC/NORAD Airforce Museum and dedicate it during the bicentennial year. He placed the command's support people at my disposal to get the job done.

I came away overwhelmed. I had no museum experience and had never undertaken such a project. When I went back and presented the order to my staff, Don Stephens stepped up and volunteered to take on the project. He and our staff together designed and modified a historic old Peterson Field Hanger and passenger terminal into what is today the award-winning Peterson AFB NORAD Museum. It took much effort and imagination on our part and lots of support from the command, but it is now an official Air Force Museum with its own staff. There are many past fighter-interceptor aircraft and other airplanes that had missions within ADC and NORAD mounted around the museum area as well as the base.

We got Don promoted for doing such a fantastic job. One of the projects that we/he did in Community Relations was converting the original Colorado Springs air terminal that was used in the 1940s into a military museum which started bringing off-the-street tourists onto Peterson AFB for a personal look at NORAD/ADC. The museum quickly grew in size and mission and is now an official US

Air Force Museum.

During this period our family was growing up and was involved in our new home.

Betty was a stay-at-home mom and kept busy as a homemaker. Steve was a student at Wasson High School playing trumpet in the band and running cross country. Sandy was a student at Washington Irving Jr. High and played clarinet in that school's band. She was also now involved in confirmation classes at Prince of Peace Lutheran Church. She and Steve had picked this church early on as they liked Pastor Don Olson who was young and cool. Betty and I sang in the choir, and I was on the church council during our early years in Colorado Springs. The church also sponsored some Laotian refugees. Our Pastor, Phil Erlander, got both Betty and me involved in that program. Steve was in Scouting, and I was the troop chairman of Troop xxx, which was sponsored by Holy Cross Lutheran Church on the corner of Murray and Constitution. Steve, upon completing his Eagle Scout project, finally had his court of honor and was now an Eagle Scout. He had applied for college scholarships and the Naval Academy. Darrel Higman, his math instructor at Wasson, suggested he apply to the Naval Academy. (Darrel was a Naval Reserve Officer and an Academy recruiter, and he knew Steve would do well in the Navy.) I did not care as I knew of Steve's love of the sea, so he got the blessing of his parents.

Steve was offered a scholarship at the School of Mines in Golden, CO, and an appointment to the Naval Academy. He chose the Navy. Life was busy, and we enjoyed living in the Pikes Peak area.

The Year 1975

1975 was a remarkable year. We were still living at 4855 Windward Circle. Sandy was now a student at Wasson High School. Steve earned his private pilot's license, received his Eagle Scout award, graduated from High School, and left for the U. S. Naval Academy.

We thought that Steve was launched, so we spent his college money on a new 1975 Datsun 280 Z car that Betty would drive to her new career at the Air Force Academy.

Betty had decided in July 1974 that we would be retiring in the Colorado Springs area and that she could help with the retired finances by working. She applied at the USAF Academy in July 1974 and started as a GS-5, part of the Cadet Personnel Services Program/ Hostess office, and by 1975, had completed her six-month probationary period and was a permanent government employee.

In the Fall of 1975, we had an interesting adventure when Steve's Parents' Weekend came up at the USNA. Betty and I drove her new Z car to Annapolis while Sandy and Steve's girlfriend at the time (Debbie) flew into DC.

We all had a wonderful time with Steve until it was time to leave, and Steve and Betty started to cry. We were a bit taken aback, but he managed to say goodbye, and we watched him sadly trudging back to his dormitory. He later told us that when he got back to his room, his roommates were also crying, so the apron strings were now cut, and he was on his way to his first career.

Many friends

During the mid-1970s, we made many friends around the Colorado Springs area. One of these friends was Colonel Gene Neilson who was stationed at Peterson AFB and lived near the intersection of Constitution and Oro Blanco. Gene owned a buildable lot on the corner of Oro Blanco and Constitution. He was interested in purchasing houses with assumable mortgages and using them as rentals but had no plans for this lot.

Troy and Betty get into real estate.

Gene planned on retiring in California. Betty and I had thought about retiring near Yosemite National Park and had purchased a buildable lot near Lake Berryessa, which was near the main entrance to Yosemite, east of Merced. Now, we had decided that we were not going back to California for retirement as the state's quality of life was deteriorating. Gene had already purchased into a senior living campus near Travis AFB and knew he was heading to California, so we traded lots. Now, we own a vacant lot on the corner of Constitution and Oro Blanco in Colorado Springs. Our new lot was a short distance away from our Windward Circle home.

A speculation "Spec" house

We decided to build a speculation home on the lot and hired a well-known contractor, Al Clancy, as the builder. Al's wife, Linda, was his decorator, and we trusted them to construct a marketable spec house. Betty and I selected the design. Al started construction on the property in the Spring of 1978.

During this time, we met Gale and Carol Gundersen, who lived in the Black Forest area northeast of Colorado Springs. They were on acreage. Gale was retired from the Navy and, like me, an Amateur Radio hobbyist or a Ham (W0PDF).

We spent a lot of time in the forest visiting and partying and decided we would like to live there. We located ten acres on North Holmes Road, purchased the land and put in electricity, well, and septic. All of this occurred in 1978.

We were now big into real estate, owning two houses (one under construction) and acreage with utilities in and plans drawn for a nice retirement home.

We had followed Gene Neilson's lead in purchasing two houses in Cimarron Hills, East of Colorado Springs, which had assumable VA loans. We planned to use these properties for rentals and thought that we could receive tax breaks by using them as such. In the ensuing years, we would purchase three or four more of these rental homes, in some cases selling some to our relatives and friends.

We then sold our house on Windward Circle, moved Sandy and her friend Kim into her first apartment on South Academy Blvd near Pace Warehouse, and purchased an old 40-foot trailer house and had it moved onto the land on Holmes Road. We moved in with the idea of living there while our Black Forest home was being constructed.

We lived in the trailer during the summer and early Fall of 1978. The house on Oro Blanco was finished that Fall and we were about to place it on the market when Betty had a problem with our Black Forest trailer.

A Mouse Problem

As the weather got cold in the Fall, the Black Forest mice started looking for a warm place for the winter. One night Betty had gotten up to use the toilet, and while she was sitting on the throne, a mouse ran over her bare feet. She jumped around and managed to kick the side of the tub and break a toe.

The next day she announced that we were moving into our new spec home on Oro Blanco.

Sandy had moved into her first apartment on Academy Blvd when we moved to the Black Forest, and now she was told to come back home and live with us at Oro Blanco. She was not happy, but we needed the furniture we had loaned her to furnish our new house and did not want to pay her apartment rent when we had plenty of room for her in the new house.

It gave her the opportunity to enroll at Pikes Peak Junior College, working toward a degree in early childhood development.

When Sandy moved into the Oro Blanco house, she was dating a young soldier by the name of Tom. He was a nice fellow and we even got to meet his parents who were visiting him while he was stationed at Ft. Carson. Sandy came home one day and announced that she and Tom were going to get married. We told her that she was too young (she was 18) and she said that they would run away/elope to tie the knot. This really concerned me as I believed them. I found out the unit that Tom was assigned to and, since I was still on active duty, I paid Tom's commander, a young Captain, a visit. A day or so later, Sandy came home to announce that her friend Tom had just been reassigned to Germany. She said he had already departed and would not be coming back to Ft. Carson. There was no more mention of marriage. Sandy then found a new job at a manufacturing company in the Springs. She lived with us for a time, and before we sold Oro Blanco, she moved into a new apartment.

We found a young woman with a dog to rent our Black Forest trailer, so now we were landlords and deeper into real estate.

Thoughts About Working in Public Affairs

My 1974/1975 years in Public Information were challenging. The Toastmaster training and the school teaching that I had done at Castle AFB were now coming in very handy. My Community Relations Division had now given hundreds of tours to over 10,000 visitors to the NORAD underground facility and had dealt with top Canadian and U.S. community leaders in planning tours, speeches, flyovers, static displays, NORAD band appearances and parades. We were doing long-distance telephone briefings to civic groups nationwide as well as answering hundreds of letters that came into the command from the general public reporting UFOs and other weird events as well as legitimate requests for information.

I completed my third year in Community Relations by helping organize the largest air show in Colorado Spring history as part of the Bicentennial celebration. I was also a state leader in Boy Scout activities, helping direct public relations for the National Explorer Olympics. I personally presented Colorado Governor Dick Lamm with the 1976 Scouting Report.

New Job

Now, in April 1976, the Chief of the NORAD Briefing Team

had been promoted to full colonel and was being transferred. I was selected to replace him. Since he had been promoted to full colonel, I saw that as a possible steppingstone to being promoted.

The NORAD Briefing Team

The NORAD briefing team consisted of the chief, who would be a USAF officer and a Canadian officer counterpart. The presentation, which was "The NORAD Mission Briefing", was given by both officers, each taking a certain part. 35 mm slides and a 16mm film were used to support the speakers. The whole presentation took about forty-five minutes, and then the team or senior officer sponsor opened up to questions from the audience.

The NORAD STORY

The NORAD Story was a presentation of what NORAD was, how the command was organized, and why NORAD existed. The briefing was done verbally by the briefing team using visual aids such as slides and film. An audio-visual operator assisted the team by using projectors to put images on a movie screen.

Normally the presentation is unclassified, but when briefing senior officers, the classification could go as high as Top Secret. The difference was that the classified briefing would include specific numbers, etc.

Cold War topics surrounded the briefing material. NORAD

was made up of Canada and the US because the whole North American Continent needed to be defended. The Soviet Union was the only country that had nuclear weapons and was considered the enemy. The North American Air Defense Command was the only two-nation military command in existence. NORAD's primary mission was to give warning of an incoming nuclear attack by the Soviet Union.

A variety of systems were used for this mission, and these systems were technically advanced as the Soviets went from the Manned Bombers to Intercontinental Ballistic Missiles.

As satellites were put into space, NORAD expanded to monitor all the objects floating around the Earth, even those that would fall back to Earth.

The final point that the presentation made was that an attack on North America by Soviet intercontinental and submarine-launched missiles could not be stopped, but the early warning of the attack given by NORAD would allow time for the US to launch our nuclear bombers and our own ICBMs toward the Soviet Union and they could not stop our force either.

Since the Soviets knew this, a launch by their strike force would result in Mutual Assured Destruction-MAD. This was the basis of the Cold War. I felt then and still feel today that this all-out nuclear war would be the end of the world. Nuclear fallout would kill the entire world population. Not a happy thought.

NORAD IN 2023

I have not kept up with NORAD technology over the past years, but I know that now we need to monitor and prepare to strike other countries that are now armed with ICBM-type nuclear weapons. I hope that the US has up-to-date technology to counter the threat.

Chief of the NORAD Briefing Team

I found that my school teaching experience back at Castle AFB came in handy as the team ended up briefing many high-ranking individuals such as Pierre Trudeau, the Prime Minister of Canada, heads of state of many foreign countries and military chiefs of staff from various services.

I gave my first team briefing as Chief of the NORAD Presentations Division in May of 1976 with Major Bill Stewart as my first Canadian counterpart. In 1978 Major Cliff Zacharias stepped in as my final one.

A tight team

Cliff and I traveled all around North America - Canada and US - appearing in front of large audiences and also on major network radio and television stations taking on-air questions. We even went to Baldwin, Wisconsin, at the request of the local American Legion post and presented the NORAD story to an audience in a local church. My mother was part of the audience.

Gee Whiz items

We carried with us one-half of a Soviet satellite fuel bottle that NORAD had tracked as it fell from space when the spent satellite burned up in the atmosphere. It was a gee-whiz presentation. We received newspaper coverage wherever we went, and that was the whole idea of our travels - to spread the NORAD story.

End of the Road

I had begun, in early 1978, to see that I had come to the end of USAF promotions. I had requested a counseling session with a general officer -- the NORAD Chief of Staff, to get his view on my future. My OERs (officers effectiveness report) had been the top ratings during the whole time I was assigned to NORAD/ADC, but the information field had few openings for full colonels, and I had been passed over for the past couple of years. The General was honest with me and thought that retiring would be the best for me. I felt that I had given my best to the many challenges set before me and that I was still young and healthy, so after a serious consultation with Betty, I put in my retirement papers.

Toward Retirement

The family was now living in our new spec home on Oro Blanco Drive. Steve was at the Naval Academy; Sandy was living in our lower level; and Betty was working on her career at the Air Force Academy. I started, at age 44, looking for a new career.

My first thought was to work as a pilot for the airlines, but they were not hiring many pilots. A new air cargo carrier, Federal Express, was hiring for immediate employment. I started working on an Air Line Transport FAA license at a school at Peterson Field, using my GI bill to fund it. I also called Federal Express and applied for a pilot's position and was told that I would be hired and that they would help get me my ATP license. They said that I would train at their home base of Memphis, TN, and my class would start in the Spring of 1979. They were just getting started, but I assumed that things would go as planned. I later learned accepting this job would involve a permanent move to Tennessee. Sandy was now a senior in high school and Betty was well involved in her late blooming career, so we decided that Colorado Springs would remain our home base.

My retirement had been approved for February 1979. This left me with some months to prepare for retirement. I had two months of accrued leave, so I would be leaving my position and stop working at the end of November 1978. I continued my briefing job with Clifford at my side and started studying for my insurance sales license as a backup if the flying job fell through.

1978 was coming to a close, and I had an exciting 1979 in the planning stage.

The Official Farewell

The final official ceremony for me was my retirement ceremony. It was held just before Christmas 1978 in the Chidlaw Building auditorium. Colonel Bob O'Brian, my boss, was my retirement officer, and our top General, CINCNORAD- Four-star General Chappy James, presented me with the Defense Meritorious Medal, the most prestigious of my collection.

Ag and Waino were there also, son Steve who was home from the Naval Academy on Christmas leave, daughter Sandy and my long-suffering military wife, Betty. She, in a sense, was retiring from military life too. There was a large group from NORAD Public Affairs and other military offices attending as well. It was a very satisfying ceremony – I was pleased.

I knew that, again, I would have future challenges and experiences. So Long Air Force – It's been great!

Chapter Sixteen

Retirement Years

February 1st, 1979

<u>LIEUTENANT COLONEL TROY L HANSON, USAF-RETIRED.</u>

I have now taken off the blue uniform that I had worn for nearly 25 years and have a new life. We are living at our new spec home at 2504 Oro Blanco Drive in Colorado Springs, I am selling life insurance for the Northwestern National Life Insurance (NWNL) company, and Betty is working her career at the Air Force Academy that she started on July 15, 1974, Steve is in his fourth year at the Naval Academy and is due to graduate in a few months, and Sandy has graduated from Wasson High School and has completed a year at Pikes Peak Junior College. She had been living, until last year, with her girlfriend Kim in an apartment on South Academy, now she is living in the lower level of our new house, and she is working for a manufacturing company and is driving her 1960's orange Fiat convertible which is the apple of her eye.

We own 10 acres of prime land in the Black Forest where we plan to build our retirement house (13880 N. Holmes Road). It now has an old trailer house sitting there which we are renting to a college student and her dog. Betty is driving her aging Z car, and I am driving the five-year-old green International Travel All. We have a reasonable income between Betty and me and little debt – the mortgage on the house is the exception. I needed to get an additional stream of income, so I got going.

A New Career

I wasted no time getting into a new career. About a year prior to retirement, I had started training in life insurance sales and now have my sales license and am operating out of an NWNL office on Galley Road West of Academy Blvd.

A friend from NORAD Public Affairs and fellow Air Force retiree, Tom Langley, who was also breaking into the business, is an agent in that office. Tom and I had been recruited by Northwestern National Life Insurance Company (NWNL) which is headquartered in Minneapolis and has an active office in Colorado Springs.

Our product was whole life insurance which, along with the death benefit, also built up a savings account and seemed to fit the folks who had families to protect and had trouble saving money. The commissions were okay, and the whole sales presentation was interesting.

Prospecting

We started out getting our sales leads by making solicitation phone calls directly out of the Colorado Springs telephone book. Computers were rare, and the internet was unknown to us, so we simply went down the inch-thick phone book and tried to get people to allow us to come to their homes and tell them about protecting their families using life insurance.

We faced a lot of rejection which was difficult for all of us to overcome. I was very dedicated, able to easily chat with folks, and soon was reasonably successful.

Sandy Moves Out

The next event occurred around April of 1979 when Sandy decided to move to her own apartment. She had been sad about having to come back home when we moved into the Oro Blanco house and knew we were planning to sell the house. She then would have to move when it sold so she moved into an apartment near Academy Blvd and Palmer Park.

USNA Class of 79

Steve's graduation and commissioning occurred in May of 1979. Betty and I flew to Annapolis and rented a car to get around the area. The ceremonies were impressive, and we found Steve to be happy with his assignment to the submarine force. He will attend many schools prior to joining the "Sea Dragon", an attack nuclear submarine based in Hawaii.

Steve had purchased a small Fiat X-19 convertible, which he used after graduation to visit grandparents in Wisconsin prior to stopping to see us on his way to his first school in Orlando, FL.

He had a friend, Lorna, whom we knew as she was the daughter of fellow church members at Prince of Peace Lutheran. She had already graduated from Colorado State and moved to a job in Miami, FL, so we hoped that they would be making contact after his arrival in Florida.

Juggling Real Estate

We were reassessing our future when a couple who worked for one of the airlines in the Springs made us an offer on the 10 acres in the Black Forest. We negotiated with them and ended up selling the whole parcel, so now we were down to the Oro Blanco house and a couple of houses we use as rentals for tax write-offs.

We were empty nesters and felt that we did not need that large Oro Blanco house, so we put it on the market.

Our First Computer??

I was quite excited about selling insurance because Northwestern National had come out with a new "computer?" which helped our sales. It was a briefcase-sized device called a dial-up modem, which was able to use the client's telephone to tap into the NWNL main computer and print out a sales proposal right in the home of the potential client. This capability did increase our sales and was a "Gee Whiz" point of sale. I was now making a small amount of money, but I was still not comfortable with the situation.

Our Oro Blanco home is sold.

When we decided to sell the Oro Blanco house, we listed it on a 90-day contract in June 1979. The days went by without even one showing, and the day before the listing expired, the Realtor brought in a full-price offer. October was coming up.

Another Move

Our next home was a rented townhouse in a development called Ocho Caballos, which was near the Colorado Springs Country Club. The building was well-designed but poorly constructed. Our unit was owned by Dr. George Merkert, who was a member of First Lutheran Church.

New Cars

Betty and I had now purchased two new cars. They both were Honda Civics, a small two-door sedan with 4-speed manual transmissions. Betty's was bronze in color, and mine was silver. They were small but well-built machines that ran like fine sewing machines.

Our First Family death

The month of September 1979 saw Betty's sister, Joanne, being treated in a pain hospital in Duluth, MN. She had, over the past years, many physical problems and was living in California with her husband Charles Hess and was under the care of many doctors in the San Diego area. Joanne seemed to have constant pain and was recommended to Duluth Hospital for extended treatment.

Betty's parents, Ag and Waino, lived just South of Superior which was only five miles from Duluth and Joanne's hospital. At this time, Astrid Horyza, Betty's mom's sister, was visiting Ag and Waino in South Range.

Waino had been having health problems for a number of years and had been in the Superior hospital from time to time. He went into the hospital again around the first of October, and Joanne called Betty on October 2nd and suggested she immediately fly to Superior as Waino was doing poorly. Betty got to Waino's bedside the day before he passed away on October 4th, 1979.

He had been hospitalized for a brief time and, as we determined later, had died of a heart attack caused by bleeding ulcers.

Waino's funeral was held the next week at Pilgrim Lutheran in Superior. It was the church where Betty and I were married.

Waino is buried at the St Francis Catholic Cemetery in Superior. He and Ag had two spaces next to Astrid's husband, Joe

Horyza. This arrangement was done years ago when Joe died at an early age and left Astrid with her five kids.

Troy to Superior

While I was getting ready to drive to Superior to attend Waino's funeral, Betty's cousin Jean Sewell called. She was visiting Denver and asked if she could ride with me to Superior for the funeral. There went my comfortable but lonely ride. Jean loved to talk and chatted away the whole trip, so I never listened to my cassette music tapes. We even shared a motel room (I told Betty!) on the way up so she could continue her chatting. Jean is a lovable character.

Ag joins our family.

After Waino's death, we were concerned about Betty's mom living alone in her country home near Superior in the upcoming frigid winter. We talked her into coming to Colorado Springs to stay with us as we thought there would be plenty of room in our rented townhouse.

A couple of weeks later, Joanne, Esty and Ag arrived in Colorado Springs from Superior driving Ag's big 1975 Dodge 4-door sedan. Lots of excitement.

After Esty and Joanne left to go back to California and we all got settled in our new digs, it became apparent that the town house was not going to be large enough for our new family situation. So, we started looking for a larger house.

In the meantime, our little family started our new lifestyle with me still working with NWNL, Betty now a permanent government employee at the Air Force Academy, and Ag getting used to widowhood and living at a high altitude.

The Rest of the Family

During this time, Betty's sister Mary and her husband Jerry were working for the TRW Corporation in Alice Springs, Australia. Their daughter Denise was married and living in Florida, and their youngest daughter Jannette, who was still in high school, was living with Denise.

A major move

In November 1979, we found a beautiful new house that was built on top of a ridge in the north end of Colorado Springs - 1033 Garlock Lane. Vic McCann was known for building unique homes, and this one was that. It had about 4,000 sq. feet of living area built on 4 levels with large windows facing west looking at the beautiful Front Range of the Rocky Mountains. There was a deck off the kitchen that looked North, over to Dublin Blvd., which was at that time the northern limit of the settled north end of the city. The home was built with Anderson Windows and had lots of quality items in it but, overall, it was, like our townhouse, poorly constructed.

We moved into our new home in the spring of 1980 and had the builder modify the second level so Ag would have a bedroom – sitting room with a nearby bathroom.

Ag then went back to Wisconsin and sold Cousin Bill Anderson the family farm. She then downsized and moved her stuff into her new home on Garlock Lane.

Our Children Marry

We had a good life in our new home, with me still selling insurance and Betty working in civil service at the USAF Academy. Grandma Ag was even driving herself around the city in her big Dodge. The home was quickly warmed as it hosted two family weddings during the first year.

Sandy and Steve Leonard decided to marry in early 1980. Sandy had been working at a manufacturing company, National Cash Register, and had met Steve at her employment. They were married at our church, Prince of Peace Lutheran, on June 15, 1980. Our Pastor and family friend Phil Erlander officiated at the ceremony. The newlyweds then moved into our Poteae Street rental house where they were living when both Dana and David were born. Sandy attended a medical trade school after her marriage while her new husband Steve continued working at National Cash Register the company where they met.later, She got her nursing degree from

Pikes Peak Community College and her Bachelor of Science degree from Regis University in Denver.

Three months after Sandy's wedding, son Steve and Lorna Charlson were married on September 20, 1980. They were also married at our home church, Prince of Peace, with Pastor Erlander tying the knot. They had, as part of their wedding ceremony, a Navy Honor Guard made up of Steve's classmates – very impressive. Steve, who received an Aeronautical Engineering BS degree from the USNA, had just finished nuclear reactor school in Idaho and the new couple moved to another submarine school on the East coast after their ceremony. After this school, the newlyweds moved to Hawaii to begin Steve's permanent assignment on the submarine USS Sea Dragon.

Ag gets itchy feet.

Ag decided to do some traveling. In late 1980 She flew on an organized tour to Australia for a visit with Mary and Jerry who were working for TRW on a satellite system. The highly classified operation was called DSP, which was monitoring the USSR for missile launches that would indicate a nuclear attack on the United States. During that visit, Ag also visited New Zealand.

A couple of months after her return from Australia, she left for Hawaii on February 5, 1981, to visit and tour. During that trip, she stayed with Lorna and Steve. A few days after her arrival, Steve sailed away on maneuvers on his boat, the USS Sea Dragon. Lorna and Ag then had a delightful visit with Lorna as the tour guide. Unfortunately, Ag fell ill and ended up in a hospital on Maui.

Ag Passes

After her release from the hospital, Ag flew to Sacramento to visit her sister Astrid. While there, she suffered a stroke. Betty got the call and flew to Sacramento, thinking it was a minor stroke. Betty arrived in Sacramento in the afternoon on a day in the Spring of 1982 and went directly to Ag's bedside, thinking she would be sitting up in bed. Instead, she found her unresponsive. Betty kissed her mom's cheek and said, "I am here." A tear rolled down Ag's cheek, and she passed away shortly thereafter.

Ag had two funerals. One in Sacramento with the California Anderson family in attendance and another at Prince of Peace Lutheran church in Colorado Springs with Mary; Joanne; Granddaughters Candy and Sandy; Great Granddaughter Dana; and Betty and Troy attending. Ag's ashes were later interred next to Waino in the St. Francis cemetery in Superior.

Life Continues

We now had the big house on Garlock Lane to ourselves. It served us well for family gatherings and office parties and for Troy's business office.

Real Estate Rentals

I had been chatting with my friend Gene Neilson and found that he was investing in houses with assumable mortgages that he was then renting out. It did not take but a couple of thousand dollars to pick these properties up, and the rents would pay the mortgage payments with some left over for maintenance and paying a manager. Betty and I decided to give that idea a try.

We were attempting to recover from the mismanagement of the Jimmy Carter presidency (he left office in 1981), and interest rates for new mortgages were in the high teens.

Selling a property with a new mortgage was difficult, but assuming a VA mortgage was easy if one had some money. The rates on the assumed mortgages were 5-7 %, and that was much below the prevailing new mortgage rates of 15 – 18 percent. We also felt that owning and renting out these homes would help give us some income tax deductions. We purchased houses on Poteae and Chippewa Court streets in Cimmaron Hills before I retired, plus a few more over a year or so later.

Now a landlord, I started getting busy managing real estate rentals. I learned quickly about repairs, evictions, legal processes and managing good and bad tenants.

Hanson Rentals

I was now in the insurance and real estate business and rather enjoying it. I started a new business called "Hanson Rentals" and set up an office in our new home on Garlock Lane. I also assisted Betty's sister and her husband, Jerry Bourassa, in purchasing rental properties and then, since they were living out of the United States, I managed them. I suddenly was a Property Manager. I found that I was not required to have a real estate sales license to get paid to do this service.

Jerry sent me referrals of other US citizens who worked with him, and I assisted them in purchasing other rental properties, which gave me more properties to manage. Things were sailing along when I found another interesting proposition.

National Travelers Life Insurance Company

My insurance sales situation changed in April of 1981. I had met, in the course of my life insurance sales, a fellow by the name of Carl Swenson. Carl had a one-person insurance agency in Colorado Springs where he was representing the National Travelers (NTL) Insurance company, headquartered in Des Moines, IA. Carl was trying to recruit me to move to his agency and represent National Travelers. One day he asked me to lunch to meet a highly successful agent who had a National Travelers agency in western Minnesota. At the luncheon, I met Larry Swenson and another agent, Duane Hanson, who was a close friend of Larry's. I got a lot of encouragement from Larry on switching companies and found Duane to have an interesting background.

Duane Hanson

Duane lived in Palmer Lake and was marketing aviation insurance. He had clients all around the United States and owned two aircraft, which he used to visit his clients.

Duane was raised in Minnesota, not too far from where I was born and had attended the U of Minnesota prior to coming out to Colorado where he had purchased a grocery store in Palmer Lake. He ran the store for some years, got interested in aviation and got his pilot's license. He then got into insurance.

Duane invited me to come fly his aircraft in May of 1981. I logged my first flight in his Piper Aero.

Now, I considered Duane's friendship and his friendship with Larry Swenson and felt like I should join the National Travelers group. I left Northwestern National Life a month later and started marketing National Travelers Life products. With the help of Carl and Duane, I became quite successful.

Monitoring Troy's Parents

My "only child" status continued to affect my life. During all of this hectic time, Betty and I felt that we needed, on a regular basis, to go to Baldwin to visit my folks. They had sold the farm back in 1967 after first calling me and offering to sell it to us for $17,000. At that time, Betty and I were in no position to get out of a successful career with the Air Force and had little interest in living or farming in Wisconsin.

The folks then sold the farm to Irv Moldenhauer, the same fellow who picked up their milk while I was still living at home in the 1950s. They then purchased a new mobile home from a dealer in Knapp, WI, just a few miles East of Wilson, and had it placed on a rented lot in the village of Baldwin, remarkably close to the Baldwin Care Center.

Their mobile home was now more than twelve years old and needed major work, so at the urging of my cousins, who were keeping a close eye on them, they sold the trailer and moved into an apartment in the Baldwin Care Center and were seemingly happy there.

They, like most of the other rural farmers, were eligible for Medicaid and would be financially and health-wise better off making the Care Center their home.

My cousins were working or volunteering at the Center, so they kept an eye on the folks. And the folks also had many of their friends living in the facility, which made my "only child" life much easier.

Betty and I committed ourselves to drive or fly commercially to Minneapolis to visit every month or so. I think the whole family was comfortable with this situation.

Now in August of 1980, we made another trip just before I made the NTL change in my career. We continued these trips, either driving, flying commercially or, later, flying our own aircraft until they had both passed on.

We have now tried to visit the Midwest each year as most of our relatives live in Wisconsin.

A New Approach

By 1982 my insurance business had matured, and I found myself coming into contact with folks who owned businesses and even some farmers and ranchers who were interested in estate planning. Therefore, I changed my life insurance marketing targets from middle-class working families to families who owned larger businesses, large farms and ranches.

Duane Hanson and Carl Swenson helped me transition to estate planning using life insurance as a funding source in the event of the death of a major business partner or family member.

It was a taxing change for me, and I soon saw the need for a Law Firm to assist me in presenting estate plans and placing them into action by using wills and trusts. Carl Swenson, my NTL manager, knew of a group of lawyers in Denver who were forming a new firm called Wagner and Waller.

Carl and I met with these attorneys, and we decided to form our own company - Integrated Financial Consultants, Ltd (IFC), with Carl as the President and me as the Vice President.

The law firm of Wagner and Waller would also have ownership in this stock company and would be listed as our lawyers. The first formal organizational meeting was held on January 26, 1982, at my new office at 1860 Dublin Blvd. in Colorado Springs. (I had moved my office from Garlock Lane in anticipation of needing more space.)

The Board of Directors were Carl Swenson, Troy Hanson, and Wagner and Waller Law Firm's David J. Wagner, William C. Waller and Barry Engel. Carl was the Board of Directors Chairman, and Barry the Secretary. As the Bylaws were signed, Carl, Troy and the Law firm each contributed $861.86 and, in turn, received 150,000 shares of the company's new stock.

On 9 June 1982, our new law firm had us sign a stack of legal documents forming the new stock company of Integrated Financial Consultants LTD (IFC Ltd). We were off and running.

In 1982, I continued to market life insurance for National Travelers and had a large life insurance sale to one of Duane's clients in Wyoming pushing me into a "Million Dollar Producer" category.

Million Dollar Producer

I had been doing some flying with Duane's aircraft since I met him in 1981, and he introduced me to Mike Stone, who had a thriving business in Wyoming. Mike's business had his company leveling oil drilling sites throughout the state, and he was busy. He owned his own aircraft, which he would use to fly to various sites, landing on nearby country roads, to maintain the heavy equipment his company used in earth moving.

Duane insured his aircraft, and I ended up selling him life insurance to fund his business liabilities. I made a number of flights in Duane's twin-engine aircraft to underwrite the million-dollar life insurance policy. It was the largest I ever sold.

A flying note - on 7/16/1982, Duane and I, in Duane's Seneca, flew to Gillette, Wyoming, where I wrote Mike Stone a one-million-dollar life insurance application with National Travelers Life. A couple of months later, we delivered the approved, in force, whole life policy to Mike in Gillette on 9/23/1982 using Duane's single-engine Piper Aero PA28 RT 201T.

This life insurance policy sale helped send Betty and me on

a pleasure trip to Europe in 1983, and it was the first time I had used aviation in my business.

Since my insurance sales in 1982 exceeded the million-dollar NTL production requirement, Betty and I were awarded a two-week Europe trip in the Spring of 1983.

We were flown to Zurich, Switzerland, where we visited Switzerland, Austria, Germany, France and England. Since Carl Swenson was the Colorado Springs NTL manager, he and his wife, Sandy, also went along. We rented a car in Switzerland and had an interesting time traveling with them in France, Italy, Austria and Germany.

Carl had spent some years selling life insurance to the American military in Germany and apparently knew that driving in Europe was tenuous at best, so I did the driving. The driving trip was challenging as none of us spoke any of the languages of the countries we visited, but we stayed in hotels where the locals took us under their wings and made sure we were well cared for. I now know why Europe is a tourist haven.

Carl and Sandy wanted to visit old friends in Germany, so Betty and I traveled alone to England, where we were lodged in a British Officers club in London, where I was required to wear a coat and tie for breakfast. We also visited with a British officer whom we served with in NORAD. It was a small world. Overall, it was a super trip, and we were fortunate to be able to enjoy it.

Ready – Set -Go

I was now the President of IFC. After we returned from the Europe trip, Carl Swenson, in April of 1983, ran into some business and personal headwinds and needed money. He resigned from his office with IFC and sold his shares back to the company. Carl continued to support me because he continued to receive his override commissions on sales I made for National Travelers Life, but he no longer had input into IFC operations.

Expansion

Back In December of 1981, I had taken some actions to prepare for the existence of IFC. First, I found a small office space in a new office building on the corner of Academy Blvd and Dublin Blvd. (1860 Dublin Blvd. Ste 2). Bill Lamphere, a CPA, sublet the space to me, and I moved my office from our house on Garlock Lane, which was about a mile away.

My business, for the last year, was doing property management and insurance sales with a small staff of people. Now I felt IFC should become a full-service company that would do real estate sales. So, in May of 1983, I started Real Estate Brokers school at the Jones Real Estate College, graduating in November 1983.

Now a Real Estate Broker

I now took on two friends who were licensed Realtors, Paul Tolleson and Roy Mann. IFC needed some administrative guidance in sales etc., so in August 1983, we hired a long-time Colorado Springs Broker, Bill Wallace, to mentor us. He worked with us for 5 months, and then I soloed.

The new IFC Division was called IFC Realty Investments. We then joined the Colorado Springs Board of Realtors, which made us a legitimate real estate company.

Increase in Flying Activity!

I started to increase my flight activity in 1983. Duane and I had an agreement that I would do some quasi-commercial flying for our business acquaintances if they would pay the expenses. I was qualified to do the flying as I had an active Commercial Pilots License with a current medical certificate. We used Duane's twin-engine Seneca, tail number 38812, which was a six-passenger aircraft.

One of my first flights had me flying Ben Doherty, President of IIS, from Centennial airport (APA) in Denver to Amarillo, TX, and back. I took my old NORAD briefer friend Cliff Zacharias along as my safety pilot. This flight was on 1/10/1983, and it set precedence for many similar flights to come.

Newly Organized IFC and flying.

IFC was operating quite well, with me being gone a day or so each week. Also, my rentals were rented most of the time and did not require constant attention. I decided I could have some fun flying again. I realized that I would be busy, but I felt I had the energy to do the job.

Duane was a good friend to allow this. I started using the airplane for my trips to Baldwin, landing at New Richmond and Red Wing as these airports were close to Baldwin. I, of course, paid the costs of operating and maintaining the aircraft.

Flying Porta-Potty

In November of 1983, Whitney and Ginger Sullivan, our old friends from the Bermuda 303rd ARS, and Betty went to Las Vegas with me. We were going to meet Betty's sister Joanne and her friend there and go to a show or two. It was a fun trip. Ginger was nervous flying in a small aircraft and brought her porta potty and put it in the back in case nature called. She actually used it when we got slowed down by severe headwinds which cut our ground speed to about 70 mph. This extended our flying time and made Ginger's idea of bringing a potty a good one.

It was an enjoyable trip and probably caused Whitney to buy a share of the airplane some months later.

Glider Flying

I had another unique flying experience that year when Betty treated me to a glider lesson at the Black Forest glider port. I logged 30 minutes of glider time. It was a great Father's Day present as I really enjoyed it.

Gambling Flying

In 1984 Duane and his wife Bonnie and Betty and I took part in a flying poker run from Arapaho to Jefferson County to Ft. Collins to Greeley and to Tri-County airports. Bonnie won the first-place award for us on that trip. My flying hobby was now a lot of fun.

Float Plane flying

The next flying thing I did was, while in Superior on a visit, go out to Barkers Island and check out in a float plane. I did not see any future use of the rating, so I did not complete the checkout, but it was fun and looked good in the logbook.

Wagner and Waller dissolve their partnership.

In 1984 Wagner and Waller ran into business problems and dissolved. They split up the practice, and the attorneys started their own practices. Barry Engel stayed on for a while as our attorney and secretary of our board of directors until resigning on 11-1 1984.

At that point, for the next few years, IFC had on our Board our friends Cliff Zacarias, Don Thomas and Paul Tolleson. After 1986, the officers and directors of the IFC were always members of the Hanson family.

STEVEN AND LORNA LEAVE NAVY

Steve's commitment to the U.S. Navy terminated in the spring of 1984. He and Lorna determined that the long deployments were not going to be good for the family which they now had started. Christiana was on the way and would arrive in September and more children were anticipated. They signed a contract with Proctor and Gamble and Steve will be in their marketing division. They moved from Hawaii to Cincinnati and started settling down. Betty and I were to have many trips to their home to greet new grandchildren and to watch them grow up.

Real Estate Business Continues

I continued purchasing rental properties for myself and outside investors and was doing the management of these properties. We finally got the Trade name registered for "IFC Realty Investments" in March of 1986, but we had been doing a lot of business in the meantime.

Integrated Insurance Services (IIS)

I also became a Director of Integrated Insurance Services, a startup insurance company in Denver.

Carl Swenson, while he was the president of IFC, had tried

to merge this company into IFC when Ben Dougherty, who owned Integrated Insurance Services IIS, suggested a merger. It was rejected by the IFC board due to potential conflicts of interest. I then became a member of their board of directors, lending my insurance experience to the new company.

IIS was the first company that I flew a charter for when Cliff Z and I flew Ben to Amarillo a couple of years back. I remained on the IIS board for a few years and was given 40,000 of their shares. However, this firm dissolved in 1990 and their shares became worthless.

I was now busy with real estate managing a large number of rentals and making some sales. I eventually had to hire a receptionist and a couple of salespeople to help out.

As we started expanding in 1983, I hired some staffers to take on some of my workload. I hired Bernadette Ables first to manage the rentals and later a lady named Karen McKinster to assist Bernadette.

My first receptionist was Cammy Kirk, and later I hired Beverly Volker, Duane Hanson's niece. After that, I hired Jannette Bourassa, Mary and Jerry's Daughter – Betty's niece.

I took on a couple of my friends who were licensed real estate salespeople – Roy Mann and Paul Tolleson, and a lady by the name of Janet Green, who handled the sales end of IFC Realty

Investments. There were some other salespeople as well, but I can't remember their names.

Betty's niece, Jannette, came to live with us in Colorado Springs on March 17, 1983, and we gave her the reception job. As time progressed, she studied for her real estate license and ended up in the sales department. We were reasonably busy, but I saw a need for a sales increase. The economy was starting to slow.

I again leased more office space from our CPA, Bill Lamphere. We started our office leasing only two rooms. We now have four offices and a reception area. All our employees were kept busy, but most of the business was property management. I knew a fellow insurance salesperson by the name of Don Bartek. He had been a Catholic priest in the Omaha area and had fallen in love with a Catholic nun from his parish. They wanted to marry and raise a family, so Don's bishop suggested they resign and move to Colorado Springs to live out their lives.

Don came to me and rented an office in our complex and ran his business from our offices. He was a great addition to our group. IFC was becoming well-known throughout the area.

Our First full-size computer

Our business expansion needed assistance with the paperwork. IBM was the first company to manufacture a full-size computer available to the general public in 1981. After IFC got organized, we recognized that having one would solve a lot of problems, so we purchased one in 1983.

The unit was a metal box with a detached 12" black and white screen. It was a tabletop model and sold for about $5000. We were among the first businesses in Colorado Springs to own one. Even the Air Force Academy offices were without computers at that time. Betty's boss knew about ours and had Betty come to the office to make a mailing list for an upcoming convention. Like the rest of us, she was just starting on computers, so she worked the entire day and did not have the list done by evening, so I told her I would finish it. I got it done a few hours later and hit the wrong button and erased the whole thing. There were curses and tears when I admitted to it, but we took the next day and completed the project.

The early computers required a lot of skill to work. The thing really did a lot of work for us later when we took on another company – Help U Sell.

V and H Construction

Betty's sister Joanne and her husband Charlie had two daughters, Candice and Chris. Candice was married to Steven Vought, and they had a son Steve. They all lived in the San Diego area. The Vought's decided they wanted to leave CA and came to visit us in 1978. Betty and I, at that time, were living in the old trailer on our 10 acres in the Black Forest, and I was still on active duty.

Steve and Candy stayed in our old 21-foot California travel trailer, which was parked on the acreage.

Steve and Candy liked the area and went back and sold everything and moved to the Colorado Springs area in 1979. They and a few of their CA friends had invested in a large apartment complex in the SE part of Colorado Springs, so they were going to assist in the management of that complex.

When they moved to Colorado Springs, Betty and I made them an exceptionally good deal on one of our rentals on Chippewa Court, which they bought and moved into.

Steve had learned the building trade in CA and was intent on starting his own business in Colorado Springs. As soon as they arrived, Steve started as a maintenance man at the CA-owned apartment complex, and Candy started working the desk as manager of the complex. Steve's brother, Don, also moved to Colorado Springs and started his own tile-laying business. We had quite a group of relatives in the area.

Steve obtained his Colorado contractor's license about a year after he arrived. Sometime after that, Steve contracted with a fellow Betty knew from the AF Academy to build a custom house in Monument, CO - the high-rent area of Woodmoor. As construction progressed, the owner made a number of changes, and Steve was green enough not to make change orders to cover the cost of the changes. After the house was complete, Candy called us, crying that they had not made any money on the deal. It was a hard lesson to learn.

Bonita Village

Now it was the spring of 1985, and I had met a fellow who needed to sell a newly approved multiple family housing development that was in the limits of the City of Colorado Springs. He wanted $35,000 for the acreage, which was off Palmer Park Blvd just on the eastern edge of the city. The development and plot plans for the eight four-plex buildings were already approved by the City Council, so all we had to do was do the site work and build and sell the units. I thought that the price I paid for that package was exceptionally low. Later, I realized that the seller had a reason to give the project away. We will address that later.

I considered that I had Betty's niece Candy's husband, Steve Vought, an experienced, licensed building contractor, ready to go, and I was again looking for a challenge.

So, Steve Vought and I formed a construction company called "V & H."

Steve was the president, and I was the vice president. I put $30,000 into the project and bought out the original property owner. Steve had no money to invest but brought his building talent. The project was called "Bonita Village." It was March of 1985.

We got V&H going quickly. We hired Larry Gilland, a fellow church member from Prince of Peace Lutheran, to design the buildings and got some bank loans to start the work. By the end of 1985, IFC Realty was showing the first buildings for sale to prospective buyers. By mid-January of 1986, five of the eight buildings were completed, and the first few were sold.

2212 East San Rafael Street, Colorado Springs

In March of 1986, Phil Erlander, the Pastor of Prince of Peace Lutheran Church (our church) and his real estate business partner Bob Stajuhar approached V&H with a proposal to trade a house they were using as a rental property to become a downpayment on one of our four-plexes. We had it appraised and noted that it had an assumable VA loan available.

Steve V. and I decided to go for it but to keep it simple, I would personally buy the property (2212 E. San Rafael St.) and apply the trade money in the amount of approximately $7,000, to the sale of one of our completed new four plexes.

V&H Finances

I now had about $100,000 of my personal funds invested in V&H, but Steve V. still had not invested anything but his labor. Steve had been drawing a salary from V&H since we began construction as he had no other income to support his family.

I elected not to draw a salary since I was hoping that the company would produce a cash surplus that would allow me later to get a return on my investment. I did have ownership of 2212 E. San Rafael, which could prove to financially reward me.

With the sale of a four-plex to Phil and Bob completed, V&H had sold another four-plex and Betty and I now owned yet another rental property. I felt this would also better secure the investment that we had made in V&H.

San Rafael

We closed San Rafael on March 7, 1986. This property would have a major impact on Betty and our lives in the future. – more to come.

While all of the V&H and Bonita village concepts were taking place, I took time to do some more charter flying.

Back to Flying

During May of 1985, I got involved in our quasi- charter business using Duane's twin Seneca.

Duane and I met, through Ben Dorherty, a fellow by the name of Richard Friedman. Richard had a startup company in Denver called EXPAN. He was a high roller and was focusing on a real estate project near Glasgow, Montana.

Richard contracted our little charter company to fly him and his wife Karen to a meeting at the old Glasgow AFB, which had been shut down since 1976. Montana's Valley County now owned the abandoned base and wanted to turn it into an industrial park with the housing area to be used for senior living. Richard was trying to get the contract to develop the housing area into a senior village.

I had heard of Glasgow AFB when I was in the USAF, flying KC-135 tankers. They had B-52 bombers and KC-135 tankers at Glasgow AFB from 1971 -1976 before they closed it down. I was told that the weather was very bad in the winter and to avoid getting assigned there. I did.

Glasgow AFB

We flew Richard and Karen to Glasgow on May 31, 1985. The weather was good, and the flight took about 4 hours.

Richard was to meet some people in front of the hangers, and we were to land on the 15,000 ft long runway and taxi to the largest hanger. As we arrived, I was talking on the radio to the air traffic control ATC controller for the Glasgow area and told him I wanted to land on the big runway at the old base. He told me it was closed, but I could use it at my own risk, and then he informed me the wind was North at 40 kts.

The runway ran NW/SE giving us a strong crosswind. It was the longest AFB runway in the US, so I thought that I would be able to play around getting the aircraft on the ground. I made a couple of landing attempts and determined that the crosswind was too strong.

I noticed that the SAC alert parking area was on the SE end of the runway, and its taxiway was heading into the wind. This was much better. The taxiway was about 3,000 feet long, which was plenty long with a strong headwind. I made a low pass to see if there were any rocks or debris on the concrete, and it looked good, so I came around and landed.

The people who were waiting for my passengers had watched us trying to land on the big runway and decided that we were not going to land. They were surprised when we taxied around the side of the hanger. They also said that an earlier charter aircraft had tried to land and left the area.

The old base was spooky. The big hanger doors rattled in the wind, and the housing was empty. There were no aviation support people around. I left the airplane by the hangar and walked with the group through the housing area. We then got back into the aircraft and flew about 10 miles into the international airport next to Glasgow village and spent the night.

I found that the new name of the old AFB base was now "Valley Industrial Park."

A couple of days later, on 6/2/1985, we flew back out with a photographer and flew passes over the base while he took pictures. We then flew back to Glasgow International Airport, which was about a mile east of the village, to take on fuel, and then took off with my original passengers and flew to a town called Malta which was about 100 miles West of Minot AFB. We stayed overnight there. I had no idea who Richard was meeting or what he was planning. I was just the charter pilot. The next day we flew from Malta to Gillette, WY, for a quick stop and then back to Denver.

I now had my first authentic experience as a charter pilot and rather enjoyed it.

A week later, we again flew Richard from Denver to Glasgow International Airport, the official name of the small airport next to Glasgow Village. This time I used Duane's friend's Turbo arrow because Duane needed to use the Seneca. Richard was now accompanied by a fellow named Raul Rodriguez. That day we stopped at Glasgow International Airport, then at Valley Industrial Park, and then back to Denver.

A couple of weeks later, on 6/28/1985, I took Richard in the turbo arrow from Denver to Granby for an overnight and then back to Denver via Pueblo. I believe Richard was also trying to take over the ownership of the ski area at Granby, as all the officers of the ski area corporation had just been killed in an attempted landing in a snowstorm at Granby.

An Aircraft Incident

On July 17, 1985, I was flying Richard to Helena, Montana,

in Duane's Seneca. It was a beautiful morning when we arrived. On the final approach, I put the landing gear down, and the nose gear would not extend. We spent the next hour attempting to get the nose gear down without any luck. I even had a helicopter fly under me and watch while I tried to put the gear down, and he said the nose doors wiggled, but nothing comes out. The tower then called me and said they had a mechanic on the phone, and he wanted to know if any work had been done on the nose gear before this flight. I told him that the nose tire had been balanced. He said that the bolt attaching the nose gear door to the actuator arm had probably been installed upside down, and we were not going to be able to get the gear to come down.

We had now used up our fuel, so I would need to land soon. I requested the tower to put a strip of firefighting foam about a thousand feet down the runway on the approach end. I knew we would damage the nose of the aircraft as we slid down the runway, and the batteries were in the very front of the nose, so I feared a fire.

Richard, my only passenger, was seated in the right front seat and was next to the entry door, so I told him that after we came to a stop on the runway to open the door and run straight out the wing and get away from the plane. I explained that I would be coming out that door, too, and did not want to run over him. He was scared, but that was to be expected.

I lined up on the final approach higher than normal and lowered the main gear. When I saw we were going to be able to glide to the runway, I shut down and feathered the propellors on both engines and used the starters to turn the propellors horizontally so they would not be damaged on sliding on the runway. I noted that the fire trucks were on the side of the runway as we approached, so I knew things would be okay right after we stopped. As we touched down in the foam, I gently lowered the nose to the runway, and we quickly came to a grinding stop. I turned off all the switches and cut power to the airplane and saw that Richard had followed my advice and was standing about 20 feet from the wing tip watching the commotion. I got out and noted that there was no fire or smoke from the crushed nose, but the foam the fire department had put on the runway had splashed on the airplane as it slid through it. Some mechanics came over and pushed down on the tail lifting the nose, and one of them jerked the nose gear doors open, and the gear came down and locked in place. A tow tug came and towed the airplane to a parking spot, and I spent the next hour filling out forms for the airport and FAA, which called the event an incident.

I called Duane and informed him about the situation, and he confirmed that he had his mechanic remove the nose wheel to balance it the night before and assumed that the bolts to the door had indeed been installed incorrectly. He said he would come up the next day in another aircraft and pick Richard and me up. He called a repair company in Loveland to come and fly our damaged plane to their facility for repairs. That company had to fly it back with the nose all duct taped and the gear down. Everyone was pleased that the engines and propellers were not damaged, which saved a large insurance claim.

The caustic foam on the windshield and paint required all of the glass/plastic windows to be replaced and a new paint job. When the airplane was returned to us, it looked like new.

Richard Friedman Snorts Cocaine.

I found out what Richard Friedman was all about that afternoon when we shared a motel room waiting for Duane to pick us up. I walked into the room and caught Richard bent over the bathroom counter, snorting cocaine. I was shocked. His credibility was now shaky, but after discussing it with Duane, we continued our business relationship. This proved to be an unwise decision.

Life Continues

Two days later, I used the borrowed Seneca, tail number 36637, to fly Betty, Sandy, Dana, and David to Minneapolis International, where we visited the folks for Mother's birthday on 7/19/85.

I determined that sometime in October 1985, the county commissioners had come to a decision at Glasgow. Since Duane's

Seneca was still being repaired from the incident at Helena, Richard had to charter a Cessna 340 from International Jet in Denver and brought, among others, Ben Dohrety, Betty and me up to Glasgow for a meeting with the commissioners at the county courthouse. I believe that Richard expected the three of us to testify to the quality of his company Expan. Fortunately, none of us were asked to speak.

I don't remember how the proceedings went, but Betty remembers the feeling from Richard, who mentioned that the meeting had bad results, which meant that Expan did not get the contract. I do remember the chartered aircraft pilot was known to Duane and me as Dick Ely.

Glasgow AFB History

A note on Glasgow AFB – I researched the base as I wrote this part of the book. Glasgow AFB was constructed and opened for business in 1957. It was first used by NORAD's Air Defense Command (I was assigned to this command when I served with NORAD in Colorado Springs), and they had USAF F-86 and F-101 Fighter Interceptors stationed there. The threat at that time was the Soviet Union Nuclear Bombers, and Glasgow was on the closest route from the USSR. By 1968 the bomber threat had diminished, and the base was closed. It was reopened in 1971 with Strategic Air Command B-52 Bombers and KC-135 Tankers again because it was on the shorter route to the USSR. It was finally closed permanently in 1976, and the whole base was given to Valley County, Montana, of which the city of Glasgow was the county seat.

Saint Marie Montana

The county eventually did turn the housing area into a small independent village they called Saint Marie. It has a creepy reputation now in 2023. I googled it. Look for yourself.

The rest of the base and the runway were turned into Glasgow Industrial Park. The runway was shortened to 13,500 ft and made active again but as a private airport. The airport that was next to the village of Glasgow was renamed from Glasgow International Airport to" Wokal Field/Glasgow-Valley County Airport."

Richard Friedman had an idea, but his company, Expan, was not qualified to convert the property as the County Commissioners would like, or maybe they saw through Richard's B.S.

Back to Reality

Duane and I had a pleasant experience with Expan on 12/4/1985. Richard had some grandiose ideas for the company, that he needed his own airplane. He contacted Piper Aircraft, who sent a new Cessna Citation #N111KR to Denver for Duane and me to test fly. Duane experienced left-seat jet pilot time and said that whatever he had spent working with Richard was worth it because he would never have had the opportunity to fly the sleek little jet.

I also got left seat time in it and thought that it was a modernized T-39 similar to the USAF one in which I closed my flying career in 1973. Of course, we now knew that Richard was a cocaine addict, and those grandiose ideas about jet airplanes would not materialize. But the demo ride was a lot of fun, and I was tickled to watch Duane's face when he was flying the little executive jet aircraft.

Moving On

1986 was proving to be another busy year for the family and me. In May, we went to Baldwin, WI, to help Dad celebrate his 89th birthday. He was not doing well health-wise, having heart problems, which eventually moved him from their apartment in the Care Center to a private room in the Care Center close to the nurse's station. Mother continued to live in the apartment just a few hallways away.

Dad had fallen and broken his ankle in the last year, and it was slow to heal, and it pained him to walk. He was depressed and told me again on this trip that he wished he could die. The Care Center was looking out for him and trying to keep him comfortable. We could only hope for the best.

More flying

On 3-29-1986, I flew Steve Vought and Henry Sosa from

Denver to Kremmling, CO, to visit a construction site. This was a first for V&H Construction.

Partners in Seneca #38812

April 18, 1986, I flew to Silver West Airport in Westcliffe, CO, and then to Denver, CO, arranging the signing of documents related to Whitney Sullivan and me buying partnerships in Duane Hanson's Seneca #38812.

I knew Whitney from our Bermuda 303rd Air Refueling Squadron where we were both KC-97 pilots, and we were both Masons and Shriners and played in the same Shrine band.

Whitney and Ginger were now retired from the workforce. Now, Whitney had been appointed as a non-attorney County Judge by Dick Lamm, the Colorado Governor.

Whitney had developed a small housing development South of Westcliffe, CO, which is about 50 miles South of Colorado Springs. He still loved flying, but I suspect he was looking for the tax write-off that ownership in Duane's Seneca would provide.

Still flying Friedman

During the month of May 1986, I flew Richard Friedman on several flights from Denver to Granby, CO. Richard's company was trying to take over the ski area there. The story was that all the executives of the ski area had died in an aircraft accident while trying to land in a blinding snowstorm at the Granby airport. The group's female vice president was the pilot.

The Federal Courts were now controlling the resort and were looking for a company to take over management. I am sure this looked like easy pickings to Richard and Ben Doherty. They were planning some kind of a move to take over the operation.

I flew a few more flights for Richard in June of 1986, and then our business with both Ben and Richard stopped.

Back to Normal

Betty and I flew commercially to Cincinnati on 18 June 1986 for a nice visit with Steve and Lorna, and the kids. We came back a week later and continued showing properties, including Bonita Village, which were no longer selling well.

Had a quick trip flying commercially to Baldwin from 18 to 20 July. Dad was failing, and I needed to comfort both Mom and Dad. This is what happens when you're an only child. Thank God for my cousins. They were acting like sisters in helping me.

My Dad Dies

Dad died on July 30, 1986, and his funeral was on Sunday, August 3. He was buried in the Baldwin Cemetery with military honors presented by the Baldwin American Legion. I did not play TAPS; I was too emotional. Mother stood up well. We remember her walking into the funeral service at Gethsemane Lutheran Church and picking her head up, and saying, "I better buck up!". She was an iron butterfly.

She soon moved from the apartment to a room with a roommate, Margaret – more stories on this later.

Finally, an opportunity to give Dewey an airplane ride.

Dewey and Shirley Wienke and their daughter Karen came to visit in early August. I finally got to give Dewey an airplane ride when I took him and his family for a short flight out of the Colorado Springs airport in our twin-engine Seneca. We stopped for a snack in Pueblo. It was a beautiful evening. I had waited a lifetime to do this.

Sandy Remarries

August 16, 1986, saw our daughter Sandy get married again. This marriage was to Mark Shtatman. She now has Mark's two children, Danielle and Matthew, as well as Dana and David, to raise. It will be a busy household.

August 21-22, another Baldwin trip to check on Mother. She is doing well with her new room and roommate, Margaret.

Help-U-Sell

To cap off a remarkably busy month, Guy Descharden, who was the owner of the franchise Help U Sell in Modesto, CA, came by to pitch his operation. I thought the idea was intriguing and decided to investigate buying a franchise for IFC Realty Investments.

I flew out the next few days to see the operation for myself. I furthered the business end of the trip by stopping in Vacaville on September 4th to call on my old friend Gene Neilson. Gene still owned four rentals which IFC managed. This included his old house in Colorado Springs, which we were also managing. I told him about Help U Sell, and he thought it sounded good. I then flew back to the Springs to think about another new adventure.

October 1986

October 1986 brought about the routine stuff. Some real estate sales but mainly real estate management problems.

One of our new rentals was giving me problems. 2212 San Rafael was rented out as a duplex. It was a unique house in the fact that it was made of a cinder block, and the power and hot water were shared by the tenants. I had trouble attracting good tenants due to the shared utility situation and consequently had a turnover problem.

The neighbors were upset with the type of people living there, and I didn't blame them. One set of tenants had gone to the Tinans next door and robbed them of their Christmas presents. However, they could not prove anything.

Rod and Terri, the policeman, and his wife, who was the El Paso County Under Sherriff, who lived on the other side of our rental, were thinking about selling and moving due to these bad tenants.

We kept evicting and trying to find decent folks to rent, but it was difficult.

Expan and Integrated Insurance- Richard and Ben

Richard Friedman and Ben Doherty stopped their business with our flight service in June 1986. We were to find out why in the upcoming month of December.

Duane and I had some indications that these guys were scammers earlier in our dealings. As I write this in 2023, I had called Duane for info on this book, and as we talked about flying for Ben and Richard, we discovered that neither had paid more than the fuel for all of the transport we gave them. I thought that they paid Duane, and he thought that they paid me. So, I was out the pilot time for the charters. (About 50 hours of flying time) and Duane was out of the aircraft rental funds.

Does Richard Go to Prison?

One snowy December night in 1986, I received a call from Richard Friedman's wife, Karen. She was terribly upset and told me that I had to immediately fly her to Granby. Apparently, there was a federal judge who saw through Richard's scam and had him arrested and jailed. I told her there was no way I would fly into the mountains in a snowstorm. That was the last I ever heard from the Friedmans or Ben Doherty. I had heard rumors of both of them being sent to Federal prison for the shenanigans at the ski lodge in Granby. I guess we were warned.

Wildhorn Ranch

In 1987, our family purchased a timeshare on a lovely old ranch north of Divide, Colorado. We used it for a few years and have great memories. It had a pool, riding stables, fishing lakes and ten nice cabins. It even had a restaurant. We had one week each year in the month of July.

After a couple of enjoyable years, things fell apart, and the help started putting marijuana in the restaurant food and other nefarious things. Finally, a father and son swamped a paddle boat and drowned, so the stables, restaurant and lakes became off-limits.

We still had the cabin and hiking trails and could hang around the lakes, so the kids had fun. I think that all our grandchildren spent time at the ranch and have great memories. People quit paying their dues, and the place went bankrupt, but those of us who kept up with our payments were finally rewarded when the bankruptcy court sold the cabins individually, and we got our money back from that sale in 2003.

Finally, on or about 2018, a large forest fire raged through the area destroying most of the cabins, but our cabin survived, and its new owner completely refurbished it. We drove up one weekend when Christiana was visiting us in Colorado Springs, and she had her picture taken on the porch in 2019. Now back to the '80s.

Transportation

In October of 1986, I found that I needed business transportation. IFC leased a new 1986 Ford Taurus four-door sedan. I got modern and had a mobile telephone installed in it, and it greatly simplified my life. We kept the car for a three-year lease. It worked out well.

Our last new car was a 1985 Ford Bronco II purchased for Betty who traded her Z car. We felt she needed a four-wheel drive to get to work at the Academy. It was a neat little car that served us well.

The Only Child Starts Thinking.

November 1, 1986, found Betty and me back in Baldwin to check up on Mother in the Care Center. Steven and Lorna had now moved to Puerto Rico. Lorna had called a few weeks prior and reported that Steve had some weird medical problem and asked what I knew about my birth parents' health background. I responded that

I knew nothing about them.

I got to thinking that since I was now near the St. Croix County seat of Hudson, I would drive to the courthouse and see if I could get my adoption papers released. They had been impounded after my birth, and I had only an adoption birth certificate which gave no information on my birth family. I had not previously attempted to get birth family information as I thought I would respect my adoptive parents and wait till they passed away before I would seek that information. Now I thought for my children's sake that I should try to open the records.

Betty and I drove from Baldwin to Hudson on the morning of November 3, 1986. I walked into the St Croix County Clerk's office and asked for my adoption information. I was directed to the Judge down the hall, and when I made the request, he said he would release them to me but come back after lunch to get them.

For whatever possessed me, I walked out of his office, got into the car with Betty, and drove back to Baldwin. I did not go back as the Judge suggested.

Steven recovered from whatever was ailing him, and I forgot about seeking information on my adoption. However, Lorna, who had been well-schooled in genealogy by her parents, started a search for my birth parents.

This event probably planted the seed that grew in me,

starting the search for my birth parents.

Lots more on this in future chapters.

Help U Sell

The Help U Sell folks had been talking to me over the past month or so and had invited me to the 1986 Help U Sell Convention in Monterey, CA, on December 5, 1986. I was wined and dined and returned to Colorado Springs the next day as a proud Help U Sell Franchisee. The rest of December was focused on me getting trained in Salt Lake City and Denver and me training my staff on doing real estate the Help U Sell way.

The Help U Sell sales way was rather simple. For paying Help U Sell of Colorado Springs a flat fee of $2450, the seller shows his own property and does the selling. He then pays the normal closing costs, but there is no commission outside of $2450. We, the Help U Sell realtor, then would do the marketing through newspaper ads and yellow fliers placed in supermarkets and places open to the public. We then help the buyer obtain financing and assist in the closing.

I felt that with the soaring prices of real estate that were increasing monthly and the high commissions that the regular brokers were demanding, we would do well. I can't remember what the franchise fee was, but it was not more than a couple hundred dollars per month. I set up a commission rate for the few agents we had and insisted that they not take any listing until I had inspected the property and talked to the sellers. We opened our doors on January 1, 1987. By March 5, 1987, our weekly flyer had nearly 50 listings from all around Colorado Springs, Manitou, Widefield Woodland Park and Alamosa. Three had been sold. The asking prices ranged from $48,000 to $173,000, and some had sold in 6 days. It really worked.

We did have some problems which were anticipated. First, the regular real estate brokers were not making many sales, and they were upset at being cut out of the business. I received more than a few hate calls that came close but did not threaten me. The Real Estate Board reminded me that I needed to place my listing with them, and I responded that I would if the sellers desired, but if their agents sold the listing, the seller would have to pay my $2450 plus one-half of the regular commission. That satisfied the board, but I never had a seller opt for the full listing.

The rest of 1986 was busy managing our many rentals and trying to sell the listings. There was one event that is worth mentioning only because it is sadly funny.

Gramma Letty Flies to Colorado Springs

We decided that Mother should come to Colorado Springs and spend Christmas with us. It was decided that Cousin Ruthie would bring her to Minneapolis Airport and supervise her boarding, and then Betty and I would meet Gramma in Denver and supervise the deplaning.

We drove to Denver Airport and waited for the plane to pull up and offload the passengers. Well, all the passengers were off and gone, and no mother! We were walking out to the airplane when two flight attendants appeared, leading Mother. They were harried. They came up and handed us my mom and said, "Sir, you must never let her fly alone again." Apparently, she had started behaving strangely as soon as they were airborne in MSP, and a flight attendant had to sit and manage her all the way to Denver. Well, the iron butterfly had struck again.

After a very nice visit with her in Colorado, I flew back by her side and found out firsthand what the problem was. The flight was in the dark, and she saw the light on the end of the wing and was convinced that it was a car. She wanted to get out of her seat to get off. She got agitated, and I had to hold her hand, and it went on. As soon as we got on the ground, everything was fine. That was her last flight. Happy New Year. A great start to 1987

1987

January started out with us taking HUS listings, showing properties for sale, and tending to the rentals. We drove to Cincinnati on January 30 and returned home on February 7. We go to Baldwin March 7-9 and again 26 – 29. I did HUS training in Denver on April

29 and back in Cincinnati on May 8-12. Baldwin July 9-14, and finally was at Wildhorn the week of July 25 -31.

On August 29, Troy hiked to the top of Pikes Peak with Betty's office mate, USAF Captain Joy Prosise. Betty drove her 1985 Bronco II to the top to give the two a ride back. When Betty arrived at the top, medics were carrying a body to the road, and Betty assumed it was Troy. It was a doctor who was trying to hang glide off the top and got caught in a gust of wind and fell to his death.

September 11-14, trip to Cincinnati; October 9-11Baldwin; October 19 – Black Monday; October 26 & 27 Help U Sell conference in Denver. Our last 1987 trip was to Baldwin from December 17 – 21.

Steve and family moved to Japan on 10-18-1987.

I was busy the past months, when not on a trip, working the rentals and showing the units that were listed for sale. Things started changing now.

Black Monday the Beginning of the End

A life-changing event occurred on October 19, 1987. It was called "Black Monday". President Jimmy Carter was out of office, and Ronald Reagan was trying to turn Carter's mess around. Carter and his Democrats had inflation raging, with housing prices going up every day. Mortgage interest rates headed toward 20%, and people were waiting for the worst when the stock market fell more than 20% all in one day. A severe recession had set in in 1982, and it was slow in recovering.

We immediately saw our sales drop to an almost complete halt. Carter remained in office until 1981, and during that time, the inflation and high-interest rates continued, and we ended up with gasoline rationing. It was going to take many years to recover from the debacle. Reagan had his hands full.

IFC Had Come to An End.

The loss of the economy signaled the beginning of the end for IFC Realty Investments and Help U Sell. I had been too aggressive moving into real estate sales, and V&H was now facing a complete loss of business and had spent their capital funding on poor decisions.

The rental business, however, continued as people needed a place to live, and landlords would continue to have an income, as would the IFC property management.

After the Crash

I continued to operate HUS after the crash. We had 12 people in our offices right after the crash. In only a few months, our lists were smaller and sales fewer, so Roy Mann and I were the only licensed salespeople, but Jannette and Bernadette hung in. Jannette now had her real estate license but was still our receptionist. Roy was on commission, but the girls were on the payroll. I had been helping IFC with my own cash and had taken a second mortgage out on our Garlock home when V&H started struggling.

I thought that Steve Vought had made some poor financial decisions when he had the company purchase a Ford pickup truck for him, and he hired a friend to help him manage the construction projects and then had V&H purchase a truck for his new hire.

V&H was originally chartered with Steve as the only one on salary. I told Steve that since I was the only one who had money in the company, I would handle the financial aspects of the company, i.e., marketing, bill paying, and financing. I expected Steve to make the construction decisions, i.e., hiring subcontractors, purchasing building materials, and finishing equipment. V&H would then get profits from building sales. They operated at a good profit until they hired additional people. Now, they had taken out a bank loan that I was attached to, so I was hanging out there financially.

In 1988, evictions and late rent payments started to increase, and it was more difficult to find qualified tenants. Because of this, our rentals would sit unrented, and we would have to go to our investors for cash so we could pay their mortgages.

Things were getting dicey. Property management was an active business, and we had a lot of properties.

1988

Our events in 1988 started with a trip to Baldwin on February 19 – 21. Then, on March 3rd, I got rear-ended while waiting for a red light at Galley and Academy in the Taurus. I received whiplash. The teens that hit me were driving their parents' car and were insured, so I recovered, and the car was repaired. Another Baldwin trip is April 22 – 24. HUS owners meet in Denver on May 11. The other HUS owners were getting nervous, too. The listing sheet for my HUS July 1988 had 25 for sale and 3 sold, so things were slowing down in sales too.

On May 22, we picked up Lorna and the children at the Denver Airport. Lorna and Christiana, and Elissa were home for the summer from their assignment in Japan. They would stay here for six weeks living with Lorna's parents or maybe rent a house. Proctor and Gamble took excellent care of their employees and gave them excellent benefits.

We took another trip to Baldwin to celebrate Mother's birthday, July 15 – 18, 1987.

1988 I cut way back on my flying. I was so busy with the real estate part of the business and was still selling insurance. I did one quick fun flight from Colorado Springs to Pueblo and back with Marrett in his own Centurion 210 on 9/18/88.

Another Try to Get My Adoption Papers.

On 7 October 1988, we again went to Baldwin, returning on the 10th. I decided to try my luck on my adoption papers again in Hudson. I drove over and walked in with the same request – open my adoption. This time they informed me that the law had just changed, and I would now have to deal with the adoption office at the state capitol Madison.

They gave me the address and told me to ask about my family's medical history. That would give me a better chance of a reply. In November of 1988, I sent the letter off to the Wisconsin Adoption Bureau. It would take two years to receive an answer.

National Leasing Net Work

On November 11, 1988, a new company called the "National Leasing Network' started up with offices in SE Colorado Springs. They specialized in leasing equipment, and I was going to represent them in aircraft leasing. Duane Hanson was to advise me, and I would work on commissions only. I thought it might generate some income, and I needed that now. I printed some business cards with the name National Aviation Lease, and the company gave me some contacts I could use to find aircraft to lease if I found anyone who wanted to lease. The company advertised, and I made lots of calls. The company was very unstable, and I soon found out the leadership was extremely poor.

I made one lease during the time the company existed, and when it shut down in 1989, the lease was successful, but none of the sales reps, including me, got any commissions.

Another Failure - Now I Am Picking Up the Pieces.

During this time, I continued to run the rental part of IFC Investments, and I sold most of my rental houses as they were costing me more than I could make with the sporadic rents and maintenance.

1988 ended with a trip to Baldwin from 12/21 to 12/23, followed by a trip on Christmas day to visit Cliff and Beverly Zacarias in Bellingham, WA.

We returned to rent out (again) San Rafael and to close out an unprofitable year. I expect 1989 to be even worse.

Help U Sell Shuts Down.

I shut down Help U Sell in March of 1989. We were no longer getting listings or sales that would support continuing the operation. Inflation was still high, and few people could afford mortgage interest rates still in their teens. I had been continuously talking to the Help U Sell Franchisor, and he saw the other franchisees having the same problem, so he canceled our contract and our debt. That was some relief for my personal situation.

We would still use IFC Realty Investments as our licensed

agency, and the rental business was still stumbling along. I started shedding management on the rental units owned by other investors. I ended up with only a few, and those would be owned by my friend.

Gene Neilson.

During the years 1987, 1988 and 1989, I continued to make trips to check on Mother and also to visit Steve and Lorna in Cincinnati.

A New Airplane in 1989

Some of these trips were now in an aircraft that a friend of Duane's loaned us to fly. The friend owned an airline tire service in Denver and had this plane to use in his business. But now, he was not physically qualified to fly. Inflation had him now doing all the work, including driving his own semi-truck across the USA to get the tires. He had used the airplane as collateral for a loan and had to keep it operational, but he could not fly the bird. So, he told Duane he could use it on his own if he would keep it insured and airworthy. Duane and I took it on. We had sold the Seneca a few years back and now needed something to fly.

Piper Comanche

We knew that maintaining an airplane was expensive, so we planned to fly it enough to get our money out of the deal. And we did. It was a PA -24- 250 tail number N7589P. A single engine Piper

Comanche 260 hp. Four passengers, retractable landing gear and quite fast.

The first time I flew 89P was 2/8/89 when I accompanied Duane on a very cold trip to MN to visit his father.

Betty and I took it to Baldwin many times as it was about as fast as using the airlines and less expensive. Our grandchildren had many trips to visit Great-Grandma Lettie as well.

Gramma Lettie's 100th Birthday

One memorable trip was in the Comanche from the Springs to Minneapolis International Airport MSP on July 14 -17, 1989, with Betty and three grandkids, Dana, David and Danielle. We went to celebrate Lettie's 100th Birthday.

We made many other trips in 89 and 90. The Comanche was less expensive to fly since it had one engine compared to the twin-engine Seneca.

Grandson David's Wonderful Airplane Ride

Another memorable trip was on 7/7/1989 when my Grandson David and I took the aircraft for an annual maintenance inspection in Newton, KS. David's first airplane ride, where he got to fly it, even in rough air. He was fearless. We stayed overnight at a cheap motel that had a pool - good times.

1990

1990 started off with a fire at the San Rafael rental.

The upstairs tenant was rebuilding a motorcycle in the living room and heating parts and cleaning fluid on the kitchen stove. The cleaning fluid caught fire, and the tenant, fortunately, put it out with only smoke and scorch marks. I evicted the tenant.

We had a lot of problems with San Rafael tenants. The neighbors were not pleased with me. Betty said it should have burned down. A few months later, the lower tenant reported a break-in. The neighborhood was falling apart.

IFC Annual Meeting

2-6-1990. We held our annual stockholders' meeting at the Dublin Blvd. office in Colorado Springs. We had religiously held these meetings and, over the past years, acknowledged each year that I had loaned the company money for operations. The Board would prepare a promissory note for the amount owed and set an interest rate for the loan. I would then cancel the previous year's note and add the amount canceled and accrued interest to the new note. In 1990, the new note totaled $34,942.98.

(This continued each year until IFC dissolved in 2008. At that point, I was fully paid back.) But now I was hurt financially and could have used the money. Things were tightening.

Eric Troy is born.

4-19-1990. Our second Grandson, Eric Troy Hanson, was born in Japan. His mother, Lorna, had been born there in 1958. Eric's father, our son, Steve, was born in Bermuda in 1957. Eric's Aunt Sandy, our daughter, was born in Bermuda in 1959. We are an international family.

Steve, Lorna and the family returned from the Japan assignment in June of 1990 and then moved to Cincinnati, OH, still working for Proctor and Gamble.

V&H Shut Down

!990 saw V&H shut down. I resigned from my office as vice president in 1989 due to Steve Vought ignoring my counsel. Steve had managed to build another house or two after completing Bonita Village, and then the economy got him.

He and his wife, Candy, had purchased a partially completed, lovely home in the country SE of Colorado Springs in 1990. The house was near his brother Don's home. After the V&H shutdown, Steve went to work for a school district in the maintenance department. Betty's niece Candy, Steve's wife, had started up a dress shop in Colorado Springs a few years after they moved to town, so they were okay financially.

Ellsworth AFB Airshow

Duane and I took an unusual flying trip to Ellsworth AFB in South Dakota on 9-15-1990 when we flew the Comanche to the base, landed on their long runway and watched an airshow. The Air Force had issued a special invitation to general aviation to come see a SAC active bomber, tanker, and missile base in full operation. Grandson David got to go with us. He had a ball talking to the other crewmembers who had their aircraft on display. I think he inherited his grandfather's b.s. ability.

This trip meant more to me than most as I had spent 20 years flying for SAC during my active-duty years and had spent "the Cuban Missile Crisis right here at Ellsworth AFB, watching their nuclear bombers and tankers prepare to go to war.

On 28 September 1990, we terminated the lease on the Ford Taurus and purchased a new Ford Tempo. It was an unusual sedan in the fact that it was front-wheel drive but had limited rear-wheel drive capability by simply pushing a button marked 4-wheel drive. This was to be an assist in the snowy winters ahead.

1991

The economy was starting to get to me as well. I had to cut expenses and moved out of 1860 Dublin Blvd. in January. I rented a couple of storage units for the office furniture and equipment and moved the IFC mail to our box at the mail center on N. Academy.

I had been busy managing the remaining rentals. I was now moving the remainder to property managers in Colorado Springs. I decided that I would not close IFC but place it in an inactive status. One never knew what the future would hold.

May 1991

The state of Wisconsin finally replies. We finally heard back from the State of Wisconsin on my letter requesting health data on my birth parents. We sent our request letter in December of 1988. The letter told me that my birth mother had three boys before me and that my birth father was already married and had a family. The only medical information included was that my grandfather had died of Bright's disease. I passed this on to Lorna, and she said that she was continuing to try to find my birth parents using the genealogy method her mother taught her.

A New Career

I met an old friend in Monument at the end of August who talked me into taking a part-time driving position with the D-38 school system. I would pick up a CDL school bus driving license and also help train new drivers. I started immediately.

In September, our son Steve got me hooked up with Proctor and Gamble to do store sets and sales. This would keep me and even Betty and some of my friends employed for the next six months.

Still flying to Baldwin

Our family logged four more trips to Baldwin during this year, including a flight on August 22 for the funeral of an old neighbor, Oscar Brandvold, in Wilson.

Our route generally took us near North Platte, NE, which we used for refueling and potty stops. We did have to land there a couple of times due to the weather, and one of those times, we left the airplane there and rented a car and drove to Baldwin. All in the life of flying light airplanes.

Poor financial planning

Our finances in IFC and V&H got Betty and me into a financial bind. I was on the hook for a second on our home on Garlock Lane and a construction loan with V&H. I had also run up a large amount of credit card debt trying to keep the businesses running. We could not see any relief coming as real estate was doing poorly, so we decided to pull in our horns and change course.

In November, we decided to move out of Garlock Lane and give it back to the lenders. We were current on the first mortgage but in trouble with the second mortgage holder due to our business failures. There was equity in the house for the first mortgage holder, but the second would come after us, but it would take a few years. We still had some financial challenges in front of us.

Our New Rental- Hamal Circle

When we knew that we would have to leave Garlock Lane, we started looking for a rental house.

We found a unique home north of Monument and close to a rock formation known as Elephant Rock. It had lots of stairs and an indoor hot tub. The top level had the kitchen and living room, and the master bedroom. The view to the south was magnificent. It went past Colorado Springs and to the front range of mountains about 80 miles away.

We were in the bird flyway, so we had birds pass through that were seldom seen in this area of Colorado. We moved into 3175 Hamal Circle on November 10, 1991. It was to be our home for the next year.

Unique experience

Later in November, I accompanied Duane Hanson up Highway 24 to a place where one of his insured aircraft customers had made an emergency landing on a highway when his engine failed. During the emergency landing, this aircraft struck a car that was also on the road. This caused little airplane damage as the car ran off the road upon seeing an airplane coming at him.

The pilot had his plane towed to the fire station nearby, where a new engine was installed in the town of Hartzell, CO. Duane and I supervised the takeoff on the US highway to return the aircraft to its home in Denver.

A Close Friend Passes

A sad day came when Shirley Wienke, Dewey's wife, passed away. On December 31, Betty and I attended her funeral in Minneapolis. We had flown to see her in the hospital there only a week before.

Murder in the family

Tragedy struck the V&H family on Christmas Eve of 1991 when Steve Vought went into his brother's home upon seeing lights inside while Don was gone on a trip.

Some gang members had broken in and were having a party. When Steve came through the door, they shot him dead. In the shock of the situation, Steve's wife, Candy Vought, blamed me for this tragic outcome as well as the demise of V&H.

Steve and I had settled our differences prior to that, but the family was so upset with me that they requested I not attend his funeral. After consultation with Pastor Erlander, I did attend. I am not sure that things have changed today as I write this in 2023.

Now, in 2023, Candy is living in Phoenix, AZ, and her second husband has died. Her divorced son Steve lives near her, and her sister Chris is in a care center nearby.

Her mother, Joanne, Betty's sister, died on June 3, 2018. Her father, Charlie, now in his mid-nineties' lives in Colorado Springs with a lady who has cared for him for many years.

1991 – A Unsettling Year

1991 turned out to be a stressful year for our family. I had overextended my ambition to be a builder, insurance broker, real estate broker, and property manager while still flying to be with my mother in Baldwin, who had turned 102 years old on July 19th of this strange year.

I had shut down everything that I had going for the past years and now was faced with my own eviction and corporate bankruptcy.

Looking Up

I started working in new endeavors to increase my income, and in so doing, I got rid of a lot of mental anguish. Betty was solidly behind me and was working in her career, which helped our finances and allowed us to turn a corner in our semi-retired lives. Forward March!

Chapter Seventeen
1992 - Life Style Change

We have now shut down Help-U-Sell and V&H, and IFC is operating out of our mail center box 451 in the north end of the city. Betty is still working at the USAFA, and I am still handling rentals for other investors and our own.

Our cars are the Ford Bronco II and an unusual 4-wheel drive Ford Tempo. Both are four-wheel drive and very much needed in the winter as the snowfall was heavy at nearly 9,000 feet above sea level.

Betty and I own 2212 E. San Rafael St and are having a challenging time finding quality renters. It has been a problem for years, and we need to do something permanent about the situation. We also own a rental on Poteae Street and are about to sell it.

I am still acting as a leasing agent for the investors that own apartments on Old Dutch Mill Road and Bonita Village. We still are managing three other houses, which we are trying to get rid of. I am the only realtor left in my company, so these properties are taking up a lot of my time. I hope to pass the management off to other management companies asap. I am looking forward to leaving the real estate rental business. It really put me under a lot of mental strain.

Driving Busses- A Career Change

I got a Class B Commercial Driver's License (CDL) from School District 38 in August of 1991. Started part-time, driving for School District 38 and a couple of other bus companies that year. Now, I find myself in greater demand for the school system and have been recruited to drive tours for Gray Line, Chuck Murphy's Colorado Springs company.

I am also busy making store sets for Proctor and Gamble and working for another company that does store sets. I am now working hard, but we are still struggling financially from the debt IFC and V&H caused me to incur.

Wedding in Bellingham

In March of 1992, Betty and I flew to Bellingham, WA, to attend the wedding of Karen Zacharias, the daughter of our dear friends, Clifford and Beverly. A refreshing break, and we were happy to visit with our old Canadian military friends.

Pikes Peak Tour Bus

In June of 1992, I started doing a very unusual bus driving job. Grayline had been, in past years, touring Pikes Peak in 14-passenger vans, and I had been driving those. They had purchased a forty-foot diesel bus that they wanted to use to increase the number of tourists they would take up Pikes Peak.

At that time, the road was gravel and had no guard rails. Sitting up high in the coach gave the impression that the bus was on the very edge of the road, and the drops were steep and long. When a car met the bus, it frightened the car driver, and the facial expressions of the driver could easily be seen from the passenger section of the bus. Quite funny.

It was a challenging drive for me, but I got used to it and had many fun trips. The bus had a PA system, and I had a mike in my hand as I drove, which concerned the passengers.

I would make two trips each day, and it was a respectable job. The greatest problem was coming down the mountain when I would run in low gear to try to keep the brakes from overheating.

In the last couple of years that I drove, Grey Line had installed an electric retarding device that made coming down the mountainside with a load of tourists much safer.

The tour would take us from 6,000 feet above sea level to 14,110 feet above sea level and required that I warn the tourists before we started up that those with heart problems should not go. I had only one problem, and that person was airlifted off the Peak and rushed to a local hospital. She recovered and went back to her home the next day. I had a couple of passenger scares, but they resolved themselves with a few breaths of oxygen administered at the top by EMTs.

The Spring of 1992 was remarkably busy with driving D-38 school trips, some Greyline work, some Inter Mountain coach work and lots of property management. By summer, I got busy doing tourist driving for Grayline, and I was shucking off the property management.

We finished off 1992 with a December trip to Baldwin, and since Steve and Lorna and family were working for Proctor and Gamble in Mexico City, we flew to see them and celebrate Christmas. We got back on December 30th and worked for Grayline on December 31 and January 1, 1993.

1993

1993 started with us living at Hamal near Palmer Lake. I continued to be employed driving for D-38 and Grayline and doing store sets for Proctor and Gamble.

We still had a few rentals to deal with, but our big rental problems were now gone with some other company managing them.

The lease was coming due on our Hamal home, so we decided to move into the San Rafael rental.

Our New San Rafael Home

The whole month of July saw us, with few exceptions doing Grayline tours and Proctor and Gamble sets and working at San Rafael.

We now rewired, plumbed, finished the floors, painted, cleaned, and put in new windows and insulation. The place was a real dump when we got rid of the tenants, and slowly, it started to look better and better.

Betty and I did most of the work. I had a friend with an EE degree talk me through rewiring since I could not get a licensed electrical contractor to even give me a bid since the house was made of cinder block and wiring would be slow, having to snake the wires through the blocks.

The county inspected my work and passed it without any redo. July was hot, and I lost about 20 pounds sweating in the attic. I even discovered the site of an ancient fire from the old wiring in the attic that went unnoticed by previous owners.

The House

After five weeks of almost constant work and to the delight of the San Rafael neighborhood, we completed our move into the property on July 15, 1993. The house was far from our hoped-for final project. Betty was the enthusiastic one. She had always wanted to redo an old house, and this house seemed logical.

The house was different, and the neighborhood was filled with mature people with few children. The neighborhood was named Knob Hill when it was platted in the forties. It was bordered by busy streets; mail was delivered to a box on the street in front of the house, and we had a nursery garden store across the street in front of the house and an alley running up on the East side of the property. Mature trees were around the house, and the house had a walk-out lower level with a bedroom, bath, kitchen and large living room. The upstairs had three bedrooms, one bath, a kitchen and a living room. There was an oversized one-car garage attached to the SE part of the house, and it had a walk-out roof accessible from the upper-level kitchen. The house was stuccoed in pink, and it had black asphalt shingles.

I ended up with the place after V&H took it in trade for a new duplex that V&H built at Bonita Village. The Pastor of our church Prince of Peace Lutheran, Phil Erlander and his partner Bob Stadjhar had brought this trade to us. I figured I had about $7,000 cash in it, and I assumed a VA loan of approximately $70,000.

1994

This year was bittersweet. Our life has changed for the better, and we now must pay the price. We continued to work hard. Betty is still at the Academy, and I am juggling the school bus driving for D-38, grocery store resetting for Proctor and Gamble, and occasionally I flew somewhere.

I did take one flight to St. George, Utah, so I could participate in a Barbershop Quartet competition. I flew 3 other singers with me using the Commanche aircraft, and we had a great time. I was a member of the Colorado Springs Barbershop Chorus for a few years and was in several concerts.

This year saw my schedule crammed with school trips during the school year, and then I moved to Grayline Tours during the summer and then back to school jobs. Later in the year, I started Driving for Ramblin Express, the Casino bus company for Cripple Creek. This started as my tour driving for Grayline Tours slowed down. I literally worked seven days a week.

I was able to take a work break and attend a 303rd ARS reunion in Tucson, AZ 6-9 October. Whitney and Ginger went with us, each driving our own car.

I also continued my Al Kaly Shrine Band association. I played in the parades when I could and played official Shrine functions when I was available.

Bankrupt

We finally reached the breaking point in our finances and filed Chapter 7 Bankruptcy in the latter part of September. The process took about ninety days, and we were out of bankruptcy by the end of the year. This situation was a business-related affair, but since I financed the businesses personally, I could not hide behind the corporate structure. In a way, this made it easier as the legal steps of personal bankruptcy are less than corporate. I took a hit on my credit rating, but we had that back to normal in about six months.

Another 1994 event was a thunderstorm on the first of October that dropped hail up to six inches in diameter. A hailstone hit a baby in the head during that storm and killed the child. Colorado is the hail capital of the United States. Over the years we lived at San Rafael, we had two large insurance claims due to large hail. We ended the year with a ten-day Mexico City visit with Steve and Lorna and their family. It was delightful, and I was now out of my mental funk.

1995

January started off with a full schedule of driving for Ramblin Express. I did a D-38 event every other week, which was normally a sports team transport.

Hooray! We were notified that our bankruptcy was discharged on January 19, 1995. Big relief! We will never go that way again.

The only company we have left is IFC, and it no longer has any business dealings. I plan to keep it open for the near future. I have terminated my real estate broker's license and do not plan on needing it in the future. I still have my insurance broker's license and will keep it active for some potential future sales.

Back to Mexico

We made a quick return to Mexico City in the latter part of

February to stay with the Hanson grandkids while Steve and Lorna went on a special vacation.

I had also started an interview process with Proctor and Gamble for a sales position but found that my bankruptcy quashed that job. I never went back to setting stores for them after that. I was too busy driving buses.

New Normal

My schedule books now show me driving buses for Ramblin and Grayline during the summer and then adding D-38 during the school year. I found driving to be fun and giving tours to be rewarding in money tips.

We started doing some dreaming and watched retirees driving their motor homes and travel trailers south in the fall. We could see retirement coming up in a few years, so we decided that we would use a pickup truck to tow a travel trailer for our snowbirding. In November, we purchased a new 1995 Toyota Tacoma pickup truck and traded the Ford sedan that Betty had used for the past many years. Betty would now drive a stick shift 4-wheel drive truck. She took to the stick shift easily as she had a 1979 stick Honda as we entered civilian life. Now Betty and I had yet another idea.

Military Reunions

Betty and I had attended some 303rd reunions and got contacted by a company that would train you how to set up reunions and how to work with hotels and entertainment organizations. We signed up and took a class one weekend and then decided to try it. The first group that we managed was a 16th Air Force reunion in Colorado Springs. While this group was underway, I got a Grayline call to do a driving tour for my old cadet class 56-D.

What a surprise, I had lost contact with them in 1954 when I had my T-34 accident and got washed back to 56-G. Small world. Betty and I accomplished a few more reunions and had a fun time doing them and even made money getting commissions from the group's hotels.

The rest of the year was spent driving for the bus companies and school district 38. We also made a trip to Baldwin in mid-December for our frequent visits with my mother. She is doing ok, still up and around, but her memory has changed over the past years, and I am not sure that she knows who I am. As we visit, there will be moments when she looks hard at me, and then, I think, knows her son.

Steve and Lorna made another move in 1995. They moved from their Mexico assignment to Puerto Rico. We look forward to a visit there as we have not yet visited the islands.

1996

This year starts as a continuation of our more relaxed past few years. I am still driving for Ramblin, Grayline and the school district. We had the obligatory IFC corporate meeting on February 6th and renewed the loans that I made to the company. The new loan stands at $53,576.86. I still hope to recover the funds someday.

Mother Dies

On February 9th, I got a call from my cousin, Winnie VanSomeron, who is the head nurse at the Baldwin Care Center. She told me that my mother had stopped eating a few days prior and was now bedridden and becoming unresponsive. Winnie advised me to come ASAP as my mom was dying. I got to her bedside the next day in the evening and found her unresponsive. I sat beside her for the next few hours, talking to her but receiving no response.

It was approaching midnight, and I had been traveling for the past many hours and was fatigued. Winnie suggested that I go to my cousin Ruth Tegrotenhuis's home, where I was staying and get some rest. She said if Mother regained consciousness, they would call me, and I was only a few blocks away. I told Mom goodbye and walked over to Ruthies.

I went to sleep and was awakened the next morning by a call that my mother had passed away at five minutes past five on the morning of February 11, 1996. She was about 5 months short of her 107h birthday.

Lettie Lund Hanson 7-19-1890 to 2-11-1996 My Eulogy

Lettie was my iron butterfly. She was my mother, and I was her son, the child that she and my dad Everett had been praying for.

She and my dad married later in life as she was 40 years old when she was married, and it was the time of the great depression. She was born less than 100 miles from the spot where she spent her married life, married to Everett, who was a dairy farmer. They realized that she probably would not be able to have children, so they went to the county and applied for a baby to adopt.

About 3 years after their marriage, St Croix County gave them a baby boy to have as a foster child. The law was that a mother giving up her baby would have six months to change her mind before adoption would place the child with the new parents.

Apparently, this child was claimed back by his birth mother prior to the cutoff point. Lettie never mentioned the name of the baby but did say, "I never did like that baby anyway," which indicated to me that she was devastated that she had lost in her first adoption attempt.

Lettie was a friend of the person who handled St. Croix County adoptions, Hanna Borge, and I imagine that Hanna told her to be patient and that another baby would be along. Sometime in the summer of 1934, Lettie's hopes were bolstered by the announcement of a baby that was due to be born in the first days of

January 1935. She and Everett applied again to become foster parents. They were told little about the birth mother but knew that she lived in New Richmond, Wisconsin, which was about 20 miles north of their farm in the county of St. Croix.

I imagine that they waited for the news of the birth with much anticipation. Both she and Everett had their families living near Baldwin, and I would think that the families were also anticipating the birth. As you have just read, the adoption took place, and that baby was given all that they had and was raised as an Only Child. That lucky child was me.

This Book

You have just heard the story of Troy, the "Only Child," and the wonderful adoptive parents that raised me. Everett and Letty Hanson are the main characters in this part of the book. Their story is intertwined with mine as they accepted God's call to raise and nurture one of his creatures. Let's review their story.

It is the story of a marriage during the Great Depression of two later-in-life, Scandinavian heritage people who were looking for a marriage filled with happiness. This involved dairy farming on their own farm and a child to raise as their own. I turned out to be that incredibly lucky child. This book is the story of successful adoption and the successful rearing of the adopted child who turned out to be their only child. Everett and Letty probably felt that they could not afford another child and wanted to give the one they had as many opportunities as they could. My parents were exceptional people. My mother was a strong-willed person, and my dad was smart and a hard worker, and both were intelligent, capable country folks.

This book tells the story of an extremely fortunate child whose birth mother and adoptive mother were solid Christian human beings who wanted the best for this new life. Now I would like to show you why I named the book as I did. Let's talk about my BIRTH families and how I found them.

Chapter Eighteen
Finding My Birth Family

My mother's death was a turning point in my family's lives. As I said earlier, I had not thought much about my only child status and was not curious about my birth family. I told myself that if I searched for them, I would wait until both of my adoptive parents had passed away.

I had made an exception a few years ago when I wrote to the State of Wisconsin requesting information on health issues of my birth family, and after two years, the state finally responded, telling me only a small bit of family history and then said there was little health data to give me. At this point, I pretty much stopped trying to find more of my history. But my daughter-in-law, Lorna, kept working on my genealogy. She knew that I wanted to honor my adoptive parents by waiting until they had both passed before I looked for my birth family.

That day had finally come. Dad died in 1986, and now, ten years later, we are about to bury my mother.

Mother's funeral

Mom was buried next to Dad in the Baldwin cemetery on Valentine's Day, 1996. The service was at her church, Gethsemane Lutheran Church, in Baldwin. The Baldwin Bulletin newspaper said she was the oldest person ever to live in the village.

It was well attended by what was left of our aging relatives with Pastors Doug and Rex Brandt, the two neighbor boys who stated that her Sunday school teaching helped direct them into the Lutheran ministry, officiating at her service.

Terry Ostergaard, my cousin, sang Mother's favorite song, "In the Garden," and I did the eulogy where I got to talk about not being sad but celebrating her long, happy Christian life.

It was a lovely service that I will always remember. Steve and Lorna were living in Puerto Rico and flew in with the children, which I really appreciated. Lorna had requested my okay to search for my birth family some years ago after we had received the Wisconsin Adoption Service letter. I had told her that I would not take part in the search until Everett and Letty passed. Lorna honored that but continued the investigation on her own.

The Search Begins.

Steve and Lorna had a couple of extra days after the funeral before returning to Puerto Rico, so they drove up to my birthplace, New Richmond, and started looking into church records and visiting the local nursing home. They found some interesting information.

They found at the Methodist church, records of a family that had two young boys and their mother living with the mother's parents. This was the John Cook family. Genevieve Olsen and her two boys, Bill and John, were listed as part of the John and Lenora Cook household, and all were members of the church. The two boys were a few years older than me, so that interested Lorna.

Steve and Lorna then visited the New Richmond Care Center and spoke to some of the elderly folks to see if they knew the Cooks. One of the folks said she had lived near the Cook family and remembered a birth around January or February of 1935. She never saw the baby and thought maybe it was a girl. That really got Lorna's attention.

Steve, Lorna and family started back to Puerto Rico later that week, and Betty and I went back to Colorado Springs.

Troy and Betty in Puerto Rico

Betty and I had planned a visit to Steve and their family in Puerto Rico prior to my mother's death and had previously made airline reservations. The day after we got back from Baldwin on February 15, 1996, we flew to San Juan and got to PR a few days ahead of Steve and Lorna's return.

They had given me a key to their Puerto Rico home, so Betty and I moved in and awaited their return. Steve was feeling ill at the funeral, and the reason they stayed longer in Baldwin was his attempt to seek medical care there.

He did not improve after arriving back in San Juan and, during our visit, ended up in the San Juan hospital with pneumonia. That gave us a chance to see the poor health care the Puerto Rican people contend with. He eventually recovered. We stayed in San Juan for 10 days visiting and helping Lorna with the kids.

The first Birth family contact

Lorna got busy with her new leads on my birth family and called me on 1 March to say that she thought she had a lead on a brother and wanted to know if she had my permission to call him. I told her to go ahead, and on March 3, I had my first conversation with Bill Olsen, and then I talked to John (aka Jack) Olsen. I have these conversations recorded on cassette tape.

Back to work

Upon our return to Colorado, I got back to my driving job, but the family excitement continued with the exchange of pictures with Bill and his wife, Laverne. My baby pictures compared to the baby pictures of Genevieve Lenore Cook Olsen, "Gen", my possible birth mother, showed a remarkable resemblance. I was also informed that "Gen" Olsen had passed away in 1982. So, these brothers, Bill and Jack, were my closest relatives.

The problem with genealogy at this time was the lack of positive proof. But for now, we were willing to believe that Lorna had found my birth mother and her family.

A Florida Visit

I had many telephone conversations, letters and picture swaps in the months following my initial contact with Jack and Bill. There were many unanswered questions that could not be addressed except by personal family contact. Not long after these phone calls, son Steve had a business trip to Miami and went to West Palm Beach and met Bill Olsen and his family.

On May 22, 1996, Betty and I flew to Miami, rented a car and drove north to meet Bill and Jack in person. We first stayed about a week visiting with Bill and Laverne Olsen at their home next to West Palm Beach, Florida. (An interesting note - back in 1956, I had trained to fly the KC-97 at Palm Beach AFB, not far from Bill's home. The base is now the West Palm Beach airport).

We then drove to Orlando, about 100 miles north, to visit Jack and Jeanne. We stayed with them for a few days and got to hear the story of my birth mother and her children.

My Birth Mother Genevieve's Story

Jack and Jeannie told me, in great detail, the story of my purported birth mother and her family. It was quite intriguing. I was also informed that I had yet another brother, John, who had been a shop teacher in Mauston, Wisconsin, and now was retired and owned a shoe store in that town.

One fact that was repeated was that my birth was unknown to all the family. They were surprised, yet they seemed to accept me as a long-lost relative. There was a reason that I was quickly and warmly accepted as a member of the Cook family. Here it is.

Genevieve Lenore Cook was born on June 19, 1905, on a farm near Star Prairie, Wisconsin. Her parents were John E Cook and Nellie Lenore Cook, who were first-generation Irish immigrants to the United States.

Genevieve (Gen) was the only girl of the five Cook children, and from the pictures I saw of her, she was a comely Irish lass. She was a tomboy and loved to drive cars, drink beer and smoke cigarettes. I would imagine she was spoiled by her family, and since her father had some money from owning a stock farm and doing extra work such as working as a mail carrier as well as having other farms, she got her way most of the time.

Gen's first indiscretion occurred when she gave birth on January 17, 1928, to a boy. Since she was single, she arranged with the family doctor to alter the baby's birth certificate to show that her brother, Winifred, and his wife, June, were the parents. (Family Adoption?) This child was given the name of John Ora Cook. John was raised by Gen's brother and sister-in-law on their farm south of New Richmond. The real father of this baby was never named and was unknown to anyone in the family except, of course, Gen.

The next event was Gen, a few months later, again becoming pregnant. This time the father's name was known to be Darrel Laramy Olsen. After Darrel found that he was to be a father, he ran away to Sioux Falls, South Dakota. Gen was having none of that and followed him. They were married in Sioux Falls, and William Clark Olsen (Bill) was born there on March 17, 1929 (St. Patrick's Day). Gen and Darrel raised Bill in town, and Gen again became pregnant a year later with another child who was born in Sioux Falls on February 14, 1931 (Valentine's Day). John Gaylord Olsen (Jack) (John Gaylord got the nickname Jack since Gen now had named two of her children John).

Not long after Jack's birth, his father, Darrel Olsen, ran away again and abandoned his family in Sioux Falls. Gen was left destitute without a husband to support her or her children. Her father, John Cook, came from New Richmond and brought the family back to his home in town, where Gen raised Bill and Jack. Their home was less than a mile from the Winifred Cook farm where Win and June's stepchild John was being raised. - Cousin John?

Gen worked as a seamstress and also as a typesetter for the local New Richmond paper as the boys grew up. After her father died in 1940, she continued to live at her parents' home, caring for her mother, Nellie, who had become an invalid. Nellie died in 1957.

The Only Child and His Brothers

(Now I continue the story, and the Olsen family listens).

Gen had another indiscretion 3 years later, in 1934, when she became pregnant with yet another child. This child was born at the Cook residence in New Richmond on January 7, 1935. She named this boy Troy Linden Olsen. Troy's father, like his half-brother John Cook's father, was unknown to everyone except Gen.

This time Gen decided that the Cook/Olsen family could not afford another mouth to feed, and Gen contacted her county welfare department and made arrangements for Troy to be placed as a foster child soon after his birth. Hanna Borge was the county official who prepared the documents to bring Troy into the foster/adoption division of the child welfare department of St Croix County, Wisconsin. Troy was removed from Gen's home on January 17, 1935, and transported by Hanna to Everett and Letty Hanson's home to begin a new life.

Untruth Uncovered

Jack Olsen's wife, Jeanne, continues the story. The Cook and Olsen family members had always called John Cook 'Cousin John," believing that he was the product of Winifred and June Cook. Jack Olsen's wife, Jeanne, somehow found out about the paperwork switch at John's birth and approached Gen and persuaded her to confess the fraud to Bill, Jack and the rest of the family. Gen did this, but Bill and Jack and John were now in their twenties, and this knowledge had no impact on their lives until Troy came along. They probably thought if it happened before, it could happen again. So, the cat was out of the bag now about me and my relationship with the family, but I had no "proof," and I, like my half-brother John Cook, had no idea who our fathers were because Gen had passed away on December 29, 1982, and took those names with her.

More relatives

During this visit, I met most of the children and grandchildren of Bill and Jack. They all seemed to love Florida and lived near their parents. I was not able to meet John Cook as he had lost contact with Bill and Jack, but Jack told me he would regain contact and put us together.

I sent John Cook a letter through the Mauston school district but never did hear back. When I met him in person, he told me he got the letter but thought it was a scam. I would have thought the same thing if I had been in his shoes.

No Longer an Only Child

Betty and I returned to Colorado Springs to continue our lives, but we now had many contacts with Olsen's trading documents and pictures. I started feeling like I was no longer an only child – I now have brothers.

Time Marches On

The rest of 1996 was hectic. Besides both Betty and me working, we had several family events, and it started with our annual vacation at our Wildhorn timeshare.

Steve and Lorna leave Puerto Rico.

Steve and Lorna, and their family moved from Puerto Rico in July. They came to Colorado Springs just as our annual Wildhorn vacation started. Betty and I had the kids at the cabin while Steve and Lorna visited with Lorna's parents, George and Ginny Charleson, in Colorado Springs.

They then left for a corporate visit to Austria, taking Eric with them and leaving the girls with their grandparents in Colorado Springs. Later after they turned down moving to Austria, they went for a short visit to Japan, again at corporate expense and returned after a week in Tokyo. They finally changed employers and signed up with the Kellogg Corp, and moved to Kalamazoo, MI. I drove one of their cars and their dog Shadow up to Kalamazoo and flew back in November.

The Rest of 1996

I had been driving for the school district since the beginning of the year, and now school was out for the summer. Grayline started their tours again, and I again drove for the company. Ramblin

Express and I had parted ways earlier in the year when their maintenance person and I had a dispute, and I had quit. I was trying to slow down and enjoy life.

Betty and I had changed churches and were now involved with Mount Calvary Lutheran. We both sang in their choir. Mel Graner, who owned a music store in the city, was the director, and he and I hit it off. I later assisted Mel in becoming a Mason and Shriner. We played together in several Shrine and local bands over the following years.

I was still involved with aviation. I had stopped flying when we had our financial problems, but now, I renewed my pilot's license by flying a Bi-Annual flight with RudyWelch, the flying service owner, at Meadow Lake airport north of Colorado Springs. Duane Hanson and I kept the Piper Comanche hangered there. Rudy rented us a hanger for the aircraft and was available to give FAA check rides like the one I just mentioned. I would be legally flying for two more years with this evaluation.

A Surprise Brother Reunion

To further cement my relationship with my new brothers, Betty and I were invited to New Richmond for a meeting of my new relatives on 23 -26 August 1996. We met Jack and Jeanne and Jeanne's family, including her mom, Irene. Bill and Laverne came up with their car and travel trailer. I had yet to meet my brother John

Cook, but my brother Jack and wife Jeanne had driven to Mauston and convinced John that I was real. John was busy with his shoe store and could not get away to the New Richmond gathering.

Betty and I flew to New Richmond in the Seneca and landed at their very modern airport. Bill and Jack got a tour of the airplane, but I did not give them a ride as they didn't ask, and we were not acting like brothers at that time.

A couple of weeks after we returned from New Richmond, Bill and Laverne came through Colorado Springs on their way back to Florida. Betty and I were really getting to know our new brother, and we were impressed.

303rd Reunion Tucson AZ

Our Bermuda Squadron, the 303rd ARS, held a reunion in the city they had moved from when the unit went to Bermuda. Our old friends Whitney and Ginger Sullivan attended with us. We had an exciting time as it was fun to meet old friends that I had flown with more than 30 years ago.

Another New Family Gathering.

Brother Bill's son William (Billy) was married in Palm Beach on November 23, 1996. Betty and I were invited. I now felt like part of the Cook/Olsen family. My status as "the only child" was changing, and I would look at my new brothers to try to see resemblances.

Betty and I flew to Orlando and stayed with Jack and Jeanne and then drove down to Palm Beach for the wedding. I got to meet all of Bill and Laverne's children and grandchildren and also met Jack and Jeannie's kids. It was a warm meeting, and I was starting to feel at home with the families.

Christmas in Kalamazoo

The end of 1996 came with a trip for Betty and me to spend Christmas with Steve and Lorna, and family. We drove our new Toyota Tacoma pickup, which performed well on the sometime icy roads. Our children had purchased a large home in Kalamazoo, and we had a lovely time with the whole family. This was the first Christmas with them living in the United States.

It was a great ending to a bittersweet year. I had completely changed the way I worked, and now we were comfortable financially again. My adoptive parents had now passed, and I was starting to realize how wonderful they were. They raised me as an only child and gave me as many advantages as they could. I hope that I honor them as I continue my life. They were deserving of the honor.

1997

The new year got off to a fast start. I was going to turn into a saltwater sailor.

When Steve was working in Puerto Rico, he continued to feed his love of saltwater sailing. Living in the middle of the Atlantic Ocean caused him to purchase a 31-foot mono-hull sailboat. He kept it at a marina on the west end of the Puerto Rico Islands. Steve had enjoyed many sails around the area and now found that his moving away from the sea would force him to sell the boat.

Selling a large sailboat in PR proved difficult. There are not many residents that have the money to purchase or maintain such a vessel. Just before his move, Steve was able to sell the boat with the caveat that he would deliver it to Miami, Florida. Steve had an idea. He would sail the boat the one thousand plus miles in about ten days to Miami. To accomplish this, he would have to sail 24 hours a day for most of the trip. He would require help. He would also need communication and assistance with navigation. Who came to mind? – dear old dad – me.

I had an amateur radio license and radios, and I had experienced using celestial navigation as I flew around the world, and I was reasonably healthy. The problem was that I knew nothing about sailing, and on a trip, with only two of us on board, I would be in command at least part of the time while Steve slept. Solution! Talk Steve's Naval Academy roommate into joining the boat in Puerto Rico and train Dad on seamanship while the boat sails to the

USA.

Joe Conyers was Steve's college roommate and was talked into joining the crew, but he could not take that much time off from his job, so Steve said Joe could get off the boat in the Caicos Islands, and Steve and Dad would complete the cruise with Dad as First Mate. Done!

The Interesting Puerto Rico to Miami Sailing Trip

I packed up my HF TS-50 radio and stick antennas, and some clothes and flew to Miami, Florida, on January 17th, 1997. After an overnight (Steve arrived at 0200 because of snow in Michigan), I flew into San Juan, PR, arriving on 18 January. We went immediately to the ADVENTURE, which was tied up at the marina at Fajardo PR, which is the Western tip of the island.

We put our equipment and belongings into the cabin and started living on the boat. The next few days were spent repairing, improving and supplying our new home to get prepared for the upcoming ordeal. During that period, Steve's Navy classmate, Joe Conyers, joined us and helped prepare the boat for the voyage.

On January 21, 1997, we finally set sail for the first leg of the trip. No stops are planned until reaching the Grand Caicos Islands.

Day 1 at sea

We left the marina at the West end of Puerto Rico at 1715Z (1000 Local) 1-21-1997. We were hoping to arrive in Miami by February 2, 1997.

We didn't know it, but it was going to be a rough trip. The weather was crappy when we left, so we chose sailing on the South side of the landmass, hoping it would be smoother. We were wrong.

We encountered very rough seas and a wind of 15 kts. The boat was pitching and rolling. None of us had slept well the previous night as the wind was howling at the marina. I had taken Dramamine, which made me feel funny, but I wasn't seasick.

The boat was moving in all directions, and it was difficult to move around. I had my own GPS and was comparing it to Steve's and found it right on track. I believe our heading was 320 degrees. We had only been on the water for five hours, and I already had bruises from being thrown around in the cabin.

As the sun set, the rain began, as did the thunderstorms. I had to disconnect the radio antenna to protect the radio from a lightning strike. I was encouraged to go below and try to get some sleep but found that I would be pitched out of the bunk. That gave me more bruises.

It was now pitch dark, and Joe was at the helm. Soon the wind picked up to 40 kts, and Steve and Joe had to reduce the size of the main sail as the boat was overpowered. The autopilot could no longer control the boat, so someone had to be at the helm continuously. Now the boat was moaning and wallowing, so the main sail was reefed as it was not needed. We were sailing on the jib and maintaining our speed of about 5 kts. We were now all in our safety harnesses and were wearing life preservers. It was simply a wild ride.

The next adjustment was to roll up the jib, and now we were sailing on the mast and maintaining speed. I had gone below to secure the radio equipment, and Steve and Joe kept yelling at me to come up as they thought I would get seasick. When I came up, I found they both were turning green, and we had our hands full with waves that were now about 40 feet high.

It was now my turn at the helm – my first time. Joe went below to try to sleep, and Steve laid down in the cockpit to keep an eye on me. He told me to turn into the huge waves and to try to stay on heading. The compass was swinging 30 degrees on each side of the heading, and I was constantly turning the wheel. I stayed at the helm for a couple of hours, and then Joe got up and relieved me, and I took his bunk and tied myself in and went to sleep. The storm continued and apparently got even worse while I slept. When I awakened, the sun was up, and the wind had died down.

Steve found the port of Myaguez on the Eastern end of the island, and we put in there to get fuel and dry out the boat.

Sailing Day 2

We spent the morning drying out and finally having something to eat. I fired up the radio, and we sent messages to our families and then started out again on the same heading, 320 degrees. We were now headed for the Caicos islands. We passed by an uninhabited island not far from PR when we were buzzed by a Coast Guard helicopter. A bit later, we encountered a Coast Guard cutter who hailed us on the radio and requested the ship master's name, rank and serial number. After an exchange of information, they moved out of the way, and we continued.

The sail into the Caicos Islands was my training time. We went over emergency procedures like man overboard and handling the boat for a recovery operation. Joe would be leaving us there, and then Steve and I would be alone for a long ride. We sail into the night, and the sea is somewhat quiet. Things have settled down; we have had some tasty food and are taking turns at our watches.

Third day at sea

My watch ended at 0600 (six o'clock in the morning). We were off the coast of the Dominican Republic when we were again buzzed by first a helicopter and then a small twin-engine jet similar to my USAF T-39 Sabreliner. Steve surmised that the aircraft were from the Dominican drug enforcement group.

I spent some time on the radio trying to get a message to Betty and then sat and looked at the most beautiful blue water I had ever seen. It was 25000 feet deep. We got inside some reefs and were pushed along by a tailwind where we had the sail out 90 degrees to the side of the boat. We were due in the Caicos tomorrow. I took a long nap.

Day four at sea

I was awakened around midnight by the noise of a sail flapping. The jib had come loose, and Steve and Joe had to get up on a leaning deck and fix it. Quite the sight.

I was glad I got to stay at the helm. During the night, on my watch, I heard a boat approaching and saw an unlighted boat pass abeam. I was afraid that we were going to be raided. Later in the night, we cruised into an anchorage in the Caicos Islands. We all went to sleep.

The Caicos

We awakened to the sight of many sailing vessels moored near us. We motored into a marina, tied up, and took a cab to the airport to clear customs. We met some retired Air Force types that had their twin-engine aircraft and their wives at the airport. One was a bird colonel, and they were enjoying cruising the Caribbean in their toys. We then went shopping at an expensive IGA market and a local hotel. Joe left us, and Steve and I left the lovely island and struck out for the Bahamas.

We entered nighttime, cruising in open water with me on watch. Sometime during the night, I saw a freighter pass by. Later that night, during the early hours of the morning, I was still on watch, and I heard a marine diesel engine sound, and it was coming toward us. Since we still were near the Dominican Republic, I thought of pirates. Steve and I had discussed this in the planning portion of our trip and decided not to carry weapons but to have extra flare pistols handy in the event of a conflict. I flashed our altus lamp around but avoided aiming it at the sound as Steve had cautioned me to simply flash our sails, and other boats would see us. I also yelled at Steve, who was sleeping below, and he simply said, "flash the light!" The sound got louder, and I finally saw a small beat-up fishing boat with one-person on-board pass by on our port side. The fisherman waved and was gone. What a relief!

I was now doing well as a crewman. Adjusting the sails as the wind changed direction and doing basic navigation.

1-27-97 at sea toward the Bahamas

We had now been sailing for five days. I ended my watch and went to bed at dawn. I was awakened from a sound sleep by a strange noise which turned out to be a whale that snuggled against the boat and blew water from his blow hole. I didn't see it, but Steve said it was about two times the size of the boat. No pictures darn!

Later in the day, we are in the Bahamas, pass through customs and go ashore and take our first showers and trim our beards. We hire a taxi and take a tour to see the damage caused by Hurricane Lily. We then go to a local hotel for dinner and a few scotches. We then go back to the boat for a lovely sleep.

1-29-97 in port on a beautiful morning

We put on fuel and water. Steve talked to Lorna last night, and she had talked to Tim, the boat buyer. He is to meet us in Nassau, so we set out to meet him. We sailed into the night, and I took the early watch, and it was so peaceful that all I had to do was look at the stars. Steve takes over at about 0100, and I go to bed. An hour later, there is a loud crashing noise, and I find Steve fixing the main boom, which has just broken. When I got to the topside, Steve was in the process of replacing the Vang (Rope) with a new one, so we were soon sailing again.

We sailed into the harbor and tied up at the dock and hooked up to shore power (electricity) and turned on the air conditioner to dry out the cabin. We then walked to a nice restaurant called the "Poop" deck and had a nice dinner. The new owner, Tim, and his wife were to meet us tomorrow, and then we would sail to Miami. We took a shower on shore and went to bed in a cool, drying cabin on our boat.

To Miami

It was the last day of January, and we were up early. Tim, the new owner, shows up on time without his wife. We are ready to cast off and get moving. We sail under a high bridge and observe a helicopter flying under the bridge right beside us. We then must stop and let a tug park a large cruise ship before we are in the open and sailing.

Prior to the trip, I had applied for a Bahama's Ham license and received the call sign C6A/MM2. When I wanted to talk to someone, I used that call and always got a lot of answers.

We sailed into the night with me at the helm, looking for a red flashing light indicating the end of the harbor. Steve comes up to confirm our location and stands with a very bright altus light shining forward. He suddenly shouts, "Hard Left," and I spin the wheel left, and we narrowly miss a mass of steel sticking out of the water. It was an unmarked hazard, and we were lucky to have missed it.

As we progress to Miami, we pass Andros Island. This is where my Brother Bill Olsen worked. We tried contacting their command post-Snapper Control, without any luck. Maybe we could have said Hi to brother Bill.

2-1-1997

We were now cruising in beautiful emerald water that was quite shallow, 10-15 feet deep. The sun has just risen, and I am doing the skippering. We are motoring and have been most of the night. Now we are not finding much wind and still need to cross the Gulf Stream, so Steve is concerned that we may not have enough fuel to motor the 30 miles we have left to go. Steve then made the decision to go to Miami Beach and take advantage of the gulf steam current. The last few hours of waiting for the engine to quit was a bit tense, but we finally cruised in front of the hotels, into the marina and directly to the fuel dock. It turned out that we still had 15 gallons of fuel which was enough for many more hours of motoring.

We were pretty tired but went into the Miami Beach Strip and encountered a real Latin party. People were everywhere, and they were all having a fun time.

By the time we had dinner and a couple of drinks, we headed back to the boat and collapsed in an un-airconditioned cabin with a blanket.

On the final day, 2-2-1997

The Dock Master woke us up at 0700, and we hurried to straighten up the boat as the new owner's wife was coming in at eight o'clock. Her parents came with her, so Steve and I left them with the boat and walked around the largest marina in Florida. There were numerous yachts tied up there, and I wondered how those folks could make enough money to support owning one.

I was leaving in a few hours, but Steve was going to have to stay to return rented equipment and finalize boat papers.

I flew back to Springs that afternoon. I probably looked like a bum with beard, long hair, and rumpled clothes. I don't think I smelled bad, as we had showered on shore during our stops on the way through the Bahamas. I was still black and blue from being tossed around during the rough weather, but nothing was broken. My ham gear survived, and I still use it today in 2023.

This was Steve and my first Father/Son extreme adventure, and what an adventure it was. I admire his seaman skills, which got us safely through some tight situations. Would I do it again? Read on.

1997 continues.

I returned to my driving job as soon as I got back from the big sail. We needed the income, and I was going to retire from School District 38 soon. These jobs fit in with the other activities we will mention now.

We attended an RV show in February and found a new concept Thor ultra lite 5th wheel trailer. It weighed in at 5,000 lbs., and our truck was rated for towing 5000 lbs. We purchased the trailer, installed the 5th wheel hitch in the truck, and, during Spring break, headed to New Mexico on our first RV campout.

We left the Springs on March 23 and watched birds migrate in New Mexico, staying at Carlsbad, among other stops. We did go to Deming, NM, and stayed at a snowbird park owned by a mutual friend. We said that we would consider this place an all-winter escape, but it did not seem warm enough to fill the requirement. It was closer to home, which could have made it somewhat desirable. We drove down to the Mexico border from there for lunch and a museum that featured Pancho Villa, which was interesting.

I recall a fuel stop as we came into NM at Raton, NM, and then a concern about running out of fuel at Las Vegas, NM. We did not carry extra fuel. This was about the only interesting problem we had on our first trip.

This trip was one of many we would do over the next years as we adapted well to RV living, pulling 5th-wheel trailers.

More 1997 trips

We towed our lite 5th wheel to Baldwin in August for a high school class reunion and then on to Mauston to visit with my new brother John Cook and then on to Michigan, crossing to Lake Michigan by ferry. This was in mid-August. I came back to Springs and to my bus driving work.

Betty Retires.

Betty had always planned to retire as soon as she was eligible. Her eligibility date was August 8, 1997. She had some leave accrued and had her retirement ceremony at the U.S. Air Force Academy a few weeks earlier, on July 23, 1997. She attended her retirement ceremony and left her office without even cleaning out her desk. Betty had over twenty years of Civil Service.

Shrine Parade in Lindsborg KS.

The Shriners held a special parade in Lindsborg, Kansas, on October 10. I participated by donning our old Al Kaly Band wool uniform and marching, playing my Baritone horn. It was hot and miserable, and the band was a bunch of old guys out of step and not aligned. We did have fun and enjoyed the hospitality of our Kansas Shriners.

We took our truck and 5th-wheel trailer to the event. As we headed West to return to Colorado Springs, we encountered the traditional Kansas strong west wind, giving us a 20 kt headwind. Our little pickup truck was not powerful enough to exceed 30 mph on the freeway – I had to keep the transmission in third gear. We had to go to Colorado a longer way to avoid the headwind.

When we finally got into Colorado Springs and were stopped at a traffic light in the middle of a hill, our truck had to be shifted into a four-wheel drive low to move the trailer. Now, I was very unhappy with our travel rig.

After we got home, our niece Jannette and her husband came over, and I was complaining about our choice of a tow vehicle. Janette's husband, Mark, was a truck driver for the city and suggested we purchase a Ford diesel pickup truck to do the towing. The following year, we did, and we were very happy with that truck.

Another trip

We finished up 1997 with a Christmas trip, driving the Toyota truck only, to Kalamazoo to be with Steve, Lorna, and family. We had a wonderful time and needed the four-wheel drive truck to handle the snow-covered highways.

1998 and on.

We now both have the attitude of a retired couple with many future plans incorporating our trailer and places to visit.

Troy will be working for D-38 until he gets enough service time to qualify for retirement, but he will not work much for them anymore, only when he is home in Colorado Springs and needs something to do. We have been looking at new tow trucks and have been trying to make a decision.

We were home in Colorado Springs in January 1998. Troy was working for D-38, and Betty was enjoying retirement working at home. We were busy planning what we would do when we left Colorado Springs for our first retirement trip this coming month.

The Geddes

We met a Lutheran Pastor and his wife last year when they came to our church, Mount Calvary, to function as a fill – in pastor while the congregation searched for a new one.

Palmer and Beverly Gedde stayed with us in our lower apartment while he served the congregation, and consequently, we became close friends. Palmer had retired from many years of pastoring congregations from the northwest part of the U.S. and had moved in retirement to winter in an RV park in Yuma, AZ. He spoke highly of the location and invited us to come and stay in the park as we began our retirement plans. We decided that we would make Yuma a stop on our first retirement RV trip. Palmer volunteered to sponsor us for a rental lot when the time came.

Our First Retirement Venture.

We decided to spend this winter on the road, living in our 5th-wheel trailer. We thought that the southwest part of the U.S. would work best for us. We considered Florida, but the distance and cost of campgrounds made us think twice about the south, and we really liked the western part of the country.

We decided to head south from home, which would get us to warmer temperatures and better weather, so we drew a plan to head south on I-25 to I-10 and then west to Yuma, AZ.

From that point, we would go to San Diego and then up the coast of California to Sacramento.

We would spend a couple of months on the road, enjoying warm weather, and then return to CO in the Spring.

To make our plan work, we would have to have a new tow vehicle, so we went to Phil Long Ford in Colorado Springs and started negotiating a new truck.

A New 1997 Ford F-250.

Near the end of January, we started looking and soon were in negotiations with a salesperson at our Colorado Springs Ford dealer for a new tan-colored F-250 two-wheel drive, four-door turbo diesel truck. We did not trade in our Toyota pickup as a friend from the bus barn wanted to buy it but needed a little time to get the money.

The dealer told us that the truck we wanted was sitting on a dealer lot about 100 miles away, so we negotiated with them to transport me to personally drive the truck down as I did not want a lot boy to ruin the engine by mishandling the drive down. I wanted to do that myself. We settled on a price of about $25,000, and I signed the contract. I told the salesman that I would be available on Tuesday of the following week to go get the truck, and he agreed.

The following Monday, I was working at the school district,

and the salesman called me to say that the dealership had sent a driver to pick up my truck and it would be ready for me the next day. I called the sales manager and cancelled the sale as they did not abide by the contract of having me personally pick the truck up. They were unhappy but had to agree when I cancelled the deposit check. Now what?

The next few days after I assured myself that the deal was off saw me drive north to the Ford dealer in Castle Rock looking for a truck. He found an identical truck again on another dealer's lot, with the only difference being the color. It was white. I found that the truck was in Kansas and negotiated a lower price with me traveling to get it. We had a deal for about the same price as the Colorado Springs dealer. Now, how to bring it back?

I was still a partner with Duane Hanson on his airplanes but had not done much flying in the past years. I called him and asked if he could fly Betty and me to Kansas to pick up the truck, and he readily consented.

On February 7, 1998, Duane flew Betty and me in the Seneca to Winfield, KS, where I took delivery of our new truck. Duane dropped us off and flew to visit some nearby relatives, and Betty and I started a long drive back to Colorado. I broke- in the truck's engine using the handbook as my guide. It said no hard acceleration and drive the first 50 miles at no more than 50 mph. Then the next 50 miles at 60 mph and then the next 50 at 70 mph. Etc. We got back to Colorado Springs in the wee small hours of the morning, but we had started our new truck to a long, free-of-engine trouble life. Now, we were just about ready to begin our first retirement trip.

Our new truck needed some modifications to tow a trailer. We installed a 5th wheel hitch in the truck bed, installed an electric brake controller, and put a utility storage box to hold tools in the front of the bed. We finished the project by installing an electrical outlet on the back bumper to send electricity to the trailer lights, brakes, and appliances. We had a church friend, Al Beck, who owned a mattress store, make a special mattress for the trailer so we would sleep well at night.

We moved clothes, dishes, towels, and food into the trailer, winterized the house, loaded our dogs into the back seat of the truck, and we were ready to go. We left Colorado Springs for our inaugural snow-bird trip on Thursday, February 26, 1998.

Our new diesel truck pulled the light weight fifth wheel with ease. It was a welcome change from our small Toyota pickup truck. The day was cool, with snow showers but nothing sticking to the road, so we cruised at 75 mph.

The first stop/overnight was at a campground in Colorado City owned by some Shriner friends' kids. Cocktails and a home-cooked dinner and bed. A good first day.

The next day proved to be more interesting. We ran into heavy snow showers covering the interstate with snow above Las Vegas, NM. Driving visibility was down to 1,000 feet in the worst of it, and I did not try the brakes. I am sure it was slippery. As soon as the showers were behind us, the day was sunny, and the road was dry. We stopped for fuel in Las Vegas, NM. Now we have two fuel tanks so fuel management would be much easier and more convenient. We would have a range of 200 miles between fuel stops now, a big improvement over our other trucks.

Spent our second and third nights at a National Bird Sanctuary south of San Antonio, NM. It was a neat place to watch Whooping Cranes in winter. After spending two days watching the birds and relaxing, we headed off to Deming, NM, where we had stayed last year with the same trailer but a small pickup. The weather is now warmer, and the sky is clear and blue.

Now on I-10 to Yuma. Driving is easy with the big truck and smaller trailer. We got off I-10 west of Tucson, AZ, and took I-8 into Yuma. We arrived in Yuma on March 4th, called Palmer, who met us, and we followed him to Rancho Bonitos, a lovely 5-acre RV park in the country south of the city of Yuma. We parked the trailer with the neighbors watching and covering their ears as our truck was quite noisy.

We then took part in the winter life of a snowbird by

attending Lenten services at Palmer and Beverly's Lutheran church and having a meal with them.

We spent the next 15 days enjoying the park and pretending that we were residents. Took trips to Mexico, bought some junk, and made a lot of new friends. We found that the Canadians, who make up about 30% of the park, pack up and go home to file their taxes now so the park is not crowded.

March 19, 1998. Packed up and said our goodbyes. We have been here since March 4th and have really enjoyed this type of life. We then left and went to the San Diego area to visit Betty's sister, Joanne. We found a small trailer park in El Cajon, CA, which was near Joanne's trailer park. We spent the next few days visiting and then set off to spend time camping on the Pacific Coast. This had been our intention as we planned our first snowbird RV trip.

We first stopped at San Onofre beach near President Nixon's home. When we were stationed at March AFB, we used to come down and camp here and watch the surfers and enjoy the sand. We had a few office gatherings back in the '60s. We now found it cold and windy. I guess we forgot about the old saying that California was cold and damp in the winter. We had to change plans.

We decided to go north through Bakersfield to another of our memory assignments, Castle AFB. We would then visit our next-door neighbors, Ruth and Moe Crawford. The temperature improved somewhat, and we ended up going to Crawford's new home in Mariposa, CA, near the entrance to Yosemite National Park. After a great visit, we went to Sacramento to be with Betty's relatives. After a few days there, we had an idea.

We abandoned our plans of snow birding the southwest. A call to Palmer Gedde set up another rental at Rancho Bonitos, and we headed south again. We went back for a final visit with Joanne and then back to Yuma, AZ and the lovely Rancho Bonitos. We stayed there another week, and while there, we purchased lot 56 and parked our trailer on what was now our lot. We started dreaming about how to improve our new winter home and ended up pouring a large cement pad next to our trailer to use as a patio and parking for our truck.

Back to Work

We left Yuma at the end of April and went back to Colorado Springs and picked up on life where we left it with me at work driving buses. This ended our first major truck/trailer snowbird trip. It was highly successful and proved to be one of many in the future.

We spent the rest of the spring and summer making short trips and parades with the Shriners and the band.

At the end of May, we took the truck and trailer to Minneapolis to celebrate my boyhood friend Dewey Wienke's marriage to Kathy. I was the honorary best man (Dewey's son

Duane got the real job). The night after the ceremony, a bad storm with high winds came through and did a lot of damage. A tree blew down at our campground, and we had to wait for it to be cut apart before we could reach our trailer. The wind blew head-on to the trailer, so there was no damage. I guess the trailer thought it was going down the road at high speed.

We continued our trailer trips in July when we towed up to Superior for Betty's high school class reunion. We spent a couple of weeks roaming around northern Wisconsin, and as we were returning home, we learned that Betty's sister Mary had suffered a heart attack and was in the hospital in Colorado Springs. Mary died a few days after we got back on August 8, 1998, and her funeral was held five days later. Both of Mary's daughters attended- Denise and Jannette.

A 303rd reunion

Our old Bermuda Tanker squadron, the 303rd ARS, held a reunion in Seattle, WA, at the beginning of September. We towed our trailer and ended up camping next to our old friend Charlie Jensen and his wife, Julie. Charlie did not stay in the Air Force but went to work as a Captain for American Airlines. Our campground was near Bellevue, WA, which was the home of my NORAD briefing team partner, Cliff Zacharias, so we had a fun time there. On the way home from the reunion, we went through Palmer and

Beverly Geddes's past home and then spent time in Yellowstone National Park. We are really enjoying retirement and RVing.

A week after getting back from Washington State, my only Hansen cousin from Baldwin, Bob, and his wife Doris flew out for a short visit. For them to get off the farm was a miracle, and we really enjoyed that visit.

Our Ultralight Trailer is Falling Apart.

We had pulled our little trailer now for many thousands of miles, and the bouncing down the road was causing the cabinets and other parts to fail. It was still under warranty, but the dealer had gone out of business, and the factory required us to bring the unit to the factory in Indiana. We decided to take it to Elkhart, IN, and then visit Steve and Lorna while it was being repaired. We dropped the trailer off on October 22 and visited our kids in Michigan for a few days and picked up the trailer the next week and went back home.

We finished the year with another trip, this time without the trailer, to spend Christmas with Steve, Lorna and family in Kalamazoo, MI. We were back in Colorado Springs in time to watch the New Year's Eve fireworks from the top of Pikes Peak. We have seen them almost every year that we have been here in Colorado.

1999 and On

Betty and I have now settled into active retirement. We are

too young to sit around and have lots of plans to improve our house and plan to snowbird to Yuma each year for the foreseeable future.

I will now, in this book, attempt to talk about the interesting events of our retirement. Hang on and enjoy.

After a couple of weeks of school driving, it was time to go back to Arizona. We arrived at Rancho Bonitos on January 20, 1999. This season we would have our old Canadian friend, Henry Rodrique, build us a 10x12 shed which would have electricity, be airconditioned and have running water. I would use it as a ham shack and office and Betty would have an extra refrigerator and cabinets there. It would allow us to get separated occasionally, which I am sure helped Betty stay sane.

Our Canadian friends, Cliff and Beverly Zacharias, decided to spend the winter in Palm Springs, California, which was only two hundred miles away. We would visit this year.

In March we took our trailer and picked up Joanne in San Diego and went to Sacramento to celebrate Aunt Esty's birthday. It was a short trip and fun.

During school spring break our grandson David and his buddy Tyler flew into Phoenix and spent a week with us sleeping in the new shed and spending lots of time at our pool. We took the trailer to San Onofre for a couple of days so they could enjoy surfing. They had a ball.

Betty and I took a bus tour with other folks from our park to San Felipe in Mexico. When we arrived our tour guide had failed to book overnight accommodation. It got solved and it was still fun.

Our April return to Colorado after Rancho B. was a long route through Las Vegas, NV, into Bryce Canyon, UT. We encountered lots of snow but got home safely.

The first part of June, I finally met my brother, John Cook, when he held a family reunion in Mauston WI. We stayed in the area and visited the Wisconsin Dells and other touristy places.

On October 13th our daughter-in-law Lorna's father, George Charleson, passed away. His funeral was held at our old church, Prince of Peace Lutheran, on October 16. We got to see Lorna and Steve again. They came back and spent Christmas with Lorna's mother, Ginny, and we got some more visits.

New Year 1999-2000 on Pikes Peak

Betty and I had a very unusual New Year's Eve courtesy of Gray Line. A group of hearty hikers called the "Add A Man Club" hike up to the summit house on Pikes Peak each New Year's Eve and set off fireworks at midnight. They then have a party and return to the city early in the morning of the new year.

This year,1999, was a dry year and the highway to the top was clear of snow. The club invited their wives to come up and party at midnight. They hired Gray Line to provide the bus to get them to and from the party.

I had, over many years, driven that bus up and down the peak carrying tourists and the company asked me if I would drive it at night on New Years Eve. Betty was invited to go along, and it was a challenge that I could not resist. To make it more interesting, the newspapers were saying that the world's computers would get messed up switching from 1999 to 2000 and this would lead to widespread power outages everywhere. No one knew what to expect, so I thought it would be neat to see all the lights go out looking out at Eastern Colorado. The weather was forecast to be clear and cold. The temperatures at the 14,000-foot elevation would be way below zero and the wind would be blowing. I anticipated a wind chill of minus fifty degrees.

We loaded our guests at about nine that evening and started up the mountain. The road has no markings and there are few guard rails and no street lighting of any kind. Betty and I were dressed as warmly as we could be, we each had parkas and boots. I hoped the heaters on the bus could keep it from becoming an icebox. We had about fifteen passengers. The drive up the mountain was without problems as the headlights illuminated the road rising before me.

We arrived at the summit about 11:00 p.m. and went inside the summit house where we found the AdAman climbers still thawing out from their trek. The fireworks were scheduled to begin at midnight sharp, so Betty and I walked outside just before midnight and looked out east.

The sky was clear, and you could see streetlights from Denver to Pueblo and as far east as La Junta. We wondered if, in a matter of minutes, we would witness the whole country go dark. It was very cold on the top of Pikes Peak, and I had not shut the engine of the bus off for fear that I couldn't get it going so we both got on the bus to watch the fireworks while keeping an eye on the country scape below us. The first of the fireworks went up promptly at midnight, and we noted that all the cities and towns we could see still had their lights on.

The Air Force Academy Cadets had designed a new fireworks rocket launcher that was to be used for the first time here on the Peak. It fired a volley of rockets simultaneously. When the time came to use it, the launcher tipped over and fired all the rockets at once. They went all directions including some that flew under our bus and exploded some distance away. It was like being in a raging battle in War. I got out to make sure that the bus was okay and then the show was over.

The drive down the mountain was a little more tense. The headlights shined into space, and I had to drive with my head out of the side window to see where we were going.

After a slow descent we made it safely to Colorado Springs and welcomed the year 2000 at home about 0300 (three o'clock in the morning). The whole evening was memorable to both Betty and me plus my passengers.

A New Century

We started the new year with a new trailer. I was preparing our Aerolite for the next trip, and I discovered that it was sitting funny. I had a mobile repair mechanic come out and he discovered that the frame was cracked and about to separate. I called the manufacturer, and they said again that I needed to take it to the factory for repair. I felt that the unit would have a catastrophic failure on the way to Indiana.

I called the dealer in Casper, Wyoming, and he told me he would give me my money back on my broken trailer if I would apply it to a slightly used full sized 34-foot Excel fifth wheel. He said the Excel was like new and had never been towed on a camping trip.

On January 10th we returned home pulling a pretty fifth wheel trailer that was manufactured about 200 miles away in Smith Center, Kansas. We left for our snowbird trip to Rancho Bonitos a week later arriving in Yuma on January 20, 2000.

I had left a recording thermometer in the shed while we were back in the Springs last summer. The high temperature during the Yuma summer of 1999 was 126 degrees. I guess that is why the

Yuma snowbirds go home for the summer.

We continued to improve our Yuma property by finishing the patio with Mexican brick and constructing a metal car port to protect our tow truck. The lot was now looking good and allowed us to comfortably live there by using the truck cover as a party area for the many gatherings that we had.

Steve and Lorna had, back in 1999, left the employ of Kellogg and had taken a new position with Pennzoil/Quaker State. They had moved to Houston TX and had just purchased a home.

A few days after we arrived in Yuma, Steve was on a business trip and stopped to see us. He shared ideas that Lorna and he had about remodeling their new place in Houston. And invited us to come see their new place and assist them in the rebuilding process.

Steve and Lorna in Houston

We left Rancho Bonitos in mid-February and pulled our new trailer to Houston and parked it by the kid's new house. On the way to Houston, we stopped at the Lackland AFB RV park and did some reminiscing.

Steve and Lorna had purchased a building that was next to Astronaut Gene Cernan's' home. The house had a 3-bedroom apartment in which they were now living, and a lower level that had been a deluxe show room for a collection of antique cars. The kids were starting to turn the building into a large deluxe home.

We helped with the demolition. Lots of hard dusty work. Betty still has the crease on her face from falling and hitting her head on a brick.

We returned to Yuma at the end of February and enjoyed park outings to San Felipe and El Golfo Mexico. Our last trip to San Felipe included David and his buddy Ryan. The pair had ridden, during Spring break, a Greyhound bus from Colorado Springs to Yuma which was an adventure of its own. When they got to Yuma, we took them in our pickup to San Felipe, Baja Mexico, so they could watch the college kids enjoy Spring Break and have fun on the Mexico beaches. We returned to Yuma and the boys got back on the Greyhound bus and had lots of stories to tell their Colorado Springs classmates on how they went to Mexico for Spring Break.

I started having prostate problems after my Air Force days and was being treated by Dr. Elliot Cohn, a Colorado Springs Urologist. I had a couple of appointments with him on the first days of April in Colorado Springs.

Automobile and Medical Problems

When we purchased our new ford truck, we sold our Toyota truck to a friend. That left Betty without transportation. I had found a newer Ford Windstar van advertised by a reputable used car dealer and purchased it. He stated that the car had just had a transmission rebuilt which made us comfortable in the purchase. We had taken the van with us on this trip to Yuma and while we were driving it in Yuma, the transmission failed. I notified the dealer I had purchased the car from, and he said if I can get it back to the Springs, he would pay to have a reputable transmission store install a new one. So, we borrowed a car tower from a Rancho Bonito neighbor and towed the Windstar to Colorado Springs to get to the Springs in time for my medical appointments. We dropped the car, attended the medical appointments and came back to Yuma a week later towing the empty car carrier. We killed two birds with one stone!

We decided to stay in Yuma until the first of May and discovered why our friends try to leave the place by mid-April. We had temperatures in the last week of April as high as 115 degrees. Our trailer air conditioner handled them well, but being outside was a bit uncomfortable. We came back to Colorado on the fourth day of May. We never stayed in Yuma that late ever again.

Life Continues

The rest of the year had me very busy driving tours, and now I am working for two school districts driving school buses.

Betty's cousin, Marlene, from Wisconsin arrived for a fun visit during the summer, and we finished the year visiting Steve and Lorna and children for the Christmas holidays.

We came back to Colorado from Houston on January 1, 2001. I was immediately immersed in my typical activities. I did pick Grandson David up at the airport when he arrived back from a visit to England to see a lady friend. He tried to reward me with some special Scotch liquor, but customs confiscated it because Dave was not 21 years old.

We spent a night in Smith Center, KS, mid-January having our new trailer tuned up.

In March, Grayline sent me to Minneapolis to pick up one of their vans and I got a chance to stay overnight with Dewey for a quick visit.

A new car came home with us when we purchased our First Nissan, a new 2001 Quest, from the dealer at South Academy in Colorado Springs. We still have the vehicle now in 2023 and it has over 160,000 miles on the odometer. I probably will die owning it.

2001

This year was the first year since we purchased our property at Rancho Bonitos that we did not spend any time there. We instead had been talking with my new brother Bill and our dear friends Dena and Glenn Rydman about a really big RV trip. I guess that all of us had read about those folks who braved the Alaskan Highway to come up to view our 50th state with our vehicles. Lots has been written and the drive has been going on since WWII. We decided to give it a try. Glen and Dena had a 26-foot diesel motor home which was small but efficient. Brother Bill had a 25-foot pull trailer which he pulled with a newer Chevy van. His tow vehicle was very capable, and he had pulled the trailer for a number of years, so he was a qualified RVer. We had our new truck and trailer and we had been trailering for the last many years dating back to California when we had our Travel All and 25-foot pull trailer with the chemical toilet.

This was to be the trip of a lifetime, and I believe it turned out that way. Betty kept the log.

To Alaska- the trip of a lifetime.

From Betty's Log: Day 1, July 29, 2001: "Finally we're ready to leave out of the neighborhood at 0900 on our way to a rest stop north of Monument to hook up with Glen and Dena. Arrived in Casper, WY, late that evening after an interesting tour of Fort Laramie. Very hot day in the mid to high 90's.

Day 2 (My input). On our way to Harder, MT with a planned stop at Little Big Horn. We did not see Little Big Horn as we had a blow out and by the time we had purchased and had installed 4 new trailer tires, it was time to move on. (I had not yet learned that once trailer tires are three years old, they are automatically replaced no matter how new they look!)

The remainder of the trip was very interesting. By August 7

we had decided that following each other was not good. Instead, we would set a destination for the day and then meet for wine and dinner in the evening. By August 10 (day12) we were in Dawson City panning for gold. I bought a gold nugget that we still have in our stash. It's worth a lot more today than when we bought it. Two days later we took a ferry ride across the Yukon, and we finally were in Alaska. August 14th. New tires on the truck! We had picked up nails and had slow leaks and I was tired of the worry. Expensive but worth it. We are in Fairbanks and visited the Fort Wainwright commissary. North Pole Alaska is close by as is Eielson AFB where my KC-135 crew operated flying in the dark in November with temps at minus 70 degrees. We were stationed at Travis AFB in California in the early 1960s when we were on this cold war mission. August 19 - day touring out of the Anchorage area. The best chance to see Mt. Denali but high overcast prevented it. Not many tourists see this sight. I have seen it from the air, but it is not the same. I wanted to take the truck to the North Pole, and it is possible sometime during the year but not done by a tourist pickup. I did start up the highway that would eventually get me there, but it was rough, and I knew it was mission impossible, so I quit. Lots of other tours and we chartered a fishing boat and went out and caught some flounder which we brought home. The water was very rough and some of the other fishermen were seasick but not Betty who hunkered down in the stern and pulled her hat down. A whale came up so close to her that she could have touched it, and she did not even see it. We were all yelling at her, but the wind and water kept her from hearing us. August 27 - now we are all heading back to the mainland. Glen got word that his brother had died and seemed very quiet. Sad for him. Maybe he could have been at his side had he not gone on this trip? September 5 - came back into the USA. Great feeling. Had some very bad muddy roads to contend with coming the last hundred miles. Stopped to visit Cliff and Beverly Zacharias and then went on to Flat Head Lake in Montana to visit Al and Garenne Cochrane from our NORAD days. After twenty-five years in the military one has friends all over the world. Great feeling.

9-11

A trip of this magnitude cannot be described in a few short sentences. The approximate 6,700 miles we traveled on this adventure went by in an instant. One needs to read the log that Betty wrote to better appreciate our experience. However, the final days of the trip are especially significant.

We arrived in Yellowstone National Park on September 10, 2001, and stayed at a National Park campground. I was up around 0800 the next morning when aa fellow RVer in a motor home waved me over to his rig. He pointed to a TV on the dash, and I saw this tall building being struck by a large aircraft and then starting on fire. I remarked that it was quite the movie when he told me it was real.

The Trade Center had been hit by two airliners and was crumbling. Confusion reigned all over the East Coast. I had just witnessed history in the making. 9-11 as it was to be known forever, was the tragedy of 3,000 lives lost due to terrorism.

That day we left the park for home and the skies were empty of airplanes. We did not know if we would be able to purchase fuel as our credit cards may be shut down. The Federal Government was in mass confusion with the President airborne in Air Force One landing at various locations where it was thought that he was safe.

We made it back to Colorado Springs on September 14th. My brother Bill and SIL Laverne were already at our Colorado home when we arrived. What a trip! What a way to get to know a brother one did not know he had until a few short years ago. What a way to cement a friendship with our Lutheran church brother and sister Glen and Dena.

Little did we know that we had more adventures coming soon. The adventure of a lifetime has ended but the memories will last forever.

Onward

Our new Nissan Quest van got exercised when we took it to Houston to spend Christmas 2001 with Steve and Lorna.

As we were returning from that trip, we got word that my

brother Jack Olsen had passed away. I am glad that I got to meet him. He was a real character. He was buried in Star Prairie, WI, with my boyhood neighbor friend Pastor Rex Brandt officiating. I played Taps at the service. Jack's wife Jeanne moved their granddaughters' cremains from the cemetery where our mother Gen was buried, East of New Richmond and placed her urn next to Jack. This funeral took place in the summer of 2002.

We started 2002 with a visit to Rancho Bonitos. Stayed for the month of January and then went back to Colorado. We did not come down to Yuma last year because of our big trip to Alaska. We went back down on March 21, 2002, and stayed until the end of March.

Betty suffered from a frozen left shoulder. After some weeks of hurting, she had surgery on May 9th. Recovered well.

Took the truck and trailer for another visit to Houston. We got to see Elissa dance in the Houston Ballet and then celebrated Christiana's graduation from High School. We all went to Padre Island for a nice campout to complete our stay. Got back to Colorado Springs on May 4th. That is a famous date as it was Grampa Everett's birthday and my 48th anniversary with the Air Force.

We left on a long Midwest trip to Wisconsin on August 1st. Set the trailer up at Bob & Doris' historic farm and operated out of there for most of our stay. We also took the trailer to Marlene and

Dale Mackey's farm at the Brule. We took a route through Sioux Falls, SD, on the way home and stopped to visit Carl and Vanice Johnson. Carl was one of my aircraft commanders when I was stationed with the 303rd ARS in Bermuda. Got back to Colorado Springs near the end of August and got right back to work driving for Grayline.

A New Horizons Band was organized in September, and I was a charter member. I had been playing with the Al Kaly shrine band since 1974 but now I was taught the Tuba and clarinet. Betty also joined it a year later, so we considered ourselves Charter members. We continued with that band until we left Colorado Springs in 2020.

Our church, Mount Calvary Lutheran, had called a new pastor, Keith Knoff, in 2000. Keith refused to fulfill his duties at the church, and I was on the church council and was charged with part of his investigation. I found that he cheated some of the members financially. The whole situation was acrimonious and resulted in 95% of the congregation leaving. Betty and I were one of the first to leave and we joined First Lutheran Church in September of 2002. We maintained our membership at that church until we moved away in 2022.

We had a Thanksgiving trip to Yuma's Rancho Bonitos in November. We were back in Colorado Springs by December 1st.

Now that I had learned to play the tuba, I played my first "Tuba Christmas" concert downtown out in the cold on December 7, 2002. Later, my tuba playing found me helping organize a Shriner Dixieland band. That band was the most enjoyable music that I ever played.

We, again, went to Houston for our Christmas celebration. I don't think we pulled the trailer, but we got back home to Colorado Springs on the first day of 2003.

Our house at 2212 E. San Rafael has been undergoing heavy remodeling since we moved into it in 1993. We now have added an extension to our bedroom to include a walk-in closet, master bath with shower, washer and dryer area and a deck extension to hold a hot tub. We had a D-38 friend do the construction, Denny Krohn. The unit was added in the Spring of 2003. We moved into the addition on March 9, 2003.

We, again, went to Rancho Bonitos with our truck and trailer. We were there from March 16 to April 9.

I have over the past years been working for School district 38 in Monument and Gray Line in Colorado Springs. This has caused us to limit our snow birding and RV traveling. We will increase these activities soon.

Another chance to get to know a new brother occurred when we trailered to Mauston the end of July of 2003. After a few days there, we moved to Superior for Betty's class reunion. We then did Brule and Baldwin on our way back home. We arrived home on August 10 just in time to get ready for another year of school driving.

Another Houston trip for Thanksgiving. I do not remember if we took the trailer. We stayed home for Christmas 2003 and enjoyed Christmas day in Colorado Springs with a temperature of 67 degrees. We were part of the First Lutheran choir and spent most of Christmas eve in the choir loft at church. Both Betty and I have sung in our church choirs for as long as we can remember. We both enjoy music and try to participate when we can.

We got an early start on Yuma in 2004 with us arriving there on February 1st. We came back on March 17 and then made a quick trip to Houston on March 20th, returning on March 27.

Our dear friend Whitney Sullivan died on April 7th. He was the fellow who moved our Oldsmobile to Florida while we were getting married in Wisconsin. We served together in Bermuda and then owned an aircraft together in Colorado. We were both Shriners, and both played in the Shrine band. Many years as dear friends. He is missed. We helped watch over his wife, Ginger, during the years that she survived Whitney. Whitney was a county judge in his home of Westcliff, CO.

Took another Wisconsin trip starting on July 7 covering

Superior, Brule, Michigan, Mauston and Baldwin. It ended back home on July 29. We are getting use out of the truck and trailer.

We attended another 303rd reunion. This time in San Antonio TX. We toured both Lackland and Randolph AFB. I was trained at both bases during my Air Force years.

Spent Christmas 2004 in Houston. Grandkids are growing up.

We started 2005 with a fast trip to Yuma to attend the funeral of our next-door neighbor Larry Davidson. Went down on February 1st and were back home on the 6th. I am working only for District 38 now. Grayline fired me last year when I scratched one of their big buses in a debacle in Denver. I got a minor ticket but the Gray Line owner, Chuck Murphy, said he can't stand his insurance bill increasing by continuing my employment. Oh well. I need to start slowing down.

Went back to Yuma again for snow birding on March 6. Stayed until April 2nd. Great time. Visited Joanne in San Diego a couple of times.

A Family Catamaran Gulf Sail

Steve was again changing employment. He is leaving Shell Oil and going to The Oreck Corporation to market their vacuum cleaners and other cleaning devices. They have moved from the house in Houston to Mandeville LA where they have a nice apartment. Steve purchased a 50-foot catamaran sailboat last year and now needs to move it from the Houston area across the Gulf of Mexico to the Slidell area of Louisiana. He has talked Betty and me into going along.

We took the truck, trailer and dogs and proceeded to the Houston area and set up camp at a Baycliff, TX, campground near the marina where Steve had his catamaran docked. Steve and Lorna were no longer living in their Houston home full-time so we thought our rig would be more secure parked at a commercial campground while we sailed across the Gulf.

Betty, Steve and I left the dock in Baycliff on June 30, 2005. The water was smooth, but the temperatures and the humidity was very high. An hour into the sail, Betty went below to our cabin in the right ama to put our stuff away and came back in 30 minutes quite seasick. The gentle bobbing and rolling got to her. She spent the rest of the cruise topside and says she enjoyed the ride.

We sailed 24 hours per day and ran air conditioners using a couple of small gasoline generators. We discovered that the Gulf is filled with oil rigs. Some are abandoned and some of those are not illuminated at night. Standing watch after dark required close attention to be sure we didn't hit an oil rig.

We ate well as Steve planned the menus and did most of the

cooking. He really took his parents for a ride.

The weather was hot, and the water was smooth all the way to Louisiana. Betty started feeling well but did not go back below deck except to shower and use the head.

We arrived in Slidell LA on July 4th and went to S&L's new apartment in Mandeville to refresh and then Lorna drove Betty and me back to our rig near Houston where we picked up our dogs and went back to Colorado. For me, it was another interesting sail. For Betty? She now knew a lot more about sailing than she wanted to know.

The Calm Before the Storm

We were back in cool Colorado and doing mundane things like school bus driving, Shrine parades and church events. We did have one concerning event occur one night.

Our neighbors to the East were Rod and Terry Goodall. They were both employed in law enforcement, Rod as a Colorado Springs Policeman and Terry as the El Paso County Under Sheriff. The night of July 16 a car pulled up in front of their house and pumped five shots into the house. Two of the bullets went through the garage wall and one struck Rods Datsun 280 Z. No one was hurt but it was frightening. Colorado Springs had a gang problem for years but did not do much to stop it. The police would not acknowledge the gangs unless pressed and the media did not cover their activity. Never found who was responsible but we over the next many years never had a repeat. An interesting fact. When we bought our house on San Rafael Street, the front picture window had a large bullet hole in it.

Hurricane Katrina THE STORM

Hurricane Katrina struck the New Orleans area of Louisiana on August 29, 2005.

The Oreck Corporation had only one manufacturing plant. It was near Gulfport, Mississippi, which was near ground zero for the hurricane.

We knew very little about Oreck, but a call from Steve revealed that the factory was quite far inland and was not very far from the area power plant which had survived the storm. The factory had a small amount of damage but would be ready to start production in a week or so. The problem was that the workers had all lost their homes and were scattered and mostly unreachable.

Steve had been given instructions to drive to the plant and see if he could get it running. He owned a large van and drove to the plant a day after the storm and had trouble getting in. He had been spending the night in the van and talking to the corporate executives via satellite phone for the past days. They had come up with a plan. They would purchase many travel trailers for living quarters and start advertising on the internet for the employees to come back and move into the trailers. The plant would have electrical power soon, but they had ordered a large diesel generator to be shipped to the plant in case the local power failed. They had also ordered a tank truck of diesel fuel and one of auto gasoline. There was a lot of activity at the manufacturing plant as the company would soon be out of business if the product was not available.

Steve asked me if I knew anyone who could run an RV Park. I thought for a minute and said Betty and I will do it. He said to load up our trailer with water, fuel, food and anything else we thought we could use and come immediately.

We dropped what we were doing and went to our friends, Glen and Dena, and talked them into going with us as we knew we would need assistance. We packed up, fueled the truck and headed to Long Beach MS, the location of the plant, on September 11, 2005. We were about to have the experience of a lifetime. Glen and Dena would be about two weeks behind us as they had some loose ends.

We arrived at Steve and Lorna's apartment in Mandeville three days later and then in Gulfport, MS, the next day. Steve's planning had taken us to an existing RV park that was operational with running water/sewer and electricity. It was called "Campgrounds of the South", and the owners were John and Betsy Retting. The location was on the edge of the city with some vacant area bordering Interstate 10. There was no traffic on the Interstate as a major bridge close by had been damaged by the storm and the

Interstate was blocked. Martial law was in place when we arrived, and the campground had an armed guard at the gate.

I talked to John, the campground owner, in June of 2023, and he told me things were going well and he and Betsy were still operating the park.

We set up our trailer and then prepared to start bringing in the 27 travel trailers that Oreck had purchased. The workers were already coming back, and we needed to get moving immediately. The park was already full of many of the folks who were there to help in recovery like us, needing a place to camp and live. John directed us to park the Oreck trailers in the vacant area next to I-10. We would have a 300-foot garden hose to keep the trailers in water and would have to use gasoline generators to provide power. He hired a septic tank pumping company to come in and empty the trailers black water tanks (toilet sludge). I had full hook ups for my trailer and Glen's rig on the edge of "Oreck Village". John started to immediately install electricity and sewer to the Oreck sites, but construction would be slow as the construction companies were fully involved in recovery operations. We would see the utilities added about seven months later.

Glen and Dena arrived a week or so later; and by that time, we had seventeen trailers in place and occupied and ten more coming in. The Oreck plant was back in production and some of the workers had a home. The manager of the plant had lost his home, too. He found only an iron decoration left on the lot where his house once stood. The 20-foot surge came in and then took everything out into the bay when it receded. The storm was devastating.

Ten days after we set up our camp and moved in 20 or so trailers, Hurricane Rita came through. The weather service advised everyone to evacuate again, but I noticed most of the other rescuers were not moving, and I did not know what to do with my new brood of trailers, so I stayed. I was stuck in our trailer for a few hours while the winds howled, and the rain came down but then it was gone and left little damage. Thank you, Lord.

Betty and I were hosting my 56-D Aviation Cadet Class Reunion in Colorado Springs in mid-October. We had to go back to run the show. Glen and Dena took over the operation on the 5th of October and Betty and I left, did the reunion in the Springs, and returned to Gulfport the 13th of November. We would not have been able to run the reunion had Glen and Dena not stepped in. Steve did all of us a favor when he arranged a financial contract between Oreck and our Integrated Financial Consultant corporation. Oreck's insurance paid IFC about $6000/month to operate Oreck Village. Betty and I paid Glen and Dena a good amount for their time and expense and IFC was able to pay off my long-time loan providing Betty and me with the ability to become debt free. The Lord had us covered.

We had many interesting events occur during our stay in Mississippi. Glen and Dena left Gulfport mid-November but Betty and I stayed until mid-April 2006 to assist in selling the vacant trailers and cleaning the sites so the campground would have additional rental capability as things came back to normal.

One final hurricane story. Oreck had a returning employee who was a single mom and had a six-year-old blond, blue eyed barefoot son by the name of David. David ran around the campground and pretty much stayed out of trouble. Betty had to take him to Day Care every day and would sit and teach him to read. David had many trials and tribulations as he grew up to the point that his only bicycle was lost in the storm and when he was given a new one by a charity it was stolen. Betty was complaining about something to him one day and he looked at her and said, "Deal with It". Wisdom from someone who at age 6 had been there. We have stayed in touch with some of these folks over the years on social media and saw a handsome six-foot young man being married. Our barefoot boy with cheek.

Back to Normal???

After seven months in Mississippi, we arrived back home in Colorado Springs on April 20, 2006.

During this year, we took a couple of short road trips to visit children. On a visit to Mandeville on November 24, Steve, Eric, and

I were at Mandeville airport where Eric had been taking flying lessons. I had Eric's CFI take me up in a Cessna 120 tail dragger just so I could say that I flew one. I made the landing, such as it was. I had not been doing any flying for the past few years and it felt good to get back to it. We then got the idea that Steve, Eric and I should take the Cessna 172 that Eric was using for his training out for a ride. The CFI said that Eric could not be pilot in command with a student license and Steve's license had long since expired. The solution was for me to be PIC but to do that, I would need a Bi-annual check ride. The CFI and I got into the 172 and went out and I made three landings (none that I was proud of). Then we came back, and I wanted Eric to fly us from the left seat since that is where he was taking his lessons. The CFI said that I had to be in the left seat since I was not a CFI. So, Eric got in the right seat, Steve in the back, and I sat in the left seat as Pilot in Command. I told Eric to do the flying and found that simply moving seats changed his perspective, so he taxied way on the right and took off on the right side of the runway and the landings were interesting. I had him make a couple of landings and then I said that I would make the last one. Well, we walked away, and the airplane could still be used. Eric and I were both embarrassed but none of us will forget the last flight that the Hanson boys had together thanks to a very understanding FBO owner/CFI at Mandeville Airport.

One 2006 driving trip was to San Antonio for a 56G Pilot

Training Reunion. When that was over, we drove to Houston for Eric's Boy Scout Court of Honor where he received his Eagle Scout award. Now three generations of Hanson's had served in the Boy Scouts of America organization and Steve and Eric were both Eagle Scouts. I made second class!

March of 2007 found Betty and me towing our trailer to Yuma for our annual vacation. When we were about 100 miles away, we got a call from Steve that Eric was in the hospital in Mandeville and could we please come there now.

We pulled into Gila Bend and had Glen Rydman come, meet us in Gila Bend and pick up some items we were bringing them. We then turned and went to Mandeville, Louisiana. We arrived in Mandeville on March 8, 2007.

We found that Steve decided to move to a company in Boca Raton, Florida to get Eric out of a dark situation in New Orleans. We again got involved moving boats. We sailed his catamaran down the inter coastal waterway into Tampa Bay and then to a marina at Ft Meyers. We drove a rental car back to Mandeville. This trip took about a week. We then decided it was too late to go to Yuma, so we went home by visiting Moultrie, GA, and the old Spence AB where I started my flying career.

Grandson David married Laurie on our wedding anniversary date of June 16. It was held at a venue site south of Colorado

Springs.

We trailered to Wisconsin in July and met brother Bill at a campground near our brother John Cook's home in Mauston. Next, a visit around Superior and Brule and finally to the Baldwin area to attend my Spring Valley High School reunion and then back to Colorado on August 7, 2007.

We had our 303rd reunion in Colorado Springs in September which Betty and I plus our Colorado 303rd members hosted.

I shut down Integrated Financial Consultants at the end of October 2007. The experience of starting up and running a productive company for all those years will forever be in my memory. Its last business operation was Betty, Steve and me operating the recovery of the Oreck company from the ravages of Hurricane Katrina. IFC developed Oreck Village to house workers to allow the company to resume manufacturing. Betty and I were heavily invested in the operation but in the end got all our investment back plus interest.

2008 finds us in Yuma on January 30. We were back in Colorado on April 21. Before we came back, we purchased a 35-foot Park Model trailer and had it installed on our lot. We decided that fuel prices were too high, and we wanted to stop RVing. Our Yuma runs are now routine. We are now old-time snowbirds.

We are busy with Shriners, music and church when we are

home. In June Steve and Eric flew in to take part in a Scouting trek at Philmont. They were on the trek for about 20 days and will have stories to tell for the rest of their lives.

We sold our fifth wheel trailer in July for $7000. Fuel prices were nearing $5.00 /gallon and we, last winter, put a park model on our lot. We made the special price on our trailer for a fellow who had fallen on hard times and lost his house. He and family were going to live full time at a campground East of the Springs. The trailer served us well. We had towed it from the Arctic Circle to southern Mexico and had put over 100,000 miles on it. We hope it will serve the new owner well.

I have been elected executive secretary of the Central States Shrine Band Association. The organization represents all the Shrine bands in the central part of the USA. We have our annual gathering in Oklahoma City in August. Lots of activity. I borrowed a truck and trailer from Colonel Boyd Van Horn to use in the parade. He even drove it for us. He was a good HAM friend and commander of the "Air Forces Flyers" amateur radio club.

I had minor surgery at Penrose hospital on November 7, 2008. Ever since I had returned from Vietnam, I had been experiencing urinary problems. I went through many procedures over the years to try to relieve my problems. A year or so earlier, the doctors detected prostate cancer, so I had elected to have the prostate surgically removed. It was larger than they planned and damaged my abdomen. The surgery this month was to repair the damage caused by the earlier surgery. I went home three hours after the repair.

We arrived at Rancho Bonitos on January 19, 2009, and walked right into our new park model. We really enjoyed the expanded living and now will install a deck and large awning. This is retirement! Dewey and Kathy came down and rented another park model near us. Unfortunately, Dewey had to have surgery for a pinched intestine. He recovered but did not enjoy Yuma much this year.

Jim and Barb Hauck came down to visit driving their motor home. A quick one-day visit.

Ron and Alta Van Someren, my cousins, had purchased a home in another park not far from us. My other cousins from Baldwin, Ron and Shirley Stone and Gene and Mary Bonnes live in a trailer park in Mesa, AZ. We visit each other from time to time.

Joanne now lives in northern Phoenix, so our traveling now has changed from San Diego to places East.

Before we went back home in April, we had two beautiful Mexican brick walls built on our lot. The side lot was challenged by the park board, so we had some personal acrimony coming up next year. We were back in Colorado Springs on 28 April 2009. Travel is simpler now without a trailer.

Our 303rd friend, Ginger Sullivan, passed away. Whitney preceded her about three years ago. We were the youngest 303rd members back in 1956, now we are turning into survivors.

We flew to Lexington VA to witness Elissa graduate from college we got back to Colorado Springs on June 9.

This month in July 2009, Mel Graner and Jim Hauck became Master Masons. I was their top line signer. They later became Shriners and played for many years in the Al Kaly Shrine band.

We rented a 24-foot pull trailer from the USAFA and pulled it to Wisconsin with our F-250 Diesel. We attended the Spring Valley High School reunion. We visited Baldwin and Superior relatives as well as Dewey and Kathy at their lake home in Turtle Lake, WI.

Steven gave us his Dodge travel van when we were working Hurricane Katrina. We are now using it to carry Shrine Band members to engagements. Very comfortable.

In August 2009, Troy was helping Christiana move to the Detroit and Washington DC area.

Colorado Springs hosted CSSA starting on Sept 8. Very busy time for me as I am still the Executive Secretary of the Band Association part. Had a great time and still have some "White

Lightning" left in my bar that was donated by Missouri Shriners.

Betty and I plus some Colorado Springs 303rders set up a Bermuda Cruise. We left on October 3 and returned on October 10. Steve and Lorna and Sandy and Bret (her third husband) accompanied us. While on the island we took our children around the island to see where they were born (the Kindley AFB hospital had been demolished) and where we lived. The trip was very enjoyable and meant a lot having our kids and their mates see where they began life.

We returned home from the cruise on October 10, 2010.

Our Christmas trip took us to the Detroit area where Steve and Lorna are now living. Steve is working for "Lifestyle Lifts" a face lift company with its headquarters in Troy, Michigan. The kids have leased a very large, lovely home there.

I purchased a very used Geo Tracker car online. The guys at Rancho Bonitos have organized a desert run group that goes exploring the vast deserts around Yuma. I needed a small four-wheel drive vehicle to be in the club. I found this car near Iowa City and put it on a dolly and brought it back to Colorado Springs when we returned from our Christmas at Steve and Lorna's. We were back in the Springs New Years Eve 2009.

The first major event in 2010 was the passing of Betty's brother -in-law, Gerry Bourassa. Betty's sister, Mary, had passed away some years earlier. Jerry left his daughter Jannette living in Colorado Springs and his eldest daughter, Denise, living in Florida. Both ladies were at his funeral. We had gone to Yuma pulling the tracker car mid-January and had to come back to the Springs for Jerry's service.

We returned to Yuma shortly after the funeral and brought the Tracker to a Mexican fellow who specializes in modifying vehicles for desert racing. He found the body was very rusty but the engine and drive train to be in good condition. He cut off a lot of the body and replaced it with boiler plate and painted the car lime green.

I then replaced the tires, brakes battery and repaired the upholstery. We used it for years and had a ball.

GRAND DAUGHTER DANA MARRIES

High lights for this year included our Granddaughter Dana marrying Mike Chrzanowski on July 17 in a beautiful county park in the Colorado Springs Black Forest area.

More events saw us attending funerals for some of our longtime friends such as Harold Nabor who was an Air Force retiree and fellow church member at First Lutheran. We also had another CSSA convention. I am stepping down from the Executive Secretary position.

We lost our dear friend and Pastor, Palmer Gedde, on

November 4, 2010. He had been at the forefront of our lives since the days of Mount Calvary Lutheran through Rancho Bonitos and finally Gloria de Cristo Lutheran church in Yuma. His wife, Beverly, will continue to live at their Yuma home until she passes.

We are doing a cruise with Jim and Barbara Hauck, Duane and Sheila Hanson and Glen and Dena Rydman. We departed the terminal in Miami on December 5, 2010. We sailed through the Panama Canal with stops at Cartagena Colombia, Huatulco, Acapulco, and Cabo San Lucas Mexico and finally Los Angeles ending on December 18, 2010. We had a great time with no sickness or injuries. We left to spend the remaining Christmas holidays with Steve and Lorna on Christmas Day 2010. We were back in the Springs on January 4, 2011.

We have started a Shrine Dixieland Band, and I am playing Tuba. We had our first organized meeting in our garage on January 6, the day before my 76th birthday. We left for Rancho Bonitos on January 21 and stayed there until April. This year we had visits from Elmo and Carol Gardner, Dewey and Kathy Wienke, and our Granddaughter Elissa. Elissa flew to Yuma from Charlottesville VA. She went on a desert run driving the Tracker and did lots of visiting. She went back on 26 February 2011. After a busy snowbird winter, we returned to the Springs on April 2. Our park model's 3rd birthday was April 3.

On April 28, 2011, I joined the Scottish Rite Consistory. Most of our Shrine Band members also belonged there so I was comfortable. Another Shrine event was Mel Graner, Elmo Gardner and me taking Mel's 1981 Oldsmobile to Lincoln NE for a CSSA meeting. The car made it, and I had to do most of the driving. We did have a good time.

On July 19th I lost my brother Bill Olsen. He was the first newfound brother I found with our daughter-in-law Lorna's genealogy talents. He was an active person all his life and we visited and traveled together after our discovery. Betty and I attended his funeral in Florida, and I was honored to play TAPS at his funeral as I had done at our brother Jack's funeral some years earlier.

I no longer feel like an only child. I have now known blood brothers for some years, and I am feeling attachments to these men. I am thanking God that our daughter in law Lorna came into our lives. Without her intense desire to solve a mystery, I would never have found my birth family.

The 303rd ARS had another reunion in Branson, MO, on September 21. We still have good turnout and its fun seeing our old squadron mates. Another reunion the end of September was my first aviation cadet class – D Class in San Antionio TX. Finally, we again spent Christmas with Steve and Lorna in Michigan, returning to the Springs on New Years eve 2011.

2012 started with the loss of another old friend, Bob Russell, who was a long time El Paso County District Attorney and Al Kaly Shrine Band member. Our Shrine Band had a lot of gigs and giggles associated with Bob and his antics.

We went to Yuma on February 7, 2012, and stayed there until the end of April.

In June of 2012, a fire that started in the forests west of Colorado Springs crept into the city eventually destroying over346homes in the NW part of the city. We had fellow church members, Ray and Arlene Avicious, lose their lovely home. They lost everything except two cars and the clothes on their backs. The wind blew glowing ashes from the inferno into our back yard. We fortunately escaped without damage. We did, however, a month before have a severe hailstorm and had about $40,000 of damage to our house. Crazy Weather.

Global warming?

We again, rented a pull trailer from the Academy and paid a visit to Wisconsin. We try to go to Wisconsin now each year to visit our few remaining relatives. We always enjoy the visits and trips. Our Ford truck continues to perform well. I got to visit with my only remaining brother, John Cook, in Mauston. I purchased some shoes from that visit. I still have and wear them today (2023).

Our daughter Sandy introduced us to her new friend, Terry

Henry. A very nice fellow. We hope for the best with them. They were married on December 11, 2011.

Betty discovered, while renewing her driver's license that she was short a small amount of work credit to quality for Social Security. She went to work for Palmer and Beverly's daughter Jackie's Dream Dinner business. She filled bags with rice. After two quarters of pay she started getting about $400 / month social security payments.

I started volunteering to drive the Disabled American Veteran's van from Colorado Springs to the Denver VA hospital. I found it challenging and worthwhile, so I am continuing to drive. It is a weekly trip year around. I am one of five drivers.

We spent this Christmas with Sandy and her now husband Terry in Cleveland TN. They just purchased a large patio home with lots of room. Terry is an accountant for a large company called Life Care Centers of America. They have their headquarters in Cleveland, TN, as well as a large senior care center which includes cottages. Sandy works for the same company as an RN traveling inspector checking their many facilities around the US for Medicare compliance. They both seem happy and are very busy.

When we left Sandy and Terry we drove back home arriving on January 2, 2012. We left for Yuma a couple of weeks later. We stayed in Yuma until March 20 when we went home to prepare to go to Elissa and Steve's wedding in Lexington VA.

Elisa and Steve Baur were wed in a small country church near Lexington VA. It was a memorable service with an older, very wise Pastor officiating. I was assigned the job of administering communion. There was a reception at a rural venue which was well decorated by Lorna and family. I remember a kind of a wild celebration where some sparklers caught on fire on the venue's deck and caused some damage. Steve and Lorna's friend, a Michigan lawyer named Jay, stepped in and saved a lawsuit.

When it was time to fly home, Betty and I got bumped and the airlines picked up the cost of our airfare plus another couple of thousand in compensation for their mess up. They then kept us overnight to fly out the next day. I missed playing TAPS for Shrine Band member Bus Hoyts funeral which really distressed me. (I have not flown again on an airline. It is September of 2023 when I write this.)

We went back to finish off winter in Yuma and then drove to Iowa City to watch Eric graduate from college. Our grandchildren are now grown up.

On June 11, our dear friend Glen Rydman passed away. The high temperatures were setting records in the 107-degree range. A terrible forest fire started in the Black ~~Forest~~Forest, burning hundreds of homes and buildings. The fire started near the property we had owned years ago and destroyed two very large homes that were built on the property we sold. It was a record breaker destroying 486 stuctures.

We drove to Branson in August to a CSSA convention. Jim and Barb Hauck had some time shares there and we stayed with them while we attended the convention. One the way home, we visited Sandy and Terry in Tennessee. David was at that gathering as he had moved to be near Sandy.

In September we took our annual trip to Wisconsin stopping at Mauston to visit my only remaining brother, John, and then to the Baldwin area to visit the VanSomeron bunch, Dewey and Kathy and then to Superior to see Betty's cousins.

In October 2013, we had yet another 303rd reunion in Grapevine, TX. We got back from that at the end of October.

On 11 December, Sandy and Terry celebrated their 2nd anniversary.

We spent Christmas 2013 with Steve and Lorna in the Rochester, Michigan, house. When we left them after Christmas, we drove to Sandy and Terry's home and spent New Years 2014 with them. We then came back to the Springs arriving on January 4, 2014. We left the Springs for Yuma on January 20, towing the Tracker behind the F-250.

Duane and Sheila Hanson started renting at Rancho Bonitos. They needed to get away from Minneapolis where they had recently moved.

While we were living in Yuma, our F-250 pickup odometer rolled 220,000 miles. It was now 16 years old. We have had no major maintenance problems with this pretty truck. (As I write this, in 2023, my son Steve inherited the truck. He maintains it well, and now it has about 400,000 miles on the odometer and still has the original transmission and engine. No major repairs have ever been made!)

We had built a deck for our Yuma park model without a building permit and got caught by the county. We hired Henry, tore down the old deck and built a better new one. It passed, and everyone was happy but my wallet.

Duane and Sheila left after staying a month, and Dewey and Kathy arrived the next month.

A New Birth Family Lead

On March 26, 2014, our newly married Granddaughter Elissa and her new husband Steve arrived in Yuma for a short visit. This visit would change my life.

Elissa was attending law school at Stanford U in California and Steve was working with the school's athletic department running a program using DNA to forecast athleticism. We were discussing finding my birth mother and boys but did not know my birth father's name due to the state of Wisconsin impounding my birth certificate. Steve Baur suggested that I use the DNA company he was working with to see if I could locate my paternal relatives. I followed his suggestion, and it changed all my conceptions.

An Amazing Revelation

After they left, I requested a DNA kit from 23andme and when it arrived, I placed my saliva in it and sent to off. A couple of weeks later I got the analysis on my computer.

It was amazing! A lot of information on me.

First, my heritage. I was about 30% Irish and 30% Norwegian. The rest was a mixture of European. The next was a list of relatives on my maternal side and another list of paternal relatives. Some names had addresses, and some just had a name. (Keep in mind that this was an early data list from 23andme. Not too many people had sent their spit in to be analyzed.) The lists showed relationships such as 2nd to 6th cousin. None revealed a father or brother. I went over the lists looking for a Cook or Olsen and came to one who listed Cook as a family name. His name was Barrett J. Williams.

I had never heard that name before but saw that his data included a family tree. I opened the list, and as I went through it, I came to the name NELLIE GENEVIEVE COOK. It also, as a group, listed her mother and father and her sons.   I JUST FOUND MY BIRTH MOTHER AND HER FAMILY!

I now have valid confirmation of Lorna's genealogy work. I truly was a half-brother to Jack, John and Bill. I was elated and called Betty to come look at the computer and see what we had found.

We called Elissa to inform her and her husband of our findings, and she had another idea. Since I had gone over the paternal listings and found nothing I could identify as my father, we needed a name.

Elissa asked me if I would give her permission, as a class project, to approach the state of Wisconsin and see if they would release my father's name. Of course, I said "Yes, go for it!" A couple of weeks later, I received a letter from the state of Wisconsin saying that a judge had ordered them to release to me the name of my birth father. They requested that I send them $20.00, and they would send me my original birth certificate. I immediately called them to confirm that the money was on the way and then asked them, "Who is my birth father?" The person on the other end stated, "THEODORE SANDS"

I have my Birth Fathers' name!

I had not heard or read the name "Sands" before. Then I

remembered…

I was going over the 23andme lists on the day they came in on the computer, and one of the search items was the area where the family had lived. I noted that one stated Eau Claire, Wisconsin. Now that was close to my birthplace, and I had attended school there. The person who listed it had left her name and phone number, and I called her the day that I saw it. We talked for a while but could not put anything together that would show me her family. Her name was Donna, and before we hung up, she said to call her anytime if I had further information.

Well, I now had further information, and I immediately called her. I told her the name of my father, and she never hesitated and said, "You have a brother in Omaha." She said his name is Gary Sands, and he is my uncle. BINGO! Now we are cooking.

I found that Donna lives in Durango, CO, and it dawned on me that we would drive through there within the next couple of weeks, so I asked her if she was willing to meet me, and she said yes. She also said she had background information on the Sands family and would bring it with her to our meeting.

Meeting Donna 4 May 2014.

We were on our way home from Yuma to the Springs, and we stopped for the night at the famous city hotel in Durango, CO. It is May 4, which is turning into a famous date for me and my family:

The Only Child and His Brothers

(1) My adoptive Dad, Everett, was born on this date in 1897; (2) I enlisted in the Air Force on this day in 1954; and now (3) I am about to meet my birth father's family member who will share with me information on my birth father, Theodore Sands.

Betty and I were sitting in the lobby of the historic Double Tree Hotel in Durango, CO, the evening of May 4th, 2014. We had arranged to meet Donna Alsdorf here at 8:00 p.m. Donna walked in the door promptly at 8:00 carrying a large manila envelope.

We exchanged greetings, and she proceeded to show me historical documents on the Sandee/Sands family that goes back more than a century. She told me that she is the Granddaughter of my uncle Bill Sands who lived in central Wisconsin and grew up on a farm south of Eau Claire near a small town called Eleva which is the homestead of the family. I found out that I have a brother Gary Sands who now lives in Bellevue NE (now part of Omaha), and she thinks that she may have met him.

I learned that Donna has lived in Durango for many years and is a professor at the local college. She has children there who are now leaving home. She is a friendly person and quickly becomes my favorite girl cousin on the Sand's side. We said our goodbyes, and the next day, Betty and I arrived home in Colorado Springs. What a trip! Thanks to Lorna, Elissa and her husband Steve, I am about to meet the paternal side of my family. I certainly am not an only child!

I Speak to My Paternal Half Brother

After we arrived back in Colorado Springs and got settled, I started the process of finding Gary Sands. I Googled him and came up with a phone number and his address in Bellevue, NE. Now, how do I approach him? I came up with an idea and dialed his phone.

Gary's wife, Rita, answered, and I told her who I was and asked to speak to Gary. She said he was at the church and would be home within the hour. I told her I would call back. I called back about an hour later, and Gary answered.

Gary was the first brother contact for my paternal Sands family, and it was May 13, 2014, over 18 years after I found my maternal birth mother's family and spoke to Bill Olsen.

I introduced myself and gave him my background, such as location, etc. I told him I was doing some genealogy on the Sands family and was having trouble finding info on his family and could ask him some questions. He said, "Sure," and away we went. Over an hour later, I said I needed to process this data and asked if I could call him again, and again he said, "Sure." We hung up, and I was busy writing.

I called Gary again the next morning, and we had not spoken long before he asked me, "What is this really about?". I took a deep breath and told him about my adoption and finding my birth mother's name but not having any luck with my father since the birth certificate had been impounded. I then told him about 23andme and my granddaughter getting the birth certificate released. I read him the impounded birth certificate. He asked me if I could overnight him copies of the important documents, including the impounded birth certificate, and I said, "of course."

Now I had verbally given him all my personal information, including my home address. Unbeknownst to me, Gary had a daughter, Julia, and a son-in-law and their family who lived near Monument, Colorado, just north of my home. He asked Julia to drive by the house that day to see if it was real.

My New Brother Is Convinced- I Am Authentic.

The next week, after Gary had received the document copies I had sent, he called the St Croix County recorder and talked him into telling him how many children were born in the county on January 7, 1935, and who the fathers were. They hesitated, but finally told him two children. The father of one of the children was named Sands. That did it! On June 26, 2014, Gary called me and welcomed me to the family. We started to make plans to meet.

His daughter, Julia, and her husband, Carlos, came by our house the next day, and after they walked in, Julia exclaimed, "You have the mannerisms of my dad, so you must be my uncle".

Gary and I met for the first time a few weeks later at his home in Bellevue. After we greeted he and his wife, Rita, Gary had us all sit down at the dining room table with me across from Gary. He looked hard at me and said, "You're freaking me out. You look just like Dad!" He then showed me a picture of our father, and I had to agree with him.

Gary had an excellent way of allowing me to meet more relatives. Each Thanksgiving, the Sand's relatives would all gather for dinner. They rented the facilities in Gary's church as the group could be very large. Betty and I were always included, and that let the others look us over and left me trying to remember many faces and names.

Over the past years, I have had visits with many of my close relatives. I visited the Sands family homestead, which is a farm South of Eau Claire, Wisconsin, near the village of Eleva. On that visit, I met the current occupants, my cousin, Joanne Sands Lehman and her husband, Jim. Joanne is the daughter of my uncle Joe Sands. She loaned me a large book called "The Sande Book," which has historical information on the family that dates back many years. I have used it to get to know my brothers and the rest of the Sands family.

We have been included in family celebrations with Gary's daughter Julia and her husband Carlos at their home in Colorado

Springs. I am slowly meeting more long-lost family members as time goes on.

The Sands family is a large group, and I am still meeting more. I thank the Good Lord for guiding me through the steps of genealogy and modern-day DNA genetic testing to show me that I never was just an only child. I always had brothers; I just needed time to find them. I now have known Gary and his close family for many years. They warmly welcomed me into their flock, and now I feel comfortable calling Gary "Brother."

Brother John Cook passes.

While Gary and I were meeting on the telephone, my maternal brother John Cook in Mauston passed away, making me the only surviving child of Genevieve Cook Olsen.

Betty and I drove her new 2014 Gold Nissan Rogue to Mauston, where I, again, was honored to play TAPS at his grave side.

The "Sande Family Book"

Now keep reading and check out the next chapter showing the main characters of my story. It has a long list of my paternal relatives. Some of the Sands' information was taken from the "Sande Family Book." You can find it by contacting one of my family members who may have a copy in their archives.

FINALLY: In November of 2015 I noticed an item in our local Colorado Springs paper advertising an upcoming college writing class that stated something to the effect, "If you have ever considered writing your personal story" take this 3-day class. I did and the instructor, Ms. Ferris Frost, a professor at Pikes Peak Community College, challenged me to start immediately as I probably did not have much time left to do my writing! It took me a few years to come to the conclusion that my story was unusual and I started to write.

I wrote this book for my descendants. I have spoken to many of my acquaintances who have told me how they would have liked to be able to read about their past people and how they lived, loved and died. This is my attempt to tell my descendants how one of them grew up and prospered.

Our Final? Household Move.

It took me about three years to finish this book. I started it when I was 85, and just after I started writing, my wife of 67 years, Elizabeth (Betty), and I heeded the call of our children, Steve and Sandy, to move near them. We sold our home in Colorado Springs after living in that city for nearly fifty years and now live in Gloucester, VA, in a new home about 20 miles from the Atlantic Ocean. We are close to military installations, which we need for our support. Our son and daughter-in-law, Steve and Lorna, live near us and now help take care of us. Betty and I are 88 years old and are in good health and are enjoying our retirement. We now belong to the Ware Episcopal Church where we sing in their choir and support their community support projects. Betty plays Bridge with some local ladies a couple of times each week and I am a member of the Botentourt Masonic Lodge, Tidewater Shrine Club and the local chapter of the Disabled American Veterans where I hold the office of Chaplain. The church has been holding services for the past 371 years and the Lodge was founded on December 15, 1778. I qualify for DAV membership from my Vietnam war experience and injury in the 1970's. We have now experienced history to the beginning of the United States of America. Betty and I are proud patriots!

There is some additional information that you may find interesting. I covered my adoptive parents' background in the preceding chapters. This next and final chapter will give you some information about my maternal and paternal birth families. I would suggest using one of the internet genealogy sources to expand on the Cook and Sands family history. There is much more information there.

Chapter Nineteen
TROY'S BIRTH FAMILY CHARACTERS

Maternal Grand Parents

Grandfather John E. Cook -1869-1940

Grampa John was born near Troy (now Aylmer), Ontario, Canada. (now you know how I got my name). His parents had migrated to Canada from Ireland. DIL Lorna found some possible ties with the famous Captain Cook.

Grandmother Nellie Lenore Cook - 1867-1957

Grandma Cook was born in Western Minnesota. Her father was a medical doctor. Nellie would ride with him in his buggy on patient calls in rural Minnesota and remembers Native American Indians stopping them to trade items. I believe her parents had ties to the Mayflower Pilgrims.

The Cooks had a farm north of New Richmond, Wisconsin, near Star Prairie, where my mother Genevieve and her four brothers were born. They were members of the Methodist church in New Richmond, and most of the family were buried in the cemetery east of New Richmond.

Cook Children

- Four boys- John, Quincy, aka Winifred, and two others. All have passed on.

- Daughter Nellie Genevieve Cook Olsen June 19, 1905 – December 28, 1982. (My Birth Mother.)

- Genevieve's children (my half-brothers)

- John O. Cook - January 19, 1928 – June 5, 2014

- William C. Olsen - March 17, 1929 – July 19, 2011

- John G Olsen (aka Jack) - February 14, 1931 – June 5, 2001

- Troy L. Olsen Hanson - January 7, 1935 –   ME!

John O. Cook - John was the first born of the maternal brothers. He was raised on a farm on the edge of New Richmond, only a few blocks from his grandparents' home, where his mother, Gen, and brothers, Bill and Jack, were raised. John enlisted in the U.S. Navy and served as a corpsman. After service, he attended Stout Institute in Menomonie, WI, graduating the same year that I started at Stout. He married his college sweetheart, Noreen, and became an Industrial Arts (Shop) teacher in Mauston, WI. He had two children with Noreen – Sandra Lynne and Tim. (Interesting note, Betty and I named our daughter Sandra Lynne. Of course, we had not even heard of John when our daughter was born.) John's second marriage was to Barbara Nagel. There were two children in this marriage – Chris and Kory. Kory was adopted. Barbara died, and then John married Debra, a young widow with three girls. John retired from school teaching and purchased and operated a shoe store in Mauston. He also drove heavy over-the-road trucks during his working years. He was a kindhearted, civic-minded person. We do not know the identity of John's father.

William C. Olsen – Bill was born to Gen and Darrell Olsen and was Gen's number two baby. He grew up in New Richmond, WI, and joined the U.S. Navy after his high school graduation. His second military career was with the U.S.AirForce. After separating from the military, he married a southern girl, Laverne Laramore, and they had four children - Vanessa, William Jr., Saen and Chris. Bill graduated from Virginia Tech and went to work for the Federal Government. He was working with Navy Seal training using submarines and their torpedo tubes for launching them when I met him. I knew Bill better than my other maternal siblings. We had a big driving trip to Alaska and some personal visits as well. His wife, Laverne, and my Betty were very good friends. Bill was very intelligent and a hard worker. He was also a good Christian.

John (aka Jack) Olsen - Jack was the second child born to Gen and Darrel Olsen. He grew up in New Richmond and went into the Navy after high school graduation. He married a New Richmond girl, Jeanne Sutliff. They eventually moved to Florida, where they had two children – John and Jeannine. Jack worked a career for Bell Telephone. Jack was quite ill when we first met and only lived for a short time, so I never really got to know him. I am told that he was the jokester of the family and a bit of a daredevil. I guess every family has one.

I have had the fortune to meet many of my maternal cousins who live in the New Richmond, Wisconsin, area. Unfortunately, my memory is fading, and I can't remember their names or even where they lived. I have recently talked to some of my brother's children, who are scattered across the United States. Most recently, I had a visit from my Brother John Cook's Granddaughter SusanWilke Brock, my Grand Niece from Phoenix, AZ. She is picking up the genealogy of the Cook family using 23andme. Perhaps she can find my brother John Cooks's birth father. Good luck, Susie.

My brother Bill Olsen's son, William Jr., lives in Idaho and has a good knowledge of his family. He helped me by triggering my memories of the Olsen tribe.

Paternal Grand Parents

Grandfather Christen Johan Christenson Sande (aka Christ Sands) - August 26, 1851- 1918. Grampa Christ immigrated from Sande, Norway, on April 25, 1869. He immigrated with a brother, two stepbrothers, and his stepfather.

Grandmother Julia Gunhil Oleson (aka Julia Gunhil Fredrikson) - October 28, 1863- 1949. She immigrated from Bergen, Norway, in 1872.

Christ and Julia were married on the family homestead near

Eleva, Wisconsin, on July 1, 1880. They had ten children between 11/1880 and 02/1902. My father, Theodore Sands, January 8, 1902-May 6, 1965, was the youngest.

Christ had a son Sever B. 4/4/1875 from a previous marriage where Sever's mother died during his birth. Sever was raised with the rest of the family. Christ changed the family name from Sande to Sands in 1910. His brothers, however, did not change their names, so the Sands and Sande families of the Midwest may be closely related. Christ was a talented wood worker, casket maker, writer and farmer. He and Julia were charter members of the Eleva Lutheran church. His most quoted saying was, "NORWEGAN BOYS ARE BORN TO WORK." Apparently, my paternal uncles, father, as well as my brothers lived by that saying. I was, however, lucky enough not to be exposed to it. Christ and Julia are buried in the Eleva church's cemetery along with many of my aunts and uncles.

My Birth Father.

Theodore (Ted) Sands - January 6, 1902 – May 6, 1965

Theodore Sands and Marjorie Olin were married on November 8, 1926. They had three sons.

•Theodore Sands Jr. - August 26, 1927-March 16, 2002

•Bruce Waldemar Sands - July 16,1929-April 29, 1976

•Gary Olin Sands - December 15. 1934-

Ted Sands, my father, grew up on the family homestead near Eleva, Wisconsin. He left home at age 16 and worked his way, walking and working in logging camps to his brother Clarence's home in Alberta, Canada. There, he learned lumber jacking by making railroad ties. He eventually returned to Wisconsin to get married and moved to a farm near Eau Claire that his wife Marjorie Olin inherited when her parents passed. Their boys were born while they lived on the farm.

My dad, Ted, was not a farmer, so he had jobs in Eau Claire. The Gillette Rubber Company moved Ted to Central City, NE when Gary was about two years old, and he rented a farm there for the boys to work on while he sold the Nebraska farmers rubber tires to replace the steel lugged wheels on their tractors. He eventually moved the family to the Bellevue, NE, area where he purchased a filling station business near the Omaha stockyards. He then started a tire vulcanizing business to rebuild auto and truck tires, which were in short supply with the war in progress.

When the family first arrived in Bellevue, they lived on a small acreage with a house and barn. This land has now been developed and is about one-half mile from Gary's present house. WWII was starting, and the Douglas Aircraft Company was starting to build bombers on land that would later be Offutt AFB. The factory had a short 4,000-foot runway that ended near the Sands family acreage. Gary remembers watching the new bomber struggling into the air on their first test flights. He also remembers some crashes.

Gary's mom turned into "Rosie the Riveter" and worked at the plant building these bomber aircraft. She also was in a small group of workers who modified the famous "Enola Gay" B-29 bomber to carry "Fat Boy" the nuclear bomb that was dropped on Hiroshima that ended WWII.

After the war, the family purchased a property in La Platte, NE, on the Platte River, where they started a sand and gravel operation. After some successful years of operation, they ran out of workable gravel land and turned the remaining land into a mobile home park. There were two houses next to the park. Bruce and his family lived in one, and Gary's parents and Gary in the other. Dad Ted was living there and operating the park when he passed away.

My Brothers:

Theodore Sands Jr. - my oldest Sands brother. After graduating from Bellevue High School in 1945, Ted started working toward a medical degree at Creighton University. He was drafted into the Army and sent to Germany, where he was assigned duty to clean up the Jewish concentration camps. He said that there still were bodies in the ovens when he arrived. He came back from the Army with PTSD but still managed a productive career in appliance repair for Westinghouse and was the owner of a Dairy Twist store in Boone, IA. He was a great outdoorsman and hunter. He married

Kitty Wilson, the girl who lived next door in the trailer park. They had no children. I never had the privilege of knowing Ted. He passed away many years before I came on the scene. I did note that his tombstone had a Masonic symbol, as did our father, Theodore.

Bruce W. Sands. - My second oldest brother. Bruce was the joker, troublemaker, and the life of the party brother. He drove a yellow and brown Ford Roadster and rode a large Indian motorcycle. I am sorry to note that I never knew him as he died at age 47, suffering from Rheumatoid Arthritis. He probably got this disease from working in cement dust-loading Redi-Mix trucks, a company where he worked for many years. He married Patricia Logan, who I did get to meet at one of the special Sands family Thanksgiving dinners. Their children were Thomas, James, Donald, Charles and Christine.

Gary O. Sands. - This brother is truly my brother. Part of this book is about our meeting when I discovered the paternal side of the family. We have had many great times together, and he has been making sure that I am part of the Sands family. Gary is the only living member of my immediate paternal family. I believe God has kept him here on earth to show me that I really did have paternal brothers.

Gary has the most interesting background of anyone that I have ever met. He was the CEO of a large corporation that pioneered vending machines and moved into concessions and catering at university sports arenas throughout the nation. He has remodeled and rebuilt many homes and has designed and constructed an award-winning solar home that exists near his present home today. It is heated in the cold Nebraska winter using solar power only.

Gary married his high school sweetheart, Rita Halterman, on June 7, 1956. Betty and I married on June 16th, 1956. This year, in July 2023, Betty and I drove from our home in Virginia to Gary and Rita's home in Bellevue, NE, and celebrated our 67th wedding anniversaries together. Three of Gary and Rita's kids – Tim, Julia, and Laura, and their spouses hosted the celebration. A memorable day. Thank You, Family,

Gary and I have similar interests, but Gary is a much harder worker and a more skilled craftsman at woodworking and building. He is a very determined person who debates with his medical doctors about the care he will receive. He generally wins!

I noted recently that he is now confined to a wheelchair due to previous injuries but gets out into the yard and digs, plants, and moves dirt and rocks riding on the chair. He maintains his own home from that chair by closely supervising his helpers and pitching in when he can. He recently painted his garage and sealed the floor by himself using long-handled brushes and his electric wheelchair.

An amazing brother. Gary and Rita have four children-

Timothy Allen, Julia Jo, Laura Jane, and Angela Lynn. All of these families are intelligent, independent, self-starting people that I am proud to call family.

I thank God that I was allowed to find and know my brothers and their families.

! Me.!

Since I am "The Brother from Another Mother" (or Dad), I guess I will save my data for the last.

Troy Lyndon Hanson (aka Troy Linden Olsen) (aka Troy Cook) (aka Troy Sande – Sands) January 7, 1935 –

Born in New Richmond, Wisconsin, at his Grandfather John Cook's home to Genevieve Cook Olsen - 06/19/1905 – 12/28/1982.

Adopted and raised on a 40-acre farm south of Wilson, Wisconsin, by Everett and Letty Hanson. (See their and my data earlier in this book).

Married Elizabeth Ann Juntti (Betty) on June 16, 1956. Children: Steven William Hanson – March 22, 1957- Sandra Lynne Hanson Henry – March 8, 1959-

STEVEN married Lorna Carol Charlson on September 21, 1980. Their children are:

Christiana Erin Hanson September 9, 1984-

Elissa Noel Hanson Baur December 29, 1986-. Elissa married Stephen Baur on Sept 21, 1983- Their children are – Jack Baur - 4/5/2017 and Juliet Virginia Baur (aka Ginny) - 11/15/2018.

Eric Troy Hanson April 19, 1990-

SANDRA married Terry Henry on December 11, 2011. Sandy's children from her first marriage are:

Dana Michelle Leonard Chrzanowski August 20, 1981-. Dana married Mike Chrzanowski on July 17, 2010. Another interesting note: Dana, a few years ago, decided to join 23andme and do some personal genealogy. She was surprised to find that she had an older brother, Jim Motes, who lives with his family in Alabama. Jim was Dana's father Steve Leonard's son and was born while Steve was in college in Colorado Springs. Jim and his family came to a family reunion for the Leonard's a few years ago and I was privileged to meet them. Small world.

David Scott Leonard - November 16, 1982- August 11, 2023. See the next and final chapter of this book.

Chapter Twenty
The Last Chapter

August 11, 2023

As I am writing this tome, I am advised that our family has experienced a tragedy. Our eldest grandson, David Leonard, was found dead in his bed on 8-11-2023. This is the first immediate family death Betty and I have experienced. We have always hoped that the parents would pass away before the children, but this case appears to end that hope. We are both devastated.

David Scott Leonard passed peacefully away on August 11th, 2023, in his apartment at 90 E. 2nd Ave in Rome, Georgia. He was alone.

His mother, our daughter, Sandra Henry, and her husband, Terry, held a brief family service for him at the Salmon Funeral home in Rome, GA, the next day, with two of David's close friends attending. His ashes will be scattered atop his beloved mountain, Pikes Peak, west of his birthplace, Colorado Springs, Colorado. His obituary is available online from the funeral home.

David was born prematurely to Sandra Lynne Hanson Leonard and Steven Leonard on the evening of November 16, 1982, at Memorial Hospital in Colorado Springs. He came into the world about two months early. His parents took him home in December, and he flourished into an active boy who won the hearts of all the people he met, including his older sister, Dana Michelle.

David's doting grandparents, Bobby and Frank Lewis and Betty and Troy Hanson, helped with his care and provided entertainment for him and his sister for David's first years of maturation. When he was five years old, his Grampa Troy took him on an airliner to meet his great-grandmother and great-grandfather, Lettie and Everett Hanson, in Baldwin, Wisconsin. While on the flight, David told his grampa, "One of the stewardesses just said I was cute," to which his grandfather replied, "Are you sure they weren't talking about me?" Dave said, "NO Way!". David was a bright lad and had never met a stranger. He was playing poker with his grampa one day, and Gramps told him, "Dave, I have lost all my money." David replied, "Shit Happens, General"! He always had a quick reply. Dave was the apple of his Gramma Betty's eye – she was his biggest defender. Dave received female attention all his life as he was first cute and then handsome.

David was my special grandson. He spent a lot of time with me, and since I was acutely aware of his cancer treatments in his early life, I suppose I spoiled him. He and his sister and cousins flew to Baldwin in my airplane to visit their great-grandparents and spent many nights in our home. They also spent time at our timeshare in Colorado, enjoying nature as only the Colorado mountains could present it. I remember Dave and his cousin Christiana camping on the shore of a nearby lake at Wildhorn, our timeshare resort north of Lake George, CO, and sitting by a small campfire. I had brought a can of gasoline to the campsite to start the fire. While I returned to the nearby cabin, David poured the whole can of gas on the fire. It flared into the air many feet and frightened the neighbors, who called the local sheriff. While the police were en route, I went back and doused the flames with lake water, and by the time the police arrived, there was no evidence of a campsite or fire. I hid behind a telephone pole and watched the sheriff drive up and down the road, looking for a fire. David and his cousin were safely in the cabin while all of this went on. Later, I was reprimanding Dave for his actions, and he said, "Boy, it was exciting, Grampa!" Dave liked exciting things.

I took him along to Kansas in the airplane, where we would have the airplane's annual inspection accomplished. I let Dave fly the bird, and even though the summer afternoon turbulence was bad, he loved diving and zooming and just having fun. We stayed overnight at a motel with a pool and had a memorable time together.

Dave came to live with us at the beginning of his senior year in high school. He now had a few kids that he hung with in the school, such as Ryan Wills and Tyler. Also Mike Chrzanowski, who later would be married to his sister Dana. They were good guys, and I suspect knew the lower level of our house well, as David probably hosted parties there while we were on trips with our truck and trailer.

I suspect that is where David got hooked up with alcohol, which haunted him for the rest of his life. The cancer treatments he received as a small child also took their toll. The chemo and radiation resulted in brain scarring, and he suffered from seizures for the last few years of his life, and I suspect that a seizure ended his life.

We hosted Dave and one of his friends two times while we snow birded in Arizona. One time, he and Ryan rode the Greyhound bus to Yuma from Colorado Springs. That trip gave the teenagers many stories to tell their friends. David was always having fun, never a dull moment.

Betty and I had the best grandparenting experiences with David and his sister and cousins. We watched David grow into manhood and experience his first workforce problems. We witnessed our cars brought back with dents and creases that teenage drivers make and had heartache when some of his life experiences turned sour. Both of us are missing his cheery greeting "Hi Gram" or "Hi Grampa." We are both rich for having had a hand in raising him, and we will never forget our oldest grandson.

On that sad note I am going to end my trip down memory lane. Writing these chapters has done a lot for me personally. I now recognize how wonderful people are. My birth mother who placed me for adoption when she was unable to raise another child; my adoptive parents who gave me everything they could; my close relatives and neighbors who had their positive input on my life; my churches and pastors who guided me through life's trials and tribulations; my military leaders for their quality grooming and guiding me through twenty-five satisfying years of professional challenges and amazing outcomes; my children, grandchildren, and now my great-grandchildren; and the girl I met at the beginning of my Air Force career who became a strong military spouse, mother, grandmother, and great grandmother to our family. I hope our future family members will read these words and know what a strong heritage they have. God Bless you all.